Marilyn Irvin Holt

The Orphan Trains

PLACING OUT IN AMERICA

University of Nebraska Press: Lincoln and London

Copyright © 1992
by the University of Nebraska Press
All rights reserved
Manufactured in the United States of
America

First Bison Book printing: 1994

Library of Congress Cataloging in Pub-
lication Data
Holt, Marilyn Irvin, 1949–
The orphan trains : placing out in
America / Marilyn Irvin Holt.
p. cm.   Includes bibliographical refer-
ences and index.
ISBN 0-8032-2360-9   1. Orphan trains.
ISBN 0-8032-7265-0 (pbk.)
I. Title.   II. Title: Placing out.
HV985.H65   1992
362.7′34′0973 – DC20   91-29155
CIP

∞

To Daniel

Contents

ILLUSTRATIONS

Following page 96

Acknowledgments

I wish to express sincere appreciation to a number of organizations, their staff, and individuals who gave particular help and support as this manuscript was prepared. The assistance offered by the following were invaluable: the New England Home for Little Wanderers, Boston; the Illinois State Historical Library, Springfield; the Nebraska State Historical Society, Lincoln; Dayton Canady, director emeritus, South Dakota Historical Society, Pierre; Kinga Perzynska, Catholic Archives of Texas, Austin; Jill Erickson, Boston Athenaeum; the Cincinnati Historical Society; Mary Ellen Johnson, executive director, Orphan Train Heritage Society, Inc., Springdale, Arkansas; and Connie Menninger, Terry Harmon, and Gene Decker, Kansas State Historical Society, Topeka. For her enthusiasm and sharing I want to especially thank Bernadine Barr, who will have completed her doctorate at Stanford University by the time this goes to press. Also, a special thank you to Nel and Robert W. Richmond—not only for being my friends, but because they had such confidence; Robert also read an early draft, offering as always good direction. Lastly, I want to thank the many people who have shared their placing-out histories; their willingness to tell their stories is of significant importance to any study of this American experience.

Introduction

In 1873 the popular periodical *Harper's New Monthly Magazine* captured with story and pen-and-ink drawing the migration of children to America's heartland. With mainstream America as its reading audience, this magazine romanticized and gave nobility to a special nineteenth-century life experience. It indicated, by the fact of publication, society's approval in general for this urban-to-rural resettlement of children and provided one small glimpse of a system that lasted for seventy-six years.

In a 1979 book the Charlene Joy Talbot character Kevin O'Rourke left his life as a New York City newspaperboy and traveled west with a group of children as *An Orphan for Nebraska*. The fictional Kevin encountered much the same experiences known to the real children illustrated in *Harper's* almost a century before.[1] This twentieth-century account of a child's migration west is just one of many to appear in recent years, indicating a continuing interest in what was known in the nineteenth century as "placing out."

The term "placing out" has given way, however, to "orphan train," and those who were placed out have now become "orphan train riders." The meaning is sure, even if the literal description is faulty. These identifiers, now common, have become a part of

American terminology, and can be traced to the 1978 publication of *Orphan Train* and the subsequent 1979 television movie by the same title. These presentations, based on Dorothea Petrie's meeting with a man who had been placed out in Dysart, Iowa, in 1894, gave to a large general audience one story of the placing-out system.[2] What these twentieth-century publications have in common with their nineteenth-century counterparts is a presentation of a subject that has received little analysis within the framework of American society, showing fictionalized and sometimes biographical accounts of an experience unknown to most.

The migration depicted in these publications was not an American phenomenon. In fact, it was not American in origin nor did it operate for a short period of time in the United States. Rather, the migration, with European precedents, had been a segment of American life since the 1850s, and had reached such a level of operation by the late nineteenth century that it could be discussed in a popular magazine.

The migration of the nation's poor from urban tenements to rural America is often misunderstood in its scope and its reasons for being. The economic and social structures of nineteenth-century America were certainly factors, but just as important were society's changing view of childhood; the treatment of the poor; the economic impact of both the Industrial Revolution and western settlement; and the benevolent impulses within the structure of government, private, and church-sponsored charitable programs.

This emigration of the poor was multifaceted. The focus was on children, but adults, particularly women suffering economic duress, were included. The emphasis centered on removing the destitute of eastern cities to western rural homes, but over time "western" states found it expedient to remove their poor farther west. And, non-western states, too, received a number of the placed out. At the same time, the mechanics of emigration changed, as experimentation, refinement of the process, and adoption of the basic formula by states and private institutions evolved.

The need perceived by urban reformers and rural populations and the premise for the system never changed, however. There was an overpopulation of poor—men, women, and children—in urban areas. State institutions, city or county poor farms, and pauper jails could not bear the burden, and private charitable organizations could only house or support a few, in proportion to the overall population of unfortunates. At the same time, the rural "west" suffered from a lack of labor. Underpopulation and fluctuating numbers of settlers created a need for workers, who could not be had in numbers large enough to break and develop the land or to support growing businesses in new towns. Farmers needed work hands, retailers and tradesmen needed shop help, and both farm and town women in these areas of new growth and settlement complained of the lack of "'help' [such] as washerwomen and kitchen girls."[3]

The solution seemed obvious. In 1855 an Illinois newspaper editor commented on the need to redistribute the nation's work force. "Our country is swarming with a population which in order to be kept from want and distress must be employed. Some general system, which shall induce a withdrawal from the towns . . . is the great demand of the times." This commentator was not alone in his solution. Eastern urban reformers and some charities had reached the same conclusion, and in New York City, Charles Loring Brace, a reformer, had "resolved to make use . . . of the endless demand for children's labor in the Western country."[4] This demand and the plight of the urban poor allowed the initiation of placing out, a system that brought the two worlds together.

It was Brace's form of placing out that became the model for all other such programs, and it was this system that removed at least two hundred thousand children, as well as men and women, from city to country. Brace and his New York based Children's Aid

Society have been credited as the American originators for the system, but other organizations, public and private, had either experimented with the idea earlier or soon followed Brace's example. Among these were the Boston's Children's Mission, the New York Foundling Hospital, and the Philadelphia Women's Industrial Aid Association.

A major evolution in the system came in the late nineteenth century when once-"western" states such as Indiana and Illinois took their cue and began to use the system for resettling their own urban poor, most of whom were children. These "orphans of the storm" were oftentimes removed farther west. At the same time that these new urban poor were being removed from states of the old Northwest Territory, institutions in eastern cities, including Brace's organization, continued to send children to the Midwest, West, South, and Southwest.

The orphan trains ceased to operate in the 1920s for a variety of reasons. Criticism of the system, a professionalization of social services, and a change in societal attitudes brought an end to the mass child migration, but not before thousands had been resettled in rural homes. Today there are living testimonials to the system. They are the last of the placed out, the last of the orphan train riders. Their stories are being uncovered and told. Often separated from brothers or sisters or, in many instances at least one parent— the myth perpetuated is that all of these children were orphans— the living reminders of this system present varied, individual stories of this American experience.

Today, studies of women's, social, and cultural history have examined more closely cultural America and have interpreted American thought. Great attention has been paid to the nineteenth-century "Cult of True Womanhood" and its definitions for feminine virtues and roles. There are today also more references and illustrative studies of the companion "Cult of Masculinity," which defined the male role at home and in public. Additionally,

within the interpretation of male and female spheres, studies have
examined the meaning of childhood and its own "cult" in nineteenth-century American society.

One point immediately apparent in these studies is that then, as
now, there were societal standards to which all were expected to
endeavor but which few could actually attain. Women, relegated by
society's standards to their sphere, were separated by class, as well as
by race or national origin. The same could be said for stereotypes
and expectations for men, as well as for children.

The cultural standards for what constituted a wholesome,
healthy childhood were, like those set for men and women, the
ideal. A museum exhibit today on nineteenth-century childhood
may depict china dolls, toy soldiers, and wicker doll buggies. This
presents what American society expected childhood to include. Of
course, not all children had such toys or the leisure to enjoy them.
There were children working in mills, collecting rags in the street,
and begging for a livelihood. This clash between the ideal and
reality was as much a jolt to nineteenth-century society as it would
be for a museum visitor today comparing china dolls with photographs of dirt-streaked, rag-clothed children.

What to do with the children of the poor played on the collective mind of American society, particularly when vocal reformers
and child-care advocates presented graphic examples of the conditions under which these children attempted to survive. In the case
of placing out, charity, economics, western settlement, and technology served to create a childhood experience based on society's
notions of what a child's "sphere" should be. Placing out was
perceived as respectable in its intent and motivation and could be
presented to the general public as an example of what good could
be done for thousands of unfortunate children. In the age of rugged
American individualism, Social Darwinism, and self-made men
and women, the advertised results of the placing-out system gave
validity to American ideals of success. That the emphasis was on

children and not adults reflected the general consensus that few adults, tarnished by their years on city streets, could be saved. Grit and determination were championed, and those who had been placed out became symbols for the ideals of the Protestant-American work ethic.

The story of placing out is told by many voices. The resettled can be heard through reminiscences, interviews, and letters. Through these, some of the relocated are fleshed out with names and life histories; most, however, remain anonymous, lost in the passage of time. Adding to the story are the organizations that used this system of relocation. Annual reports, circulars, and magazine and newspaper accounts provide the viewpoints of institutions and their managers. Even their rhetoric, most often containing religious images and solemn platitudes, is useful, establishing the mind-set of those who supported the system. No one source completes the picture, but the parts brought together paint a view of what placing out was, how it operated, and what one experienced if chosen to ride the trains to new homes.

For this study of placing out, those institutions that relocated children, women, and some families across state lines and in the manner set down by Charles Loring Brace and the New York Children's Aid Society will be considered. The workings of the Aid Society and of some other institutions are clear and documented, but there are blurred edges in the history of placing out. Some institutions and aid societies called their activities placing out when in fact they were a form of in-city or in-state foster care or traditional indenture practices. In addition, each state had private and public institutions that offered for adoption or indenture children within the home state. In fact, institutions, particularly the public ones, were authorized to allow such placement of their charges. There are some references here to these institutions, but only as examples of available options and of the continuing organization of programs for the poor. Since placing out focused on children, from infants to older teen-agers, emphasis is on this group. Some mention of adult placements is made, particularly those of women during times of economic crisis. This is ultimately the story of child relocation, however. Not included here, except as examples of other forms of child care, are missionary and government programs for Native Americans, such as boarding schools and orphans' homes. These programs did not follow the prescribed method of placing out, and most Native American children were not placed out into homes by these educational or charitable efforts.

The focus here is the placing-out system instituted by the New York Children's Aid Society, its imitators, and its reasons for being and end. Of interest is the system in which "homeless waifs [found] themselves in comfortable and kind homes, with all the boundless advantages and opportunities of the Western farmer's life about them."[5]

CHAPTER I

Ideals, Demands, and Motivations

To thousands of far-off homes these outcast waifs have come as messengers of peace to heal grevious heart-wounds. —*Jacob A. Riis, "Christmas Reminder of the Nobelist Work in the World"*

"SHE possessed fine, intelligent features, though her face exhibited no light shades." She was a child of the streets. Without gloves, hat, or shoes, the girl of six or seven crouched against the winter wind and begged near Trinity Church on New York's famous Broadway. Tears streaked a dirty face and over one eye was a soiled bandage. Thus was described in a nineteenth-century short story, "The Beggar Child and Church," an outcast waif of urban America. Whether the girl actually existed was of little importance to those who read of her plight. After all, the child was a "literary orphan," one of the most popular figures in literature of the 1800s. Literary orphans were sentimental subjects, the stuff of which not dreams, but morals, were made. Stories and poems routinely portrayed the orphan who, after much suffering, received his reward. The reward often came as death, with the suffering child finally finding peace after a world of troubles. This was the certain fate for "The Beggar Child," but the reward also could come as salvation at the hands of an adult. This was a popular theme in the books by Horatio Alger, where poor orphans and street boys moved up in society with the help of some understanding adult. Such was the case of the title character in *Jed the Poorhouse Boy*, who, it was discovered, was not an orphan at all but a lost child of landed gentry. Improbably, the story saw Jed searched out by an adult and returned to his rightful place in society, saved from his life of poverty. For an Alger character there was always a happy ending, but only after the lessons of perseverance and "right" were learned. Reading audiences responded to both happy and tragic endings, for with each the orphan served to teach a lesson and to pull at the heartstrings.[1]

The orphan image drew warm sympathies when viewed through the pages of a book or magazine; there were no harsh realities to intrude. Sometimes, however, truth met fiction. In 1894, Alger's orphan character Julius the Street Boy left the squalor of New York's tenements in the company of other children. They were headed for a new life on the western plains. The story was fiction, but the means of Julius's emigration was a real-life organization, the well-known New York Children's Aid Society. As Alger explained his character's circumstances, "Julius . . . goes west in one of the companies which are sent out periodically under the auspices of the Children's Aid Society, an admirable Association." With his emigration, Julius would have the opportunities to become a self-made man, one of the "respected prosperous citizens . . . of the West."[2]

The particular experience of the literary orphan Julius was in reality duplicated by thousands of boys and girls—the true orphans, street waifs, and indigents of America's poorer classes. What literature portrayed was in a larger context a keystone to nineteenth-century views of children and childhood and what could be done to "reward," to save, the children of the poor.

In the mid-nineteenth century, a number of America's charitable institutions embarked on a grand plan to remove the urban poor

to the country's rural areas, and the majority of those being resettled were children. Nothing quite like this had been attempted
before, but the idea seemed a necessary solution for dealing with a
growing poverty class in eastern cities. Known as placing out, this
system of emigration was a response to tremendous social pressures
and demands in both cities and agricultural communities. For it to
be successful, however, placing out had to rely on what Americans
believed about themselves, as well as on the changing influences of
technology and the country's westward expansion.

The existence and acceptance of placing out reflected many
facets of developing social thought. Life in nineteenth-century
America was not static. Its form and definition were ever changing
and varied materially and culturally between the frontier and the
more established Eastern Seaboard settlements. To bind themselves together Americans created their own cultural mind-set for
what constituted the ideals in society, and perhaps one of the most
fundamental of these was the definition of what embodied good
family life and childhood.

During the nineteenth century there was a revolution of sorts
regarding what society believed to be the nature of children and the
time of life called childhood. Influenced by the roles established for
men and women within society and the social climate created by
industrialization and western settlement, children and their special
world of growing up were given new emphasis. Evolving ideals
about the roles of men and women and their place within the family
unit created societal attitudes toward children. These became a
rigid set of expectations for a positive childhood experience that
would create happy, productive adults capable of contributing to a
prosperous America.

Discussions about children and childhood created by the mid-
nineteenth century a general consensus of what Americans believed
children to be. Early in the century there were still remnants of
eighteenth-century thought that clung to the idea of all children as

sinners. In literature, such as the 1818 series *The History of the Fairchild Family*, children were most often portrayed with "wicked" hearts requiring large doses of strict Christian training. There were also those who stood by the Reverend Jonathan Edwards's edict that children were "not too little to die . . . not too little to go to hell." In opposition to this viewpoint were eighteenth-century philosophers and educators, notably Jean Jacques Rousseau and Johann Pestalozzi, who stressed the "naturalness" of children and their lack of innate depravity. These more enlightened ideas found an audience in America, and by mid-nineteenth century and the coming of the Victorian age, a change was noticeable in American society's view of children and childhood. Once considered miniature adults, the bearers of original sin, children came to be viewed more often as sweet innocents. This change in attitude was of fundamental importance. As long as people believed that predestination decided life's outcome, there was little one could do in changing one's circumstances and character. Child rearing and education focused on the repression of the great evil that lurked in each soul. By the 1850s, however, public objections to the idea of a child's potential being limited by original sin were more open and frequent, and for the more progressive thinkers, the argument was closed in that decade with the publication of Catharine Beecher's influential *Religious Training of Children*. When Beecher came to the question of a child's original sin, she made short work of the subject by an outright denial of its possibility.[3]

The purity of children became an increasingly powerful theme in American thought, as reflected in the literature of the day, and it fell to the mother, within the family unit, to protect this innocence with "those lessons of virtue and wisdom which are not of this world." Children were dependent on the adults around them for direction and instruction. With what scholars have today termed the "Cult of True Womanhood"—society's dictated role for women in their sphere of domesticity—there came to exist a "Cult of the

Child." This recognition of childhood dictated that children were different from adults and gave a whole set of standards by which the quality of a child's experiences were judged. If women were to be the mainstays of home and the defenders of respectability, guidelines had to exist for their roles as protectors of children. Child rearing demanded thought and creativity. In the ideal household the child would follow the example and teaching of the mother, and she, in turn, would encourage deference to the perfect father. The role of the father was as breadwinner and quiet support for the family. His may have been the final word, but men were warned: "The father does need to know enough to be a wise father. The chief part of his wisdom should be to leave the managing and directing of child training to his wife." Women and men had their roles; children theirs. Thus, childhood, a time of gentle nurturing within the maternal sphere, became important not only in itself but within the defined expectations for women.[4]

These dictates for feminine, masculine, and child roles were the goals for which American society was to strive. The broad middle class accepted these mandates and was most influenced by them through popular literature, sermons, and group pressure. Within the general discussion of spheres, there were complaints, however. Some segments of society overlooked or were ignorant of acceptable norms. The wealthy upper class did not always conform to expectations, especially in child rearing. Children of the more well-to-do were given over to the care of nannies and hired teachers. Physically and emotionally these children often were separated from their parents, and their elaborate dress was seen to make them objects of show and wealth, not children. At the other end of the social scale, it was nearly impossible for the lower classes, particularly the marginally employed or destitute to replicate in their households the roles prescribed by society. Women worked outside the home, children were often left unattended or were sent to work, and father figures were not always present. In addition, there were the immigrants who brought with them cultures and behavior patterns not necessarily in tune with those of middle-class America. Also contrary to what society said childhood should be were elements of violence and abuse, even in the best of homes. America wished to see itself as a child-loving and protective society, but realities too often proved the opposite. Nevertheless, the ideal remained, setting standards for what constituted family life, acceptable conduct, and childhood. These social dictates became stronger, not weaker, as the century progressed.

Along with the development of rigid expectations for family life and its separate spheres, the Victorian era saw the expansion of ideas concerning social structure, beyond the family unit, and the make-up of the human mind. Americans argued the evolution of the species and its implications for man and his social organization. Within this dialogue, there was an intensive change in society's view of a child's "evolution" in physical and mental development. Popular magazines for women, once devoted to fashions of the day and moralizing "women's stories," began to give more space to the subject of child development and the mother's expected contributions. *Godey's Lady's Book*, well known for its fashion and home furnishings sections, provided as early as the 1850s advice on proper reading material and games for children, and by the 1870s the magazine's "Fun for the Fireside" provided mothers with ideas for instructing and entertaining the child at home. Also to appear were touching stories and poems with children as the focus. That many of these, such as the melodramatic "Cousin Helen's Baby," centered on the death of an infant or young child indicates another recognition of children's growing importance in society, as well as their perceived innocence. Indeed, the public's acceptance of published memorial poetry, illustrated by such lines as "Children in snow-white caskets, Laid away to their rest," and the material trappings in which one grieved for a lost child became cult forms in themselves.[5]

By the late nineteenth century, the concept of childhood as we understand it today was firmly rooted. By the end of the century the period defined as childhood had become extended beyond the age of five or six, recognizing the adolescent as a member of the child, not adult, world.[6] Within this context of growing up, children were to have a time to be innocent, to play, and to learn.

The literature on child rearing became extensive. Parents, particularly mothers, were advised as to the child's proper diet, clothing, education, discipline, and the need for fresh air. Receiving great emphasis was home education, particularly instruction in Christian principles. Children, tabula rasa, were to be educated, not coerced, to do "right." The message, whether stated in flowery prose or authoritative pronouncements, remained the same: "Home . . . is the cradle of the human race; and it is here the human character is fashioned either for good or for evil." Women accepted this mandate, even those who exhibited unladylike behavior as they fought for the vote, prohibition, and social and economic reform. A continuing theme in all of these arenas, particularly for prohibition of alcohol, was the protection of the home and the creation of a better world for children. Not only were homes destroyed by adult intemperance, but children, particularly of the lower classes, were thought to be drawn to drink. The concern expressed by a missionary in Boston was echoed by many: "rum-shops [are] kept open, in defiance of the law, where youths . . . from eight to twelve years of age [can be seen] intoxicated." It was woman's duty to challenge such threatening perversities; always, however, keeping sight of the bounds of woman's role in the social scheme. Thus, women's protests were made acceptable when placed within the context of preserving the bastions of American society, home and family. The Woman's Christian Temperance Union kept this theme in mind, as did other reform groups. Even in the often-perceived radical elements of the Populist movement women kept their priorities as dictated by society. As one Populist supporter urged women to become activists in the Farmers Alliance cause, she also recognized her assigned domestic duties and rejoiced in life's child-rearing responsibilities: "O Mothers! What a work for you."[7]

A Christian upbringing, the shaping of little souls, was of utmost importance. Magazines for a female audience and "mother's books" connected this upbringing with parental responsibility and advised accordingly. Spanking had its supporters, but parents were counseled to consider first if this form of punishment would produce a kind, responsible adult. Indeed, lines were being drawn between what constituted discipline and abuse, and these were more clearly detailed when Jacob Abbott's *Gentle Measures in the Training of the Young* (1871) argued that the rod was not needed if mothers incorporated proper discipline into child training. The burden of raising children fell to the woman, and a whole list of unacceptable practices filled child-rearing literature. Bribery with sweets or other treats was a decided mistake, for it would create a child whose character was "mean, creeping, [and] cowardly." Additionally, mothers were warned against making their children objects of display, dressed in clothing representative of adult finery such as silver-buckled shoes or an imitated Parisian gown. Such child fashions conveyed the wrong messages of what was important in life, as well as restricting physical movement so important to a healthy body and limbs.[8]

Christian education maintained a level of great importance in the raising of children, but there was a new interest in the development of children's intellectual abilities. Parents once had been warned that attempts at early reading or writing were harmful to small minds—they simply could not absorb too much information. Indeed, Lydia Child's authoritative *The Mother's Book*, published in 1831, counseled, "excitement in reading is a sort of intellectual intemperance and like bodily intoxication it produces weakness and delirium."[9] Educators by mid-century, however, were reevaluating early childhood education, and by the 1880s, professionals had revolutionized educational theory by accepting the premise that children not only could, but wanted to learn from an early age.

Discussions on many aspects of child rearing were decidedly for an at-home audience, but some components of child development received broad public recognition. First, it was generally accepted that fresh air was a beneficial ingredient to emotional outlook and physical health. In the poorest sections of a city, however, fresh air was a commodity in short supply. Streets that served as open sewers and housing that provided none of the basics for sanitation or personal hygiene created an environment in which infectious diseases spread rapidly, death by exposure was common, and health services were almost nonexistent. Among the most affected were the children, and by 1890, when reform movements and health care more often targeted the tenements, 40 percent of all deaths in New York City were still those of infants and children. To counteract these harmful and life-threatening influences of tenement life, benevolent societies in metropolitan areas took the fresh air edict to heart during the latter portion of the nineteenth century. Assuming that middle- and upper-class children in the city had the opportunity through holidays and family outings to sample country life, individual contributors and charitable foundations supported programs that sent children of the urban lower classes to the country for at least a few weeks each summer. By 1891 over ninety-four thousand children from New York City alone had experienced life in the country. That dedication to the fresh air ideal continues today through New York's Fresh Air Fund, which advertises, "When a city child first gets a taste of life in the country, something magical happens."[10]

The nineteenth century also witnessed a great public interest in child education. Beyond home instruction and schooling for the middle and upper classes, of particular note was an innovation imported specifically for children of the poor. This was the kindergarten movement, which, on its introduction into the United

States from Germany, was intended for the lower, not middle or upper classes. The premise for this form of early education was based on the belief that children were one with nature, innocent and pliable to the shapings of a positive environment. In America the first kindergartens were established in working-class and poorer districts of urban centers, and by the end of the century the idea had spread westward. Special schools for teachers sprang up across the country, and if California's Pacific Kindergarten Training School may serve as an example, the message repeated time and again was that of caring for and instructing "luckless children." By the latter decades of the century, this included children in America's more rural areas. In Kansas, for example, the Soldiers' Orphans' Home at Atchison had a kindergarten department by 1890, and in 1893 a kindergarten for poor blacks was established in Topeka. Whether in country or city, kindergartens had taken hold, and the movement reached its zenith of acceptance when, in 1893, it was decided that the Children's Building at the World's Columbian Exposition in Chicago would feature a kindergarten. The intent was to demonstrate the educational benefits for the poor. Visitors could view children trying out the parallel bars or exercise rings in a gymnasium—a reflection of the importance placed on physical activity and the Fresh Air Movement—or in the classroom learning a useful skill such as stitching. The child participants were members of America's lower classes, although the more well-to-do children visiting the exposition with their parents could take part in gymnasium activities.[11]

By the late nineteenth century, American society had made a rapid transition in its perception of children and had a firm view of what childhood should be. It also would seem that there was a general agreement on the innocence of children and the ability to manipulate their environment to produce responsible adults. In an industrial America, it seemed obvious that children benefited from the open country environment. Their lungs were filled with fresh air, not the soot of factories. Their minds were cleared from the impressions of squalor and, by implication, sin and vice. And in the country there was wholesome work to build both body and character.

In general, there was, as with the roles of men, women, and children, societal conflict over what provided a good living environment. Cities were glorified as centers of culture and commerce, and western settlers attempted to duplicate in their new towns the eastern cities left behind. On the other hand, there was a general agreement among rural and urban dwellers alike that cities were representative of a sinful, shameful, and degrading life, whereas physical and moral health were inherent qualities of rural America. Many would have agreed with the Iowa settler who wrote in 1859, "though we often lament the want of society I could not help thinking it much better for the children to be surrounded by the works of the divine hand than to be in the false and corrupt society of this day." Over the years little changed in this attitude. Twenty-five years after the Iowa settler expressed her sentiments, a woman in Kansas noted her own sacrifices and loss of her eastern home. For her, however, the move was essential: "One and all realize that in the youth of our land lies the hope for clean, useful and good men and women, and to-day finds mothers in prairie homes, who left comfortable ones. 'We came because of the pitfalls there for our sons; temptation awaited them everywhere, and we dared not stay.' "12

Some "westerners" would have disagreed with this outlook and would have disavowed the idealization of "an agricultural surrounding . . . [being] the best preparation for adult life." One had only to point to the wickedness of some western communities or general lawlessness in isolated frontier regions to argue about moral health. There were also the harsh day-to-day realities of trying to make a home in newly settled areas. A woman writing on the Illinois frontier of 1819 observed, "I think I never realized the necessity of a life of preparation more." In agreement was another Illinois woman who saw her family's settlement as a "stern experience," the retrospect of which was "preferable to the reality." No matter the time or place, hardship and survival were recurring themes in western rural life. When her family went to Iowa in 1869, Julia Preston assumed that her new home would duplicate the one left behind. Stunned by what she faced, her thoughts turned to "the big, white house, the shady yard, the fruit trees and the level well-tilled fields. How different from this forbidding hut, with its downstairs room of rough logs, stained with water and smoke."[13]

Despite the demands of rural life, particularly on the expanding frontier, agricultural society on the whole presented to the nation "a poetic idea that defined the promise of American life." The frontier farmer was idealized, and it was held to be true that life in the west fostered independence and self-reliance. Americans were told and wanted to believe that there was a place where "family name cuts but little figure. It's the character of the man that wins recognition." Agrarian society, romanticized as classless, was believed to allow an individual to seek his or her own fortunes based on personal abilities and talents[14]—to rise as Alger's fictional characters did, by their tenacity. It was the perfect setting for the urban poor to begin over and reach their potential.

This romanticization of the pastoral life was an extension of America's westward movement. Always there had been some who reached to the edges of settlement and beyond. Under Jefferson, exploration of the vast continent had taken place, and with Jacksonian democracy the ownership of property was declared the right of free men. By mid-century the idealization of rural America reflected expansion as well as changes brought by industrialization. Growth and manufacturing may have been seen as the natural progression of things, but the financial benefits were offset by an increasing urban population, an influx of immigrants as laborers, and a litany of social ills created by industry and urbanization.

Some wondered at the outcome and reflected on the more rural America of the past—the villages, the hamlets, the honest yeoman. Others attempted to remove themselves from this new world of machines by forming utopian communities or moving to the frontiers of western settlement.

For most laborers in the east, however, removal to the west was not necessarily a viable option; such moves took capital. Numerous spokespeople and commentators on American society encouraged western emigration and resettlement of eastern workers during times of economic downturns or threatened labor unrest. Such relocation would provide a "safety valve," maintaining high wages and peaceful class relations in the urban, industrialized centers of the east.[15]

One could argue that this theory of the west as a safety valve in labor relations also served the placing out of poverty-stricken children and adults. In the short term such placement would alleviate eastern cities of costly institutional care, and in the long term it would remove those who may have become discontented, threatening urban areas with crime and violence. Those who believed that rural life could stave off a rash of social problems brought on by industrialization continued to preach the virtues of country life. It did not stop the machines, but it did reaffirm basic values, believed to be preserved in a nonurban America.

Obviously, those most affected by the worst in the urban world were those who had the least defense against it—the children of the poor. In 1848–49 an estimated ten thousand vagrant children roamed New York City; further, in eleven of that city's wards at least three thousand minors made their living by stealing. Certainly, New York was not alone in such startling numbers. Boston, for example, reported in 1850 as many as five hundred boys, between the ages of seven and eighteen, in jail. That many had been incarcerated for small offences such as selling newspapers without a license did not lessen the impact of such numbers. To comment that these children were being robbed of their "pure and sunny years of childhood" was, if anything, an understatement. Children stole, collected rags, sold newspapers or handmade flowers, begged for themselves and their families, and otherwise attempted to find ways to survive. One girl placed out by the New York Children's Aid Society in 1895, for example, recalled her life in the city as a round of going to the docks to pick coal from among the leavings. The work was backbreaking for this eleven-year-old, especially when her heavy bundles then had to be carted the long distance back home. To make ends meet, there were also those who worked in factories or sweatshops and some who sold themselves as prostitutes. They were living proof that the city was a vile, corrupt place.[16]

Their numbers and the certainty of an increase were an unsettling prospect for the city of New York, as well as for other metropolitan centers on the Eastern Seaboard. Certainly the waves of European immigrants reaching eastern cities accounted for a general increase in population, but of equal importance in numbers was the American rural population drawn to factories, trades, and shop work in the cities. This was the time of the farm girl drawn to wages in mills and garment factories, of young men and families unable to purchase land or sustain life on a farm and willing to try their luck in the city, and of a growing industrial complex that demanded cheap labor. The new city inhabitants, whether immigrant or native-born, did not necessarily come to the city poverty stricken, but the margin for survival and the line between the laboring class and the destitute was thin and too easily crossed if tragedy struck. Hard times, factory accidents, unwanted pregnancies, lost wages, illness, or the death of the family breadwinner could easily reduce one to abject poverty.

Such suffering can be measured in many ways, but a simple gauge is the number of public institutions established for the care of a destitute population. In 1825, New York State had only 4 orphan asylums; just over forty years later, in 1866, the state had 60 such institutions, both public and private, and these did not include increased numbers of almshouses, asylums for adults, or county poor farms. The situation was true all along the Eastern Seaboard, and as the western states developed, they too created their own institutions for the poor. Nationwide, numbers rose during the 1800s. When the federal government conducted a survey in 1877 of charitable organizations for children, it noted 208 orphan asylums in the United States. Also to proliferate during the century were infant asylums and hospitals and industrial schools for children and teen-agers, but the orphan asylum became the most popular form of child care in America. With the increase in these institutions came the argument that they offered "child rescue," or salvation, from an otherwise dismal life. The San Francisco Orphanage Asylum Society in 1899, for example, noted, "It is our aim that each child *we* shelter and protect may look back to the days they spent with the asylum as the happiest of their lives, for it was a home to them when they had no other" (italics in original). As this organization illustrates, asylums were not limited to eastern cities. They could be found in all sections of the country by the end of the century. Many were sponsored by church denominations, and some were for specific groups of children. Among the broad range were Baltimore's Hebrew Orphan Asylum, Philadelphia's Home for Destitute Colored Children, St. Mary's Male Orphan Asylum in Rochester, New York, and the Asylum for Orphan and Destitute Indian Children in upstate New York. Seemingly, every religion, ethnic group, and circumstance was addressed by some orphan asylum, but not always understood was the designation of "orphan." The images created by the literary orphan and the definitions given to living counterparts were often blurred in the public mind. As one writer in the 1870s pointed out, orphan asylums were not just for those completely bereft of family: "Soon the word *orphan* became expanded in its significations to include half-orphans, and later, to embrace destitute children having both parents living, many of whom were in a condition yet more unfortunate than orphanage" (italics in original). Thus, orphan asylums became refuges for destitute children, many given up by their parents or removed from homes deemed unsatisfactory by welfare officials.[17]

The majority of orphan asylums were private charities, and these attempted to supplement public institutions. Private asylums commonly indentured minors, but it was the public sector of poor relief that not only indentured but incarcerated children and teenagers for vagrancy, jailed them for small offences, and sent them to industrial schools, reformatories, or juvenile asylums—the modern-day equivalents of youth correctional facilities. Institutions were expected to offer some form of training to their charges, providing a future means for their self-support. The Hudson County Almshouse of New Jersey, for example, had such a mandate, but with only two teachers employed for over two hundred children, the effectiveness of any educational program was questionable. No matter their failings, these forms of institutionalization were considered by much of society to be improvements over eighteenth-century practices. These had allowed indenture but additionally contracted out the poor as gang labor. Also common in the 1700s was the auction of indigents to whoever would bid for their physical toil. Newton, Massachusetts, was not unusual when in 1793 and 1794 the area's poor went to public auction; of the fifty-four given over to the lowest bidder, seventeen were minors. Viewed as unenlightened by the mid-nineteenth century, auction and gang labor were dismissed, but their replacement, institutionalization on a wide scale, had its problems. Reformers worked to improve conditions, particularly in publicly funded institutions which usually had the worst reputations. By the end of the century, however, one could argue that reform and public outcry had resulted in little improvement: "Children were packed like sardines in double cradles; were cared for by pauper inmates; and were indentured to people whose credentials could hardly receive a proper investigation."[18]

There were skeptics who questioned the redeemable character of lower-class children, which may explain in part the designation of "worthy" or "deserving" for official categories of public relief. Among the worthy were the orphaned and widowed and those too old or sick to work. At the opposite end of the spectrum were the "unworthy," those labeled as able to work but too depraved by drink, laziness, or other vices to deserve assistance. These designations were subjective, even when states attempted to give them official definition. It was often difficult to decide just who was or was not a member of the class labeled as the worthy poor. Children were worthy, but many engaged in questionable petty trades. Flower selling, for example, was believed to be a common front for prostitution, although many young girls and teen-agers innocently made a small living from this trade. Some children were labeled "delinquents," but the definition could mean any child or teen-ager who habitually used profane language, frequented saloons or pool rooms, wandered "railroad yards or tracks," or who had the "idle and immoral habits of smoking cigarettes and other things." Considering the urban environment and the close proximity of the worthy poor to a criminal element, it is not surprising that many children fell in with bad company, patronized disreputable establishments, or engaged in crime. Reformers and city missionaries still believed, however, that children could be saved from their environment and its influences if reached before bad habits became chronic. As class distinctions, based on wealth, were drawn more sharply during the century, there was both denial of and belief in redemption. This attitude reached beyond stratified official discussions and into the mainstream of public thought. When a *Godey's Lady's Book* review of children's literature, for example, dealt with the book *Philly and Kit* (1856), with its slum-children characters, the reviewer wrote that it stretched the public's imagination to believe that there were "such curiosities as honest newsboys, innocent apple girls, industrious organ grinders."[19]

As a rebuttal to those who voiced doubt, social reformers and educators spoke convincingly of what could be accomplished. Charles Loring Brace, a founder of the New York Children's Aid Society, argued that these children could be productive citizens if removed from their environment of poverty and squalor. Emphatically he argued that it was to society's advantage to recognize the potential of these children. Raised in the proper setting, they would benefit themselves and society; allowed to remain where they were, they would become the next generation of parasites. Joining the chorus were Jacob Riis in *The Children of the Poor* and Kate Douglas Wiggin in *Children's Rights,* among others, who effectively presented for American society the argument that poor children shared common bonds with their middle- and upper-class counterparts. Transcending class distinctions, these children were the same in spirit. As Wiggin so touchingly described the sad attempts to duplicate society's material standards, she drew a contrast and a responsive cord: "[The kindergarten girls had] such dolls! Five cent, ten-cent dolls, dolls with soiled clothes . . . dolls made of rags, carrots, and towels." Added to this realistic representation were the often sentimentalized accounts found in the popular press, notwithstanding *Godey's* review of *Philly and Kit.* The publication *Frank Leslie's Illustrated Newspaper* often carried stories of eastern charities and the plight of the urban poor. Usually, institutionalized adults were presented as "lazy, improvident, and vicious," but the newspaper was sympathetic to the children of poverty. To its readers, *Leslie's* brought the stories of real street waifs and orphans, and in the case of a "bright little waif of the lodging-house" named Maggie the portrayal was nothing short of a miniature Madonna, comparing the child to a religious portrait by the Spanish artist Murillo.[20] There may have been those who disavowed Wiggin's practical illustration or *Leslie's* poetic portrayals, but the strong belief among many that children in an environment of poverty shared the same qualities of children in more hopeful surroundings could not be ignored by the American public.

It is not surprising then that within cultural standards and attitudes towards children and childhood, the belief in rural values and the prevailing conditions for social welfare, permanent immigration of the poor to rural areas was deemed a satisfactory, if not crucial, solution. The realities of poverty and its institutional consequences alone could have induced Charles Loring Brace and his contemporaries to consider placing out as an alternative. When the changing cultural attitudes towards childhood, as well as the importance placed on proper environment are considered, it would seem that the system was essential if children were to have the sort of childhood that would put them on the road to "right," give them a moral foundation for life, and make them productive citizens. There was acceptance of placing out, for it fulfilled several needs. It removed children from the streets, relieving public officials and private organizations from caring for the indigents. It allowed society to assure itself that children were being given an opportunity for self-improvement in a more healthful environment. It satisfied the call for labor in the west, and it gave promise of providing Christian guidance to these innocents.

In mid-nineteenth-century America, religion was a part of society, a factor in individual lives, creating the fabric of values against which Americans judged themselves. Religion was accepted, if not expected, to be inherent in everyday living, and during the 1850s a revivalist spirit swept the country. This "religious awakening . . . overwhelming every other interest,"[21] was partially a response to a new and frightening world moving towards increased mechanization and a growing political crisis with slavery and sectionalism at its core.

Work in the home and foreign mission fields—developing frontier regions were considered to be part of foreign mission work—

was supported with missionaries sent to new states and territories and to Indian groups within the continental United States. Within urban areas there were city missionaries who worked with the poor and newly arrived immigrant groups. Charities, day schools, and the very important Sunday or Sabbath schools—created for special instruction and appreciation of "God's Day"—were established for the lower classes by these city missionaries. When this religious zeal was commented on by Alexis de Tocqueville, his conclusions of the 1830s were as applicable, if not more so, in the 1850s: "[There is] no country in the whole world in which the Christian religion retains greater influence over the souls of men than in America."[22]

This concern with religious life and the support for mission work produced an expectation that Christian people would involve themselves with charitable works. Financially, church congregations, both Catholic and Protestant, supported foreign and home missionaries, and individuals gave to charitable organizations. Relying on this visible support and on the belief of duty to give aid to good causes, the placing-out system came into being.

Christian charity and the responsibility of providing children with the tools for religious living was an announced function of placing out. In fact, Brace would have said that his placing-out plan was not one of social control but of moral control, exposing children of the poor to basic Christian instruction. On an individual level this meant something as simple as providing Bibles to those being sent to new homes; in one placing-out account specific mention was made to the Bible given by a Children's Aid Society agent and still in the possession of the woman who as a toddler was brought to Kansas over seventy years ago. On the larger scale, it must be considered that the entire placing-out system relied, to a certain extent, on the charitable impulses of families who took these children into their homes. That human response was underlined as placing-out organizations involved ministers and respected citizens, and later, Catholic orders and priests, in the effort to remove children and some adults to rural locations. Indicative of the program's focus was an 1857 newspaper story that reminded its readers, "charity begins at home." Families in the northeastern Illinois towns of Aurora, Geneva, Elgin, and "other points along the railroads" were urged to open their hearts to children arriving from New York and Boston.[23] Those who took in children or found employment for placed-out adults were perceived as performing a Christian duty, and those who served as agents and promoters of the system were viewed as serving in the home-mission field.

It is not surprising that many involved in the system were ministers. The guiding hand in the system's development in America was a minister, as were many of the agents who escorted children to new homes. Women also were involved either as caretakers in orphanages or asylums, as contact persons in western communities, or as placing-out agents. Their activities generally were viewed as an extension of woman's domestic, maternal role within society. As one author stated it, women's involvement in social and charitable works was simply a reflection of the "mother instinct in the young woman."[24] Many women, restricted by society's dictates of acceptable roles, viewed this work differently, seeing it as an avenue for a career outside the home. And within the Catholic community, which had its own emigration program by the end of the nineteenth century, women as members of a religious order combined secular society's expectations of woman as nurturer with the religious demands of service and duty to fellow human beings.

The religious, charitable aspects of placing out cannot be dismissed as idealized justifications for the system. The concerns were real. The belief in doing a charitable act was accepted as a practicality, and without the religious overtones, the system would not have gained general support within American society. That Christian, charitable arguments worked hand in hand with economic realities did not constitute a deliberate attempt to gloss over a system that would later be criticized for the very Christian, decidedly Protestant, beliefs upon which it once flourished. From the beginning, the placing-out system acknowledged the economic factors that contributed to its success, and a later historian recognized that it was "evident that the problem of labor supply entered into this charity."[25]

The call for agricultural labor was ongoing as the "western" states sought to develop their commercial and agricultural potential. Here, the term "western" is illusive, for as settlement moved westward so did the boundaries. In the 1850s, however, "west" generally conjured in the eastern mind the states of the old Northwest Territory, although by mid-century settlement had opened immediately beyond the Mississippi and along the Pacific Coast. The states of the old Northwest had shed much of their primitive frontier life, but the opportunities to build and expand on agricultural and commercial enterprises were just coming into their own. Much of the agricultural economy remained subsistence family farming, and centers of commerce remained in small towns and hamlets, many of them along river routes. Changes were coming, however, with new railroads, canals, and improved roadways that opened these states' vast interiors to outside markets. As one man raved over the prospect of the Illinois-Michigan Canal, fashioned after Ohio's canal projects, "What would be the value of even the fertile Prairies of Illinois, remote from her large rivers without a canal?"[26] Improved transportation facilities expanded markets, giving farmers a reason to increase production and diversify crops for an outside market, and town entrepreneurs had an opportunity to reach a broader clientele. As importantly for the future of placing out, an urbanization of the west had begun.

One element lacking in this new growth was a supporting labor force. Farm labor, domestics, and shop help were at a premium as a mobile population moved ever westward. A common complaint in the settled regions of the old Northwest Territory was the loss of population to western emigration. People simply would not stay put, and it might be suggested that in light of the general mobility of the population, the acceptance of relocation for children is more understandable. They were just one segment of a country on the move. An Indiana newspaper in 1857, for example, noted that railroads were "daily landing passengers in our city [Indianapolis] destined for Kansas. The tide of emigration is strong. Indiana and Ohio are losing members of the better class of their population."[27]

To alleviate the lack of a permanent labor supply, some westerners called for officials of eastern cities to send workers "where labor and employment is in demand." This would benefit the country and its "development thereof." In central Illinois, newspapers observed, "The improvements in the West require more laborers than can be obtained" and acknowledged a "great demand for domestics in this region." The scarcity of women and girls for farm and domestic work was a continuing topic in the agricultural press of the 1840s and 1850s, and local newspapers commented on the need for such labor in their regions: "Thousands upon thousands of women and girls can find full and profitable employment in families in the cities and country. . . . Women who understand house-work need not be out of employment a day in the West." Ohio newspapers appealed for girls to work on farms, and in Wisconsin it was said that a hired girl could earn seventy-five cents a week, but milking and gardening were required. In Indiana it was accepted that "girls are always in demand." Seemingly the needs were so acute that local action was taken, as in the case of an Illinois merchant who traveled to New York City hoping to recruit newly arrived German girls "to come West and live in the families of Sangamon County farmers, who [were] equally in need of help." Charities also noted this need, and in 1851, Boston organizations complained that in numerous adoptions, "the real motive for taking girls [was] to make servants of them rather than daughters." The desire for female labor was not short-lived. When the black migration into Kansas began in the late 1870s, one woman wrote the state's governor, "I wish to get one of those colored refugees to help about housework would prefer one from twelve to fifteen years old." Later, in 1915, a state-supported orphanage in Kansas noted, "The majority of people who take girls from here only take them for domestics." Still, the complaint persisted that "the unending problem of the home life . . . [was] that of obtaining adequate assistance in the performance of household work."[28]

According to some, the lack of domestics was not just a matter of having another helping hand. It was a matter of life or death. The absence of help, especially for the farm wife, was blamed for the early deaths of women who had to shoulder too much of a burden. Commenting on these circumstances was a woman who wrote to a Nebraska newspaper:

> *In most instances the wife with a family of children needs hired help fully as much as does the farmer for his work. . . . If there is a mountain of housework to be reduced by her hands unaided, she must of necessity neglect the work of child-training or exhaust the energy which she should have laid up for years to come. How many others have gone to an early grave, who might have lived in health and usefulness if they had not tried to do the work of two or three women.*[29]

The need for adult labor was a recurring theme, but boys and girls could serve just as well. Here it might be expected that social pronouncements for the perfect childhood and the child as laborer would clash. In fact, there was little debate when it came to child labor on the farm; sentimental values assigned to childhood coexisted with the positive perception of the child as a "productive" contributor to the farm family's interests and needs. As one historian of childhood in the far west has noted, "[On] the farmer's frontier, children worked at every stage and at every task of production, from the first assaults on the land to bringing in the crops."[30]

This could be said for children in the rural economy as a whole and generally applies to those who were at home with parents. The worth of a child's labor was recognized, on the family farm it was a necessity, and within the concept of a childhood it was accepted that such work would create responsible adults.

Before the advent of placing out, child farm laborers in families other than their own came from few sources. Some were local orphans or the destitute who were indentured by their guardians, local orphanages, or the courts to farmers or tradesmen. In Hamilton County, Illinois, for example, a woman indentured her son and later petitioned for a court reversal when she became able to care for him, and from 1839 to 1850 seven orphaned children were indentured by the courts in Sangamon County, Illinois. In a time when there were few choices in the care of the unfortunate, indenture was a respectable alternative and certainly preferable to the spectacle of impoverished children or young adults trying to eke out a life for themselves. As an accepted custom, the legal mechanics for indenture were carried with westward emigration. Ohio, the first area of the Northwest Territory to become a state, borrowed its early poor-relief legislation from eastern statutes, particularly those of Massachusetts. Ohio laws were later copied by Michigan and Illinois, and these in turn were borrowed by Wisconsin and Iowa as they achieved statehood. With each newly created legislative body, indenture was considered an accepted practice. Among the first laws of Kansas Territory, for example, were those that dealt with the right to bind out as "apprentices" the destitute and orphaned. Borrowing what they knew of indenture laws in their home states, territorial legislators in 1855 decreed that such apprentices were to be given a basic education and had the right to appeal to the courts if badly treated; one sobering note to the law, introduced by the territory's southern contingent familiar with slaveholder prerogative, was the acquittal of anyone who committed homicide in the process of "correcting" an apprentice.[31]

Another source of child labor in rural communities was the "rented" child. Parents in dire straits took this option. Unlike those who were indentured, rented children were sent to farmers or tradesmen and the parents took the child's wages until he or she reached the age of majority. In a rural community, however, the labor pool of rented or indentured children was never large, as illustrated by the only seven indentures in an eleven-year span in Sangamon County. This was true even when cities of the "urban frontier" endured calamities that resulted in a rise in the orphaned population: Chicago, as an example, suffered six successive years of cholera epidemics from 1849 through 1856, leaving a number of orphans who were placed in rural homes "where labor was scarce." Children were used as they were available, but the complaint still could be heard that crops were standing in the fields "from lack of laborers to gather it."[32]

These conditions persisted as the territories beyond the Mississippi were settled, became states, and saw major migrations of North American–born and immigrant populations. Kansas, which became a state in 1861, with a population of about one hundred thousand, had by 1875 a population of over five hundred thousand. The Homestead Act of 1862, the sale of railroad lands, and other congressional acts that encouraged land claims provided a means for gaining cheap farms and ranches. The panic of 1873, the grasshopper plague of 1874, and droughts could not displace those determined to stay, and despite the hardships the state saw its wheat crop increase from over 2 million bushels in 1870 to over 13 million in 1875. Corn harvests more than quadrupled during the same period. Kansas certainly was not alone. Similar adversities and patterns of growth could be found throughout the central and southern plains.[33]

The new western states saw a concentration on specific crops. In the 1870s hard winter wheat was introduced into Kansas, and by 1900 harvests had become so large that threshing outfits were shipped into the state from Illinois and Iowa. At the time it was estimated that twenty thousand men were needed to bring in the bountiful crop. Wheat was a staple of Nebraska farming also, but that state saw an emphasis on sugar beet production, with the state offering a bounty to farmers who turned over their acreage to this commodity. The crop was introduced in the 1880s and by 1922, eighty-eight thousand acres, with a yield of 12.12 tons per acre, were in sugar beet production. Many of those harvesting this crop were children working with their families as migrant laborers.[34] These little "helping hands" were in fact critical to the sugar beet industry, and the need for additional labor was so great that the Standard Cattle Company in Ames, Nebraska, hit upon a scheme early in the 1900s to use child labor taken from state institutions. Writing to Kansas Governor William Stanley, a vice-president of the Nebraska company inquired:

> *In the maintenance of a very large agricultural proposition at this point including a sugar factory and 12,000 acres of land, we can at times use children to very good advantage, either boys or girls. I can make arrangements for young girls so that they will be amply protected and taken care of. If you will be so kind as to refer this letter to some official who can furnish me a list of State charitable institutions so that I can correspond directly, I shall be grateful.*[35]

The governor's reply is not extant, but the suggestion underscores the acceptance of tapping a potential labor force—minors under the guardianship of state charities and, one may presume, also those under the care of private organizations.

Agriculture in the central plains could be productive. Certainly the introduction of mechanized farm equipment and improved farm implements aided this production and reduced some need for hand labor, but mechanization did not eliminate the need for farm workers. The sheer numbers of acres in production and the tonage of crops harvested accentuated the continuing need for a farm labor force that was not always in immediate supply. In these once-frontier states, boys and girls could still serve as farmhands and as domestics, and placing out used the demand to send "future laborers where they [were] in demand [relieving] the overcrowded market in the city."[36]

Encouraging increased farm production and emigration were the railroads, which by their development and growth in the 1850s proved an economic boon to the nation. Eastern manufacturers that had once shipped goods west by water or overland routes could transport materials much more quickly by rail, and the western farmer had a means of shipping commodities to urban centers. The significant impact of the railroad in American life led one writer in the 1880s to comment, "To-day, easy transportation makes regions populous and wealthy, which once were uninhabitable."[37]

With rail development came the promise of new settlers, and emigration was actively encouraged by rail companies anxious to sell their railroad lands and gain the increase in freight that would follow when new farms and towns had grown up along their routes. Among the promoters for new settlement was the Illinois Central, which was successful in its use of advertisements and agents in New England to bring colonies of extended families and town populations to farms along its route. Also attracting settlers to their railroad lands in central and eastern Illinois were the Great Western Railroad and the Chicago and Alton. The same patterns of railroad promotion could be found west of the Mississippi after the Civil War, when the Union Pacific and the Atchison, Topeka & Santa Fe, among others, launched major promotional campaigns for foreign emigration: in Kansas alone, the Santa Fe is credited for the Scandinavian, German, and Mennonite populations that came to the state beginning in the 1870s, and in Nebraska the same ethnic groups could be found settling along railroad lands. Advertisements, in many languages, and railroad agents in foreign lands painted glorious pictures of America's heartland and offered discounted rates to prospective settlers. These discounts extended beyond the price of a ticket, as the five major railroads of the Western Trunk-Line Association had rolling stock labeled specifically as "emigrant cars" and offered special rates for "emigrant movables" such as household goods, farm implements, and a limited number of livestock. Aiding the railroads were state boosters who published guidebooks meant to lure prospective settlers to a particular region. These guides provided grand descriptions of farm opportunities and, as in the case of a Nebraska publication, gave explicit rail routings from the East Coast, Chicago, and St. Louis.[38]

Promotion of railroad lands and the accommodations given to new settlers assured increased land development and farm production, as well as town settlement with the attendant services. The rail companies, with a vested interest in agricultural success, also aided by shipping trees into the plains states, introducing new strains of crop seeds and, in the case of the Burlington, the Union Pacific, and the Atchison, Topeka & Santa Fe, spreading the word of "scientific farming" through a variety of educational programs. Railroads revolutionized "the prevailing social and economic practices of the day,"[39] creating new markets, new communities, and new demands for labor to build upon the promising opportunities.

As importantly, expanded rail service had a direct impact on the existing forms of indigent and orphan care typical of the time. As long as rail lines were limited, any attempts to transport the eastern poor to rural communities was confined to in-state placements or nearby areas with rail service. If a venture farther afield was planned, costly and time-consuming overland or river travel was necessary and an unacceptable option. The coincidence of rail expansion in the 1850s with a plan to send the urban poor to country homes assured such a plan's success.

Writing of an early placing-out experience in which an "emigrant" car carried children to Michigan, a New York Children's Aid

Society agent was less than happy with the public conveyance: "At the depot we worked our way through the Babel of one thousand Germans, Irish, Italians, and Norwegians, with whom nothing goes right." Evidently not much went right for the agent either. Once on the train the situation was worse, at least from his point of view. "Irishmen passed around bad whiskey and sang bawdy songs; Dutch men and women smoked and sang, and grunted and cursed; babies squalled and nursed, and left no baby duties undone." From the report it is difficult to decide if the agent was appalled for the sake of the children under his charge or for himself sitting elbow to elbow with the immigrant masses. In fact, the agent found himself in a peculiar situation. The placed out more often traveled in cars reserved just for them, but on this occasion none had been available.

A somewhat happier experience, and one that highlights the important role of railroads in this enterprise, is an account from an agent for the New England Home for Little Wanderers. Traveling to northern Illinois in 1869, a company of thirty children began their route "by the Vermont Central, Ogdensburg and Lake Champlain, Grand Trunk and Michigan Central Railroads. Seven sections of a sleeping car were reserved for [them] by the Vt. Central, and every attention paid to [their] wants by the conductors of the train." When bad weather seemed to assure missed connections, the agent was highly gratified that "the gentlemanly conductor of the Michigan Central held his train at the junction for more than one hour and this enabled [them] to reach Chicago at midnight Saturday."[40]

These groups, like other companies of settlers, received discounted rates. One historian has written that railroads withdrew their offer of reduced rates in the 1860s and 1870s, and that may have been true of some rail lines. However, with the onslaught of settlement west of the Mississippi after the Civil War, it is unlikely that lines such as the Santa Fe or Union Pacific withdrew that option just at the time when they were encouraging mass emigration to western regions. There is also evidence that at least some eastern rail lines continued to generously serve the placing-out system into the twentieth century. It was not until 1906, for example, that the board of the New England Home for Little Wanderers received notice from the New York, New Haven and Hartford Railroad that reduced fares no longer would be available; the federal government's more stringent enforcement of interstate commerce acts made continuing accommodations impossible.[41]

In 1850 there were 9,021 miles of track in the United States; by 1875 there were 74,096; and by the end of the century, the number had increased to 192,556 miles, with 1,224 operating railways.[42] Placement of the eastern poor corresponded directly to expanding rail service. First limited to the eastern states with rail connections to metropolitan centers, placing out was extended in the mid-1850s to states of the old Northwest Territory with their growing miles of rails. When railroad companies began to build west of the Mississippi after the Civil War, these regions drew the attention of placing-out institutions. Increased miles of track, moving ever west, south, and southwest, allowed the transport of the eastern poor farther along the line, and railroad hubs such as Chicago, St. Louis, and Kansas City became the staging grounds from which the placed out, brought that far, could be sent to final destinations. As one man, seventy-two years after his placing out experience, recalled: "We boarded the . . . train somewhere close to New York City [in 1915]. The train had four coaches with about 40 orphans each. In St. Louis, Missouri, the train was divided and the coaches went to four different states, Kansas, Missouri, Oklahoma, and Arkansas. My coach went to Berryville, Ark."[43]

Railroads moved the country west, and among those emigrants to travel the rail lines were the children of the poor. They went to rural communities and to farm homes where life was believed to be pure and the work fundamental to building mind and body. As one commentator in the early 1900s noted, "That the farm home is an ideal place in which to build up the lives of growing boys and girls has become almost a trite saying."[44] It was, however, accepted as truth. Resettlement of the eastern poor was to provide them the advantages that society said children should have. Emigration from eastern cities would save them, make them respectable men and women, and would in the long term benefit society by depleting the mass of urban destitute. This was the object of placing out, the great crusade of nineteenth-century America, and leading the way for this system of resettlement was the New York Children's Aid Society.

CHAPTER 2

A Plan for "Little Wanderers"

They put us all on a big platform in some big building while people came from all around the countryside to pick out those of us they wished to take home. I was four years old, and my sister was only two. . . . It was a nice train ride, and we were fed mustard and bread during the trip. —Margaret Braden, placed out in South Dakota, 1914, from "Orphan Train Sisters Find Good Parents"

*P*LACING OUT in America was given form by Charles Loring Brace. Born in 1826, Brace was the product of nineteenth-century values and of old New England traditions. His family was comfortable in its financial and social status, and Brace grew up in Hartford, Connecticut. There he was influenced by the sermons of the renowned theologian Horace Bushnell who believed in the naturalness, the "unconscious influences," of child rearing, deemphasizing the use of threats and coercion in the shaping of a child's character. Bushnell also may have played a role in Brace's decision to become a minister. Graduated from Yale in 1846, Brace then attended the Yale Divinity School and the Union Theological Seminary, but after completing his education, Brace was not sure that a church ministry should be his calling. He leaned toward missionary work and had his first introduction to life as a city missionary at

New York City's Five Points Mission. That experience was of great importance to Brace's career, and he maintained ties to that institution and the Five Points district after leaving to become instrumental in founding the New York Children's Aid Society in 1853.[1]

With the Aid Society as the vehicle, Brace devoted his life to working with the poor. His contributions were many and during his lifetime his tireless efforts brought him recognition as an urban reformer. Brace also received some measure of notice for his writings, whose topics ranged from his experiences among the lower classes to analyses of life in foreign lands and ancient civilizations. One theme that held a particular fascination for him was the evolution of civilization, or perhaps more accurately, the forces that led a civilization from one step of development and culture to another. Because of this interest, Brace was a student of the theories of Charles Darwin and greatly admired this man, whom he came to know. Seemingly Brace was intrigued by the implications of Social Darwinism, and, as evidenced by his *Dangerous Classes of New York,* believed that society could be greatly changed, if not brought down, by a growing poverty class. As Brace's writings illustrate, he did not follow the school of evolutionists that argued for "natural" events to take their course. Brace disavowed survival of the fittest. Rather, he was convinced that society could create artificial social structures for improving the lives of the poor, and he sided with the evolutionists who argued for intervention programs that would change and benefit all society.[2]

Brace was convinced that just as humans had developed through an evolutionary process, their behavior could evolve, and be shaped, for the good. There was one qualifying point, however. After becoming a city missionary and working with adults at Five Points and later New York's Blackwell's Island, with its penitentiary and workhouse, Brace became convinced that any effort "to reform adults was well-nigh hopeless." He therefore directed his energies to the salvation of children. His life's work produced numerous social-welfare programs, and by 1894 the New York Children's Aid Society supported forty-five major activities in New York City and its environs. Included among these projects were twenty-two industrial schools; six lodging houses (five for boys, one for girls); a farm school; and a children's summer home on Long Island. These accomplishments, which gave help and support to many thousands of young lives, have been overshadowed by Brace's best known legacy—placing out.[3]

Although Brace later wrote of placing out as if no other person but he or any other country but America had used the system, it was an imported idea. Indeed, he was not the only American to have an interest in the system's possibilities. At least two contemporaries are known to have considered placing out as an option for dealing with the urban poor. Robert M. Hartley, of the New York Association for Improving the Condition of the Poor, and John Earl Williams, of the Boston Children's Mission, advocated the system; the association with which Hartley was involved established the New York Juvenile Asylum, a later advocate of placing out, and Williams was to become treasurer for the New York Children's Aid Society. In fact, the Boston Children's Mission, founded in 1849 and incorporated in 1864, began a modest in-state placement program under the direction of Williams in 1850. It was Charles Loring Brace, however, who gave the concept definition in America.[4]

What these men idealized was a theory for removing the urban poor to the less populated and more rural areas of the country. Abstractly, they viewed placing out as a solution. They might personalize their arguments with sad human examples, but they were in fact creators of a particular view of what should be done with the poor, and more often expressed concern in terms of the immediate effect of the poor on society. Familiar with traditional forms of charitable support, they knew that from the Colonial period children and adults had been indentured and that the institutionalized were commonly used as farm laborers to earn their keep. They shared a belief in the code, "labor is elevating and idleness is sinful." Additionally, these men seemed to have little concept of life in the expanding west. Brace's writings point to an idealized view of rural life, not unlike that expressed in popular thought. Supposedly the unlatched door of the country home offered hospitality to friend or stranger, and class or circumstance of birth had little meaning. The rigors of frontier life evidently went unrecognized, and as importantly, these city reformers seemed blissfully ignorant of the urbanization of western cities such as Cincinnati, Indianapolis, St. Louis, and Chicago. No longer frontier outposts, these were by the 1850s centers for commerce and transportation. Equally ignored was the far west, with its influx of emigrants, gold seekers, and entrepreneurs. Brace and his contemporaries certainly were aware of westward expansion but seemed oblivious to the growth of cities like San Francisco, which established its first orphan asylum in 1851, in part to house children orphaned on the Overland Trail.[5] Instead, the focus of these men centered on eastern cities, and their romantic notions of the west remained steadfast.

Those who considered the idea of placing out were well aware of established forms for assisting the poor. Brace and his colleagues simply added a new dimension. It is quite possible that Brace shaped his ideas while on a trip to Europe in 1850. At that time he toured England's "ragged" schools, which were based on the principle of reform rather than simple incarceration of children, a revolutionary idea for the times. No doubt Brace and contemporaries were already familiar with this work, but for Brace the experience of seeing programs in action allowed for a formulation of strategy. Also, Brace could not have failed to learn more about the British system of "transportation," a well-known practice used as far back as the early 1700s. Under this system the country's less desirable citizens were shipped to North America, Capetown, and

Australia. Initially, transportation was a punishment whereby convicted felons were removed from their home country. By the time Brace saw the system, a new component had been added. Along with convicts, the poor, particularly women and children, were being resettled. The government transported many and gave approval to the British Ladies' Female Emigrant Society to send more women out of country. The frontiers of the Empire needed labor, and in some cases prospective wives for male settlers. Transportation became a way to supply that demand. Children and women were sent successfully to Canada and Australia, and at least one foray was made into the United States when London's Home and Refuge for Destitute Children, in 1869, resettled twenty-one boys to the English colony of Wakefield, Kansas. In addition to what Brace saw in England, he encountered another form of relocation in the German states. There he observed a program established by prominent citizens, known as "The Friends in Need," which placed vagrant city children with rural families. He also may have come into contact with the work of Pastor Andreas Bram, which did the same thing in Neukirchen, Germany. Bram's work was inspired by his sermon text "The Christian Family-Parlour is the Best Reformatory," a theme not unlike that taught by Bushnell.[6] It seems that Brace borrowed the basic idea of supplying labor while at the same time removing the destitute from high population centers, and tailored this to American society, sending thousands of children to experience life in the West.

The New York Children's Aid Society was not founded with the sole purpose of instituting placing out. Brace actually hoped that the organization could improve conditions for children in the city. Because of his involvement with placing out, Brace was sometimes labeled as anti-urban, but today he is rightfully viewed as a reformer who hoped to teach survival in the urban world. For Brace, and many of his contemporaries, resettlement in the West was only one alternative in offering aid to the poverty class. Constructive protection and education of children within the city was of major importance, and one of Brace's first concerns was providing safe shelters for the city's newspaperboys. Thus, lodging houses were established, with the boys learning self-help by paying, when they could, a small fee. Brace spent days on the streets rounding up "little laborers" to offer them safe harbor. What he witnessed in these wanderings was most troubling, and in attempting to meet the horrific needs that he saw, the Aid Society established its industrial schools, kindergartens, night schools, sanitariums, and summer homes. These were means by which children's lives could be improved through self-help and the development of character, the principles on which Brace based his philosophies for elevating individual lives and the general well-being of society. In one of the Aid Society's first circulars, Brace developed his thoughts in a four-point statement of purpose: "Individual influences and home life as better than institutional life"; "Lessons of industry and self-help as better than alms"; "The implanting of moral and religious truths in union with the supply of bodily wants"; and "Entire change of circumstances as the best cure for the defects of children of the lowest poor."[7]

As a Christian and a missionary dedicated to his calling, Brace believed that it was impossible to see the circumstances of the children of the poor and not do something. And, like most missionaries, Brace was sure that no reform was possible for individuals or society unless religion played a part. Poverty itself was not a sign of individual moral failure, but to defeat the cycle of destitution and general moral decay in the cities, a religious awakening had to occur. Brace called for public support of the Aid Society's endeavors, arguing, "As Christian men we cannot look upon this great multitude of unhappy, deserted, and degraded boys and girls without feeling our responsibility to God for them."[8]

The plea for Christian charity went hand in hand with a warning. Brace's writings, whether a society circular or his notable book,

The Dangerous Classes of New York, paired charity with the caution that these children, left unattended, would some day threaten society. "The class increases; immigration is pouring in its multitude of poor foreigners, who leave these young outcasts everywhere in our midst," warned Brace. "These boys and girls," he wrote, "will soon form the great lower class of our city [and] if unreclaimed, [will] poison society all around them." The solution was "a means of draining the city of this class." Brace certainly had real concern for what happened to the children of the city, but his writings went beyond a simple appeal for help. Harking back to what Brace believed about social evolution, there was a desire to impose control over the possible ramifications of a growing underclass. Thus, Brace asked that support, financial and spiritual, be given the Aid Society to "drain" the potential threat. Meanwhile, he began the process "by communicating with farmers, manufacturers, or families who may have need of [child] employment."[9]

In 1853 the Aid Society began to send some teen-agers to jobs with "manufacturers" in Connecticut, New Jersey, and Massachusetts. The work included such trades as manufacturing, which was usually mill work, and printing. Receiving much more emphasis was farm placement, with the first attempts being cautious expeditions to upper New York State. The success of these early placements encouraged Brace, and in the society's first annual report, published in 1854, he proudly announced: "We have thus far sent off to homes in the country, or to places where they could earn an honest living, 164 boys and 43 girls, of whom some 20 were taken from prison, where they had been placed for being homeless on the streets." After these first placements, children soon went to Pennsylvania and Rhode Island, and a few placements were made in the upper New England states of Maine, Vermont, and New Hampshire.[10]

From the beginning, some of the placed out were removed from institutions such as asylums and prisons. Some were taken off city streets or docks. Others, learning of the program or having been in contact with the Aid Society through its lodging houses, volunteered for resettlement. There were also poverty-stricken parents who turned their children over to the Aid Society with the hope that a home outside the city would give their children a better life.

Aware of the need for laborers in western states, the Aid Society organized more groups, and within two years Ohio, Michigan, Indiana, and Illinois were receiving children from the New York Children's Aid Society. The first group to arrive in a state of the old Northwest Territory traveled in March 1854 to Dowagiac, Michigan, escorted by Aid Society agent the Reverend E. P. Smith. The choice of Dowagiac, a "struggling village only six years old," as the first site for western placement has no explanation other than the presence of transportation, the Michigan Central Railroad, and the evident need for farm labor in this land, where settlement homes were compared to "rock eggs on the desert sand." From this rather inauspicious first settlement, Michigan continued to receive the eastern poor, sharing with Ohio, Indiana, Illinois, Iowa, Missouri, and Kansas approximately 90 percent of those resettled by the Children's Aid Society.[11]

Placing out was seemingly simple. "Little companies," consisting of between five to thirty children, were organized. With an adult leader, an Aid Society agent, they were then taken to rural communities. The manner of placement was a selection process, overseen by the agent, with families or "employers" choosing from among the group of children. Accounts from those placed out and Aid Society reports name a number of places in which this selection process took place. Always it was a commodious setting, usually the largest the town had to offer, since room had to be made for the children and their prospective families or employers. Often the setting contained a stage or raised dais. Therefore, among the first impressions children had of their new community was the interior of the train depot, a local church, city hall, school, opera house, or the county courthouse. A scene reported in Hebron, Nebraska, had been repeated time and again in countless other towns. When twenty-two children arrived in the winter of 1890, a local church was packed to capacity with townspeople and farmers. Of the children, the town's paper noted, "There was not a dull, apathetic boy in the lot [but] the greatest contest was for the possession of a sweet-faced, modest girl of 14. There were as many as a dozen wanted her."[12]

As accounts of the process attest, the children's first reactions to this placing-out experience were personal and individual. Arriving in Benton County, Arkansas, one boy recalled: "We were taken from the train to the Methodist Church. Speeches were made and folks were asked to take an orphan home for dinner. Later that afternoon we were brought back for the selection process. . . . I felt sorry for the others because some of them were not chosen. I know now how it must have hurt them to feel that no one wanted them." Some certainly suffered the pain of being overlooked in the first encounter, but at least one placed-out boy took matters into his own hands and chose his new family when he reached Arkansas. He would not allow himself to be taken by just anyone: "I refused to go home with two different farmers . . . but I was fortunate I did not. The two boys the farmers adopted were hardly more than slaves to them. . . . Everyone seemed to think I was a very bad character and I was left alone on stage that day alone, with no place to go. . . . A 60 year old couple heard about me and . . . persuaded me to go home with them. . . . as it turned out, I had the best home of all the orphans I had come with."

Agents sometimes coached children in ways to make themselves more appealing, but an account of a 1910 experience in Missouri is somewhat unusual in that it records a sort of show-and-tell, with the children expected to perform: "Each one had a little act. It was like a show. One boy told jokes and did acrobatic tricks." The selection process could be humiliating and bewildering. One boy sent to Missouri later recalled feeling as if he were part of a slave auction, with farmers inspecting muscles for farm labor, and a girl sent to the same state remembered, "The man that chose me kept encouraging me to go to his wife, but I didn't like her. So I bit her."[13] From such beginnings the children of the poor found homes in new communities and began what the Aid Society hoped would be a fresh start on life.

The selection process was the standard placement procedure, but there were variations. Some of those sent to country homes knew in advance who was to "employ" them. These were older boys and girls whose labor was requested via mail or telegram to the Aid Society. By the turn of the century a number of boys were receiving agricultural training at the Brace Farm School, established in 1894 in Valhalla, New York. Clearly they were preparing themselves for rural employment. A graduate of the school, sent to Beaver Crossing, Nebraska, wrote that he was happy with his farm work, but observed: "I would like [it] if more of the boys would come out here, but if they are sent they must bear in mind that they got to work and work hard. There are no holidays here nor can they quit work at 4.30 like they do at the Farm School." These workers were placed out, but as with young men who reported $18.00 to $30.00 per month from farm wages in Nebraska at the turn of the century, it was understood that they would be receiving pay for their labor. The laborers were not indentured, but the distinction between being a laborer versus a member of the family was understood. This was the circumstance for two brothers who had gone to the Brace Farm School in 1911 after the deaths of their parents. Sent to Northwood, Iowa, in 1913, they did not work out with their new employer and were removed to other homes of employment in Pratt, Kansas.[14]

Another variation occurred when individuals who wished to adopt a child contacted the Aid Society or other New York organizations directly. Rather than wait for a group of children to arrive in their town or being too far off the track to have the opportunity to select a child, these individuals acted on their own initiative. One example is Henry Kuhn, who during the 1880s served as an Indian agent in Indian Territory (present-day Oklahoma). Evidently he had heard of the program but was unsure of whom to contact. So, as a former newspaperman, he wrote another, Whitelaw Reid of the *New York Tribune*, who had sponsored at least eleven emigration parties containing children taken largely from the Aid Society's lodging houses.

> *I have a family consisting of wife and two grown daughters and would like to get a boy and girl to raise and give them a home, where they will be cared for and trained to habits of industry and a good english education assured them.*
>
> *If you will be kind enough to inform me if there is still an organized plan either under the auspices of the "Tribune" or other wise of sending orphan children to homes in the west and what is required of persons desiring to take such, I will be glad to respond and can refer you to Senator Ingalls of Kansas—Col. D. R. Anthony, "Leav. [Leavenworth, Kansas] Times."*[15]

The placement process was also diverse in that some of the placed out traveled alone, not in companies. This was especially true if they were to go to a requesting family, such as that of Henry Kuhn, if they were older boys and girls, or if they had been engaged by an employer prior to their arrival. Such a case was that of Harry Colwell, who came to Leonardville, Kansas, when a farmer there contacted the Aid Society. Colwell traveled with a society group and agent as far as Chicago, but once there he was on his own to make rail connections in St. Louis and Kansas City.[16]

Early in the system, there were a few instances of groups making at least part of their journey by boat or horse-drawn conveyance— in one circumstance the placing agent hired a sleigh in Indiana when snows blocked the rail line. These forms of travel had their limitations, however. Children became seasick and overland transportation other than rail cars was costly. Therefore, companies soon went exclusively by train; any delays were waited out. The adult leader would debark the children at points along the rail route and place the children in homes. If all were not taken in one place, those remaining would ride to the next stop, and so on, until all of the children had been placed. Brace himself did not travel with these groups. Rather, adults, many of them clergy, served as agents. It is obvious, however, from agent reports that Brace knew many of the children being placed out, at least during the program's early years. When an agent's report referred to a child by name, it was assumed that Brace knew of the child being mentioned. Brace used these reports and agent accounts in the society's annual reports, and in reading these one comes away with mixed views. It is apparent that the agents were pleased with their successes and were dedicated to their mission. The accounts of children gathered up in New York and sent west also presents a disturbing mental picture: a street cleaner rolling along, picking up children in its wake and then those children being packed off on a train to a place of which they, and possibly Brace, had never heard. Brace and those working with him, Aid Society "visitors," did in the early years scour the streets for likely placement prospects. This form of operation changed rather quickly, however, as the Aid Society learned from experience, streamlined the process, and began to work with other charities and institutions in the resettlement of the poor.

Although it was intended that the society would keep track of the children placed out, during the early days of the system some children were rather haphazardly left with whoever expressed an interest. Sometimes an agent sought a local contact to screen applicants for children beforehand or to set up a local arrangements committee, but there were concerns that the local contacts were perhaps "too easily influenced" by prospective employers who offered a "gift" for gaining first choice from among the little laborers.

Additionally, follow-up visitations were casual, if they occurred at all. During its early years, the Aid Society relied almost exclusively on correspondence, not visitation, to keep track of the placed out and to learn of their new home conditions. This proved unreliable and the society lost contact with many children or failed to transfer those in unsatisfactory homes. One could argue that with the numbers being resettled—in the forty-year period between 1853 and 1893 a reported 84,318 children were placed out—the probability of keeping an accounting of all was near impossible. Some were returned to parents and others to institutions, but of those who remained in new areas, not all could be accounted for. That proved true in many instances, as the records for Kansas placements illustrate. The first group of Aid Society children arrived in Kansas in 1867, brought that far as railroad lines moved west. By 1893, placements numbered 960 in the state. Of this number, despite the society's claims of careful correspondence checks and visitations, 94 could be listed only as "whereabouts unknown." Such situations were of concern to the society, and there were attempts to maintain a more responsible accounting.[17]

From its trial placements, the Aid Society and its agents learned to establish planned destinations with advance advertising of a group's arrival. It became the agents' duty to "travel through remote farming districts, and discover where there is an especial call for children's labor." This may explain why the Reverend James McLaughlin, a graduate of Illinois College in Jacksonville and a student at Brace's alma mater, the Union Theological Seminary, returned to central Illinois in 1860 to deposit many of his charges. It was an area with which he was familiar and where he was known to the local community. His visits were reported on approvingly by the local press, which noted that the Aid Society was "rapidly becoming a favorite organ of Christian philanthrophy and benevolent enterprise." McLaughlin preceded his visits with newspaper advertisements that stated: "If any of our readers . . . desire to get boys who will render them valuable service on their farms, they now have the opportunity." In addition, McLaughlin promised, "I will bring *no bad* children with me" (emphasis in original).[18]

The image becomes one of persons, unknown and uninvestigated, showing up at a train station or town hall to cart off a child to a new home. Those situations existed, although the society attempted to be more responsible and organized in its placement process. On a practical level, the system did not work as well if agents had no "local arrangements" person or committee to advertise arrivals and to screen applicants for children. Therefore, local committees were given the responsibility of announcing impending arrivals, interviewing prospective families or employers, and notifying the society of children who had to be removed from their new homes. The composition of the local delegations varied from community to community. Whereas committee responsibilities in Burlington, Kansas, were taken on by the local bank, the Howard, Kansas, committee was made up of nine men, one of them a minister. No matter how the locals chose to form a group, the duties were taken seriously. Knowing their areas, committees made concerted efforts to advertise well in advance of society placements. This allowed farmers in outlying areas to plan for a trip to town. And, through local newspapers, prospective receiving families were reminded, "Those desiring boys [must] send in their names to the committee early."[19] The local committees, however, had no concrete guidelines for what constituted an acceptable home. The Aid Society implicitly expected that a child's new home would provide a good Christian environment, but willingness to take a child seemed the only practical requirement. Thus, children were placed in two-parent families—some with children, others that were childless—with single women, and bachelor farmers or tradesmen. A committee's decision for placement, therefore, varied from community to community, with local values and knowledge of the persons applying for a child deciding which homes would receive Aid Society children.

Local involvement no doubt contributed to a more congenial atmosphere when children arrived in a community. It brought an air of responsibility to the local citizenry. Those who served on the local committees were viewed as publicly accountable, although they had no legal power for overseeing the treatment and living conditions of the newly placed children. There was, however, a vested interest in seeing that these child emigrants were well treated. If the committee did not do its job or if numerous complaints of abuse reached the Aid Society, the society could send these badly needed laborers elsewhere. This did not always assure that each of the placed out received the best of care. Many did not. Such a possibility, however, did impose a certain amount of responsibility on the receiving community.

The sum of all aspects of the system were glowingly detailed in an 1873 popular magazine story written by Brace:

> *On a given day in New York the ragged and dirty little ones are gathered to a central office from the streets and lanes . . . are cleaned and dressed, and sent away, under charge of an experienced agent. . . . When they arrive in the village a great public meeting is held, and a committee of citizens formed to decide on the applications. Farmers come in from twenty to twenty-five miles, looking for the "model boy" who shall do the light work of the farm. . . ; childless mothers seek children to replace those that are lost; housekeepers look for girls to train up; mechanics seek for boys for their trades. . . . Thus in a few hours the little colony is placed in comfortable homes. . . . If changes should be necessary, the committee replace the children, or the agent revisits the village, while a steady correspondence is kept up by the central office with the employers.*[20]

Twentieth-century placing-out accounts sometimes mention experiences occurring just prior to train embarkation. These support, with variations, the general picture painted by Brace and provide some additional details. Sent to Nebraska at the age of four, one man recalled the Aid Society as "a great, monstrous building." There his group was gathered, as Brace said children were, but at least in this particular instance there were no beds. Those about to be relocated slept on the floor. Another child, sent to Nebraska in 1900, recalled: "We all had that outfit [new clothes resembling a uniform] and we were all in one room each one taken separately for the picture." How common a picture-taking session might have been is difficult to decide, but this girl's further account brings into focus some mundane, but necessary, departure preparations. This girl's hair, and one may assume that of others, was cut very short. Brace did not provide such particulars for his readers, but it is likely that the cleaning and dressing referred to served other purposes besides giving a fresh, new look; baths, haircuts, and clean clothes disposed of lice and other body parasites. Remembering the overall scene of preparation, this same Nebraska-bound girl wrote: "We were a noisy bunch, and the house mother was very patient with us. I don't think we knew where we were going, just a happy crowd of children, tho' the older ones cried."[21]

Once the placed out reached their destinations, correspondence was, as Brace assured the public, an integral part of the system. Children were encouraged to write to the society, as were the receiving families. In 1871, the Aid Society's assistant secretary, J. Macy, estimated that annually he wrote from eight to ten thousand letters and received about two thousand pieces of correspondence in return from children or their employers or new families. These letters served to mark the child's progress in his or her new home: "I have a good mother and father. . . . I am learning a lot. . . . When I came [to Iowa] I did not know how to take the halter off the pony and did not know how to harness or hitch up a horse. I do now."

Many letters were chatty descriptions: "I am going to tell you every thing about my new home in Illinois. Illinois is a very pretty place. I live in the northern part of the state, in Ogle County, a town of Byron." Other correspondence served as affirmations of the rightness of placing out: "I will tell you I was glad to get out here [Missouri]." Although one placed-out girl later remembered that the Aid Society strongly warned against writing to friends or family left behind, early letters published by the society indicate that there was contact: "I do not write many letters, only to mother."[22]

The inability of correspondence, however, to serve as a reliable gauge of new home life was recognized, and agents became responsible for visiting placement homes. How often, and if these visitations regularly took place, especially during the early years, is unclear. The return by agents to towns previously visited, always with another group in tow, may indicate that the agent used the opportunity to make these visits. Towns in central Illinois were visited repeatedly, as were the Nebraska towns of Schuyler and Stromsburg. And, in plotting placements in Kansas, return visits to such towns as Fredonia and Leonardville are apparent. It also would seem that return visits did not dampen the locals' desire for children. Of the 1895 arrivals in Fredonia, it was noted that "the applications for them [the children, 15 boys, 2 girls] are twice as great as can be supplied." In fact, often overlooked in the history of placing out is the number of families who took in more than one child. The Kansas farmer who took in Harry Colwell had an earlier positive experience with taking in a New York orphan; thus his request to the Aid Society for another. When placements were made in Fremont, Nebraska, in 1918 the Tingelhoff family took in three children, none of them related, and a girl placed in South Dakota recalled that her new parents took in a boy who had not "worked out" in his original placement home.[23]

Visitations might have been infrequent and some of the placed out may have disappeared from sight, but the Aid Society never intended to simply place children and hope for the best. To use a phrase from another child charity, the Cincinnati Children's Home, turning over children to a family did not end a charity's concern. It retained the role of "prior guardian."[24] To carry out its responsibilites in this area, the Aid Society developed a cadre of agents. Among these were ministers, married couples, and men and women who had chosen social work as a career. Some of the agents' duties remained constant throughout the system's existence. They were to locate congenial communities, work with local committees in screening applicants and placing children, escort the children on their trip from the east, and report to the Aid Society on the general progress of specific and regional placements. By the last decades of the nineteenth century one could also add the responsibility of making regular visits to the placed out. The need for such checks was recognized, but agents found the duty demanding. The rigors and frustrations of the job were recounted by Agent A. Schlegel in 1885:

> *As our emigration work increases, the importance of visiting the children in their homes becomes more and more manifest; but it is an immense undertaking. These children are often in homes ten or twenty miles from town or railroad, and can only be reached by long drives, and often a whole day will be consumed in visiting a single child. Sometimes changes are made without notifying the Society, or a child may leave the home provided for him, and seek another for himself, and much time and labor is thus expended in following him up.*
>
> *The plan adopted is for the agents to revisit, at the end of six weeks, the company taken out by them on their previous trip. By this means, if an error should possibly have been made in the locating of a child, there is an immediate chance to rectify it.*[25]

Despite the mandate to make periodic visits, Schlegel, and it may be assumed other agents, chose not to check up on all of those relocated. Of his 1885 visitations, Schlegel reported that he had gathered information on a number of the placed out, but he "did not visit them," he wrote, "as these large boys are well able to look out for themselves, and I desired to devote as much time as possible to the smaller children." Schlegel, however, did not visit all of the homes that had taken in younger children, determining that in one case his call would be "unwelcome"—a conclusion that should have led him directly to the home. In other instances he accepted secondhand information on the welfare of the placed out. Time simply did not allow for a visit to every placement, but of those who were visited, the agent made a thorough report on their progress at home and in school.[26]

Agents were hard pressed to cover the great geographic distances, as well as to deal with the very human dimension of escorting groups of children to their new homes. One has to wonder how agents managed to herd children on and off trains, maintain discipline, feed their charges, and react to accidents or illnesses en route. Contact with agents sometimes was remembered fondly by the placed out, but at least a few had less than complimentary words for the agent who brought them west. Howard Hurd, placed in Stromsburg, Nebraska, remembered his lady agent this way, "You remember that witch in the movie *The Wizard of Oz?* The one who rode the bicycle? Well, that's her." Other placing-out accounts either overlooked the agents, or the children retained no memory of the person who guided them out of New York. Of his group's travel during the winter of 1884 to Alma, Nebraska, one placed-out boy made no mention of the agent but reported an eight-hour layover between trains in Atchison, Kansas. This boy, being older, was made a "chief steward," responsible for younger children who went off and "played baseball, skated on the Missouri river, and had a walk through the town." Another child, placed out in 1914, later recalled: "We were three days and two nights getting out to Nebraska. They took out the seats and put them back crossways to make beds. . . . We had milk and bread and red-jelly sandwiches three meals a day. . . . To this day, I don't eat jelly." The agents probably were less concerned with the impressions they made than with the number of duties with which they had to contend. Therefore, it is not surprising that the Reverend W. C. Van Meter recorded with pride and relief his "slow," but successful, seven-day journey with twenty-seven children from New York to Peoria, Illinois. The trip had been a blur of delays and missed rail connections, and Van Meter had no assistant to help in looking after the children.[27]

Among the agents, four may serve as examples of Aid Society employees. Concentrating on Kansas placements was Anna Laura Hill, who had a teaching certificate from a Pennsylvania normal school and who began work with the Aid Society in 1902. She was noted as the escorting agent for a group to Clyde and Sterling in 1911, several placements in western Kansas in 1912, and placements in Abilene in 1920, and in McPherson in 1911 and 1924. Employed by the Aid Society during the same time period and working out of Sedalia, Missouri, was the Reverend J. W. Swan, who escorted children to that state, as well as others, and made visitations. One woman recalled Swan as the agent who escorted her and her brother in a 1923 group of fourteen children taken to Monroe City, Missouri. Another woman, placed out at the age of three in a southwestern Missouri home, recalled that Swan visited her every year, the last time when she was fifteen. Swan was also in Kansas. In 1908 he, with Agent Hill, had the responsibility of placing twelve children in Sabetha, Kansas, where one hundred fifty families had applied for a child. A counterpart to these agents was Clara Comstock who, after teaching for eight years at the Brace Farm School, became a western agent in 1911. Comstock was with the Aid Society for forty-three years, working in the society's in-state foster-care program after placing out ended.

Although these agents had designated territories, they sometimes worked in other western states. An arrival of children in Mitchell, South Dakota, in 1914 was preceded by a visit from Clara Comstock, and on the day of placement Comstock was joined by Hill and the Aid Society's superintendent of emigration, Robert N. Brace. One of those placed out that day in Mitchell later recalled that there were "two lady-agents" who kept a "check" on the group's seventeen children. This placed-out girl was taken by a family in Parkston, South Dakota, and her sister went to a family in Storla. Both considered themselves "fortunate to have been given to wonderful parents." In addition to these agents was P. C. Morgan, who apparently worked in Arkansas and Oklahoma during the early 1900s. One placed-out child remembered both Morgan and Swan as being present at his placement in Berryville, Arkansas, and even recalled, "Mr. Morgan visited me several times and knew that I was very happy." Morgan took his responsibilities beyond placements and visitations. He adopted at least one of the placed out, and when a child was not immediately placed or when he voluntarily left or was removed from his new home, Morgan temporarily took the child into his family.[28]

During the latter years of the system, the society boasted of a "resident agent" program, but when such agents were put in place and how long the society opted for such a program is not clear. In 1880, Brace wrote of Charles R. Fry as a "resident Western agent." Agent A. Schlegel may have been another, as he was responsible for visiting and reporting on placements in Kansas and Nebraska. Schlegel, however, also was active with society placements in southern states. In 1893 it was announced that there were three resident agents—in Kansas, Nebraska, and Missouri—but six years later an article noted: "The society employs at present three placing agents, who are also visiting agents, who cooperate with agents in the West temporarily employed, as their services are needed. . . . Besides these paid agents there is in each town a local committee . . . who have agreed to look after children in any trouble until the agent, summoned by telegraph, can arrive."[29] Evidently, the designation of resident agent was not necessarily based on assigned duties or tenure with the society and changed as the situation demanded.

One noticeable aspect of the system was the lack of legal documentation for child placement. There was only a verbal agreement between the Aid Society's agent and the adult taking the child, although each was supposedly given a card on which the agreement was printed. The society agreed to remove the child and pay his or her fare back to New York if the employer was not satisfied, and the society reserved the right to remove the child if the new home proved unsatisfactory from the viewpoint of the society's agent. For the employer's part, there was an agreement to provide proper care and education for the child. There was no indenture by the New York Children's Aid Society. An adult who accepted the child might have taken legal steps later to indenture the new charge, but Brace did not approve the practice for his organization. Additionally, individual families may have adopted a placed-out child, but no adoption requirements were made by the Aid Society. Brace could not, of course, support the legal adoption route, since many of the children were not orphans, although it is unclear if all of the receiving families knew that. For example, an agent wrote in 1856 of little Mary who had been "adopted as their own" by a Peoria, Illinois, family. She would, he assured Brace, have everything life could provide; the agent went on to ask Brace to pass this wonderful news to Mary's "weeping parents" who had given her up so gallantly.[30]

It may have been in reaction to the indenture of children by other institutions that Brace insisted that the Aid Society not legally bind out children. This was a major difference in the way the society viewed its work and the way in which public, and some private, institutions viewed theirs. Indenture was a common practice, based on the English tradition of families binding out their children as apprentices until they reached fourteen to eighteen years of age, most doing menial labor for other families or learning basic trades.

Brace, however, believed in both sides of the bargain having the option of ending a relationship. Perhaps to Brace this sort of arrangement represented his belief in rural democracy, but the plan in action did not always meet with his expected results. Some of the older boys and girls simply left the family with which they had been placed. One young man informed the society, "When Mr. Brace sent me out West, I got a place in Indiana and lived there for eighteen months. . . . I am now in Illinois." Another young man, sent to Seneca, Kansas, spent one night in his new home, then, as he put it, "lit out and got another home, but I only staid there two days." The lack of legal responsibility also allowed the employer to turn out a child. What was needed as an extra work hand in harvest season was an unnecessary mouth to feed when winter set in, and many employers simply sent the children along their way or loaned them out to someone else: "I have sent T—— to live with my half-brother, who is a farmer."[31]

The instances of the placed out moving about were unforseen when the system began. Those relocated to new homes were supposed to stay where they had been placed, only to be removed by a society agent when necessary. The Aid Society, however, could do little about the possibility of movement once the placed out reached their destinations. Usually there were no explanations for why a move was made or a child sent elsewhere, and one can only guess at the motives involved. Families or employers may have decided that they had taken on a burden, rather than a new family member or helper. Some of the placed out may have been less than model in their behavior, making it difficult for families to live up to their part of the bargain. Some may very well have been delinquents headed for more trouble, and among those who simply packed up and left may have been the adventurer or the young man or woman looking for a better job or a city environment where they felt more at home. There is no doubt that some of the placed out ran away from homes where they daily faced physical abuse or neglect. The Aid Society occasionally reported on the problem of transfers and runaways, but seemed powerless to control such instances and, more importantly, to understand why they occurred.

By the turn of the century the system had changed somewhat in its methods of demanding responsible treatment of the placed out. This may have been a result of rising criticism, but it is also likely that experience had altered the Aid Society's work. Although in an earlier time, the agents may have verbally expressed the society's expectations or handed out a card on which these were printed, by the late 1800s newspaper statements and sometimes handbills formally offered the terms of placement before a group's arrival. An 1899 newspaper announcement, for example, noted, "Boys under 15, *if not adopted* must be retained as members of the family until they are 18 years of age, and they must be sent to school regularly" (emphasis added). Boys over fifteen years of age were to be "treated as members of the family, [and] kept until 17 when they [would] be allowed to make [their] own way."[32]

That the reference excluded girls is not surprising. As Brace and the Aid Society concentrated their efforts in New York City to aiding boys over girls, so too did their placement work concentrate on finding homes for boys. It may have been easier to place boys in some regions of the country, but domestic labor was equally in demand. There is no doubt, however, that boys made up the bulk of the resettled; between 1853 and 1893, girls accounted for only 39 percent of the placements. This may be in part a result of Brace's uneasiness with adolescent and teen-age "street-girls," many of whom displayed an overt sexuality and knowledge of worldly ways unbecoming a "lady." Brace considered them to be "a class by themselves," and was particularly uncomfortable with these girls who seemed "to be children, but with woman's passion, and woman's jealousy and scathing tongue" and who seemed to exhibit very little of the "wonderful qualities of womanhood." Without doubt, Brace was imbued with the beliefs of nineteenth-century society and its dictates for women. Females were supposed to be shielded and protected, but Brace's sympathies were stretched to the limit when trying to see street girls as innocent maidens worthy of help. Sharing Brace's exasperation were Mr. and Mrs. E. Trott, who supervised the society's only lodging house for girls. Mrs. Trott was a toughened veteran of the tenements, having taught at Five Points Mission, but she found the girls a great frustration and wished that all would be sent west where they might learn ladylike, domestic ways. That all were not placed out indicates a suspicion that the girls were beyond redemption and would promiscuously misbehave, bringing shame to the society and its plan.[33]

Whether aimed at placement of boys or both sexes, the published requirements for accepting the placed out indicate a significant change in the workings of the system during the latter portion of the nineteenth century. There was now the possibility of adoption. This official allowance came relatively late in the society's operations, and indicates a change in its basic procedures. No longer were most children being taken directly from city streets. Rather, the society removed children from private orphanages and had the approval of New York City government to take children from public institutions for placement. The legality of the children's status was not questioned, since they were foundlings, orphans, or had been turned over to an institution's guardianship by a relative or officials of the city or county. The Aid Society became the instrument by which the children were resettled, but it was not the agency that transferred guardianship—the releasing charity or asylum was the legal guardian. Adoption also may have become more common as the western states passed statutes that recognized this option. Kansas, a state since 1861, enacted its first adoption law in 1864, and Illinois passed into law the legal theory of adoption in

1867, although it had been possible to secure guardianship through legislative private laws from the time of statehood in 1818. These examples are common. Adoption was not early addressed by state statute in areas other than those where French or Spanish civil law had been introduced; the first state under English codes to accept adoption as a legality was Massachusetts in 1851, and as late as the 1920s social workers were still trying "to learn the extent to which the procedure [was] resorted to and to interpret the effects of adoption as a method of social treatment."[34]

In reviewing Aid Society reports and the backgrounds of those who were placed out between 1870 and 1929, it is apparent that most, if not all, had been charges of some charity before being removed by the Aid Society. A 1914 society announcement of placements in South Dakota, for example, noted, "The children are well disciplined, having come from various orphanages." The Aid Society also documented, in 1921 and 1923, Nebraska placements of children who had been turned over to the society by "up-State [New York] county" institutions. Although these were not identified, they were most likely county poor farms or local orphan asylums. And, in a group of nineteen sent to Kansas in 1895, three boys were former inmates of the Yaphank Poorhouse. Additionally, the personal stories from those who were placed out name a number of institutions working with the Aid Society. Harry Colwell, who went to Kansas in 1899, was about fourteen years old and under the care of the Orphan Asylum Society of New York when he was asked if he would like to go west with an Aid Society group. Believing that the "'West' meant cowboys and Indians, a chance to ride horses and to participate in all sorts of exciting adventures," he agreed. Another to feel the lure of the west was John Wallace Price, who, by the age of seven, had seen several foster homes. Asked if he would like to go to Nebraska, he agreed when an Aid Society agent promised that he would see "cowboys, Indians, and buffalo." Not given any choice but going to Kansas in Aid Society groups were Virginia Howard, removed in 1910 from an orphanage in Elizabeth, New Jersey; Annie Schuckhardt, taken in 1909 from the Salvation Army Brooklyn Nursery and Infants Hospital; and Thomas Armstrong, removed in 1887 from the New York Home for the Friendless, sponsored by the American Female Guardian Society. Another named institution was the Sheltering Arms Nursery, New York. Three-year-old Alfred Bauman was taken from that institution in 1906 for placement in Hopkinton, Iowa. Clearly, the New York Children's Aid Society had a working relationship with numerous charitable organizations. In fact, the Orphan Asylum Society (which had operated an orphanage since 1806 for Protestant children, including Tuscarora Indian charges) in 1875 noted a long association under which "A large number of our boys [went] West . . . under the watchful eye of the Children's Aid Society."[35]

Brace's organization served as the means by which county and city institutions could place out children without establishing their own set of agents and network of contacts within rural areas. The number of organizations that actively cooperated with the Aid Society also indicates the general acceptance among eastern charities of the system, its tenets, and its results.

To finance its relocation work, the Children's Aid Society relied on a number of sources. By the end of the nineteenth century, the society received some state funding, but this money supported educational programs such as the night schools and kindergartens. For emigration, funds were sought from generous donors, as well as church congregations and charitable groups, such as ladies aid societies. Brace traveled and lectured to raise the needed money, and solicitations through the society's annual reports reaped more, a portion coming from western residents. Brace also noted that when children were placed out, receiving families or employers sometimes paid the society for the child's train fare. Additionally, there were contributions from receiving communities, and in some cases the placed out later attempted to repay the society. One such individual wrote, "Now I want to know what it cost the Children's Aid Society to send me to Sibley, Iowa. I would like to pay the Society back. . . . I think it is my duty, as a debt I owe."[36]

Since accounts differ, the cost of placement per child is difficult to determine. In 1880, Brace stated that it cost $15.00 to send one child west, but two other estimates published during the same time period ranged from $8.04 to $30.00. Supposedly the latter figures were based on information received from the Aid Society. The differences may rest in what was counted as costs, such as food and clothing for the trip. Some children, despite Brace's rosy descriptions of scrubbed and newly clothed groups heading off for a great adventure, were not given such amenities. An employer in Delaware wrote the society that his New York boy had arrived, bearing "about him the unmistakable evidence of the life he . . . led— covered with vermin, almost a leper." For this placed-out child, taken off the docks of New York, the cost to the society was the price of a train ticket. For the majority of those placed out, however, the society did pay for clothing, food while en route, and transportation. It should be remembered, however, that firsthand accounts present images of meager fare, with bread, jelly, and mustard as staples, and the costs for transportation were not necessarily large, as that probably was given at discount. Despite frugal travel, there were debts to pay. Meanwhile, gifts to the society, according to Brace, became "less and less." In 1880, Brace, in a plea for funds, noted: "We are continually forced, also, towards the newer and more distant states, where labor is in demand, and the temper of the population is more generous, so that the average expense of the aid thus given will in the future be greater for each boy or girl relieved."[37]

This prediction proved correct. In 1894 the cost of sending one child west was reported to be $25.00; by 1901 the cost had risen to an average of $38.13 per person relocated.[38] How much, and even if, financial support to the Aid Society's relocation work diminished is impossible to tell. Financial statements given in annual reports or in other publications include records for money spent in all aspects of the society's programs, without always making distinctions between exact monies spent for placing out and those for in-city programs.

Despite financial concerns, the system continued, and from 1853 to 1929 the New York Children's Aid Society placed out at least 150,000 of the eastern poor. Who these placed out were and where they came from is not completely a matter of record. Then as now there were questions of family and national background. In 1870 a country schoolteacher in Warren County, Indiana, wrote that among her students was a placed-out boy. He was a favorite and was seemingly able to respond to any situation; when the school caught fire, he was the one who climbed to the roof and put out the flames. Of this boy, the teacher wrote: "One of my best boys was a New York waif. He was sent west with a lot of other children, who were adopted by people in this, and adjoining Counties. George is tall for his age—13. He has a very good face and good manners. I wonder about his parentage. I have been told that he now has a very good home."[39]

The Indiana teacher was not the only one to speculate on the children's background and family. Prospective families and employers were assured by an 1857 newspaper in Illinois that the children were "mostly American born, [with] no fault but poor parentage and limited education." The Aid Society's annual reports also provided some idea of children's background—"Charles H. Ulhman, a German orphan boy who had been selling paper" or "Alexander B——, American orphan [who] had been to sea." A comprehensive listing of placements by ethnic group or parentage, however, was not maintained. Since many of the children were themselves unsure of their parentage, such an accounting was not possible. It has been estimated, however, that within the thirty-year period of 1860 to 1890, as many as 94 percent of the placements were of American-born or German, English, or Irish immigrant children. The number of placed out Italian children, who were Catholic, and of Jewish children, primarily from Germany or Russia, has been put at less than 1 percent. There is no doubt, however, that some children from these religious and ethnic backgrounds found new homes in the west. Among the first group taken to Dowagiac, Michigan, was "a little German Jew, who had been entirely friendless for four years, and finally found his way into the [Aid Society's] Newsboys Lodging-house." Nevertheless, the numbers of relocated Jewish and Italian children remained small and may be attributed in part to the family patterns of immigrant groups in the latter portion of the nineteenth century. Although children of Italian peasants were often victims of the padrone system, which enslaved and brought these children without their parents to America, studies of immigrant family groups in which both parents were present suggest a higher proportion of stable family units for Italian and Jewish families, compared with American-born or Irish immigrant families. This was true even if the parents were unskilled or semiskilled laborers and members of America's lower classes.[40]

These studies suggest that children of Italian or Jewish heritage were to a degree more protected, either by family or community ties, and less likely to be destitute or homeless and therefore candidates for placing out. Family cohesiveness had a direct correlation to who was or was not placed out, but it was not the only factor in determining likely prospects for emigration.

The ethnic backgrounds of those placed out reflect in part Brace's personal prejudices. Brace believed that American and West European cultures were superior and that children from those backgrounds were more acceptable to receiving communities and families. When writing of children who came to the society for help, Brace gave approving descriptions of children such as the "yellow-haired German boy ... with such honest blue eyes" and the "sharp, intelligient Yankee lad [who] comes in to do what he has never done before—ask for assistance." To the Mediterranean and East European born, Brace was less receptive, particularly as he feuded with the Catholic community over placing out and as he believed Eastern and Southern European groups less advanced and civilized. In fact, when there were instances of Italian children being placed, the Aid Society pointedly described their earlier conditions, proving, at least to some minds, that this group was inferior: "Eugene M——, eleven years old, [was] found locked in a vacant room in a wretched tenement, deserted by his Italian parents." After a stay at New York's Home for the Friendless, the boy was sent to a "superior home" in Kansas.[41]

To a degree, Brace's prejudices were those of American society. Robert Hartley, writing for the Association for Improving the Condition of the Poor (AICP), expressed much the same thoughts, particularly against Catholics, and despaired of the "accumulated refuse" that "had landed in New York." Reformer Jacob Riis did not share such sentiments, but he certainly observed them. Writing of New York's Fresh Air Movement, Riis noted that rural communities were not willing to open their doors to just anyone: "Sometimes a Catholic community asks for children of that faith, sometimes prosperous Jews. No one asks for Italian children. . . . Prejudice dies slowly. . . . Against colored children there is no prejudice."[42]

For "colored children," as well as the Chinese, American Indian, Spanish, Turkish, and Slavic children, there was virtually no placing out. Although society reports for the first ten years suggest that a few children with these heritages were relocated by the Aid Society, the numbers were in the tens, not in the hundreds or thousands as for the American or West European children. There were, of course, fewer of some ethnic groups on the Eastern Seaboard, and Brace put his efforts into relocating children he believed most easily placed. He may have felt that Native American children were best left to the government or to the missionaries, and to have resettled blacks at any time would have led to accusations of dealing in slavery. And, although Brace never voiced the sentiment, he may have felt that blacks had their own relocation systems, either through the African colonization movement or through organized black colonies that settled after the Civil War in midwestern states such as Kansas and Wisconsin.

Somewhat ironically, the prejudices of those who oversaw the placing out of urban children ran counter to an implied benefit of placing out. The ill-informed, immigrant poor would be placed into communities and homes where they would learn the importance of honest work, American values, and Christian virtues. In reality, those most often sent to rural communities were the least likely to need acculturation into the perceived melting pot of society. Instead, those sent out by Protestant organizations were of backgrounds most easily assimilated into both urban and rural cultures.

Another aspect of implicit prejudice is that shown by the selection of receiving communities. Generally, it is believed that children were taken to any town that would accept them, but Protestant placing-out institutions in fact may have chosen regions on the basis of religious doctrine. While some western frontier regions may have had reputations for lawlessness and were pictures of less than moral health, the late placement of children in southern Illinois, as an example, suggests another form of bias.

Southern Illinois had been accessible since 1856 by way of the Illinois Central Railroad, but the region was ignored for placing out until late in the century; that is, except for one poorly received visit by placing agent the Reverend W. C. Van Meter. That the area was overlooked until after the Civil War may have been based on its make up—factors that were also present in southern Indiana and Ohio. Southern Illinois had a mixed population of French and German Catholics, New England Presbyterians and Methodists, and southern state Episcopalians and Baptists. Despite its rich ethnic mix, the region's character was shaped by settlers from the slaveholding South. In the 1850s the most active placing-out institutions had strong connections to the Congregationalists and Presbyterians, two denominations with good ministerial results in central Illinois but poor missionary accomplishments in the state's southern area. Frustrated, ministers blamed their failure on the resident population: "Most of the people were Baptists. . . . Sunday schools and temperance societies were not popular." All in all, missionaries found southern Illinois an "ungenial soil for Puritan and Presbyterian institutions." One missionary wrote, "An obstinate hostility to education, together with other jealousies and prejudices equally unreasonable, have often baffled the most earnest endeavors for the people's good." Among the "unreasonable" prejudices was a southern proslavery viewpoint where, although Illinois was a nonslave state, citizens used indenture to bind blacks for their lifetime allowing a form of slavery to exist. Yankee boosters warned that few eastern emigrants would arrive to take up Illinois Central land if local citizens did not become "thoroughly anti-slavery," and it is possible that few placed out children would be sent to an area believed by eastern ministers to be both proslavery and unwilling to be proselytized.[43]

This circumstance presents an interesting suggestion about those communities receiving the placed out. Perhaps a willingness to take children was not the only requirement. It may have been that an area or community had to meet certain standards of "correct" moral and religious environment. In the broader spectrum this may explain Protestant charities' lack of interest in placements in Catholic communities, although these certainly existed in the western states. Thus, religious prejudice may have not only determined who would be resettled, but decided which communities would receive and provide wholesome homes for the eastern poor.

Placing out gained momentum in the 1850s, but when the nation was thrown into its great Civil War, it might be expected that this national conflict ended or at least curbed the practice. Trains were needed to carry supplies and troops, and the general condition of the times would seemingly demand a singlemindness towards the war's conclusion, not towards the needs of children. The war, however, had an opposite effect. Instead of stopping the flow of children out of metropolitan areas, it created demands to continue, if not increase, the placement of children in rural America.

The war's economic impact on northern industrial centers was tremendous, and these reverberated on the children of the poor and the lower classes. An increased number of children were drawn into factory work, replacing men who had gone off to war. At the same time, the absence of a provider and the loss of men in battle and to the diseases associated with camp life produced a population of destitute women and children who once had been supported by a husband or father. These dependents, many now orphaned or widowed, were forced into the job market and low-paying jobs— when they could be found. Many could find no honest means of support and turned to prostitution and other crime. The numbers by the end of the war were staggering. Boston had an estimated six thousand vagrant children, and New York at least thirty thousand. With these numbers, it was little wonder that juvenile delinquency increased. An inspector of Massachusetts prisons estimated, "It may not be extravagant to say that one out of four of the many children in our prisons have near relatives in the army." By war's end, Massachusetts' state board of charities also noted a steady increase in the number of women imprisoned; the majority had been jailed for small crimes or for being homeless. They were "the mothers, the wives, and daughters of men who had gone South with the armies of the Union." Their plight was the plight of their children. Deprivations created a tremendous burden for charities, and in New York City alone the war years saw the child population in almshouses rise 300 percent. Responding to the situation's critical implications, as well as taking war profiteers to task, William Cullen Bryant, the well-known editor and publisher, suggested: "Or instead of dressing a few children in silks and jewels, and robbing them of the freshness and charm of youth by these vanities, why not spend the money in sending the homeless children of the city to comfortable farm houses in the West, where they will be trained to industry and virtuous conduct, and grow up good citizens?"[44]

The Aid Society needed no prompting to continue its emigration program. The war's effect in the western states had produced additional demands for labor. Farm workers were the principal enlistees in the army, and farmers and farm hands enabled states to meet their quotas in the call to arms. In the old Northwest Territory an estimated 680,000 men left farms to go to war. The number from Illinois alone totaled 259,092. Perhaps the contributions of these western states was best expressed by an Indiana clergyman who purportedly prayed: "Oh, Lord, had the East done as well as the Hoosier state in furnishing men to put down this rebellion, we would not be under the necessity of calling on thee."[45]

While these states had great pride in the number of men in military service, the men's absence created a severe shortage in manpower on the home front. In fact, Brace estimated that about one thousand boys and young men, placed out earlier by the Aid Society, went off to war as western enlistees. The drain of labor created an uninterrupted demand that these workers be replaced, leading Brace to note: "In spite of the calamities inflicted by the war, and the absence of heads of families, the West had never contributed [financially to the Aid Society] so liberally, or called for so many children." The Aid Society attempted to answer the call, as well as to alleviate the rise in child destitution and juvenile delinquency in New York. In 1863 the society placed out 884 children, and in 1864 the relocated numbered 1,034. These figures did not maintain the status quo, but instead surpassed the pre-war years, when the highest number placed in any one year, 1855, was 863.[46]

One historian writing on childhood in America has concluded that the Civil War served as a dividing line in not only the nation's history but for children's history. A loss of a national innocence led adults in their desire for a less troubled time to project an aura of virtue around childhood. Children were seen as the only hope left to the country.[47] This analysis provides a psychological framework in which to consider the continuation of placing out during and after the war. The innocence of children was to be preserved, and their protection became a national mission.

Other than encouraging the relocation of children, the Civil War, along with Reconstruction and the continuing settlement of the West, brought about new avenues for placing out. There is some evidence that children were sent to Virginia before the war, but it was not until Reconstruction that the southern states received a growing number of urban poor. When compared with Aid Society placements in the Midwest or even New York State these numbers were not great, however. By 1893, for example, Alabama had received 24 children from Aid Society placements; Georgia, 235; Florida, 258; Mississippi, 181; and Virginia the largest contingent with 1,448. These smaller numbers were also true for far western placements. Oregon, by 1893, had received only 26 children, and Washington a total of 114. Meanwhile, Montana, Wyoming, and Utah had received only 30, 6, and 7, respectively. The Aid Society also visited the Southwest, but evidently not until after the turn of the century, when placements were made in Texas and Oklahoma. After the Civil War, Brace toured the far west, and although he cautioned, "For Heaven's sake let the weak and half-educated and unlucky beware the Pacific coast," 254 children were sent to California.[48]

Through two more wars, the Spanish-American War and World War I, placing out continued. In both, "a considerable number" of those already placed out enlisted and did "good service in the camp and field."[49] Most importantly, however, the circumstances of war continued to create a belief in the need for and the goodness of placing out. This was especially true during the First World War.

Although America did not officially enter the war until April of 1917, its industries and farms had been producing goods for Europe at an increased rate from the time hostilities began in 1914. Children and teen-agers, particularly boys, who might have been placed out during this time were drawn instead into war production or military service. By 1916 the situation had become such that the Aid Society was in the peculiar position of having too "few boys for the farms."

> *War conditions have reduced the number of boys available to help farmers in busy June days, and has cut the number of boys seeking permanent homes by more than a half. . . . Owing to industrial conditions, the Children's Aid Society reports itself unable to find enough boys to meet demands. In May forty-one young men [Aid Society charges] between the ages of 16 and 21 enlisted either in the United States Army or Navy . . . [and] munition factories are asking for and taking large numbers of New York boys.[50]*

When war did come, children and teen-agers continued to fill production lines and to work on farms, many times replacing adult workers. Social agencies and charities feared a rise in juvenile delinquency, as there had been during the Civil War, and there was increasing concern that more abuses of child labor would occur in factories. While reformers and social workers kept watch, however, there was no question that placing out would continue as the country went to war. There may have been fewer young men to send to farms, but younger boys and girls were still available. Depleted manpower seemed to demand that the system continue no matter what national or international conflicts arose. In fact, such upheavals encouraged the system, and the underlying theme continued to be the salvation of children from the ravages of poverty.

Through social turmoil and war, placing out continued. Not even the death of Charles Loring Brace in 1890 ended the system, for he had turned over stewardship of the Aid Society to his sons, Robert and Charles. Robert N. Brace had been a civil engineer with the Northern Pacific Railroad before taking up charitable works, first as a parole officer with the New York House of Refuge and then as a placing agent with the New York Children's Aid Society. In 1901 he became superintendent of the society's emigration department and retired from society work in 1931. Meanwhile, Charles L. Brace, a construction engineer for several western railroads, succeeded his father as Aid Society secretary and served in that capacity until his retirement in 1927. The brothers' work continued the many society service programs and established new ones, such as a foster home department.[51] Despite a dedication to in-city projects, the sons ensured that Charles Loring Brace's plan for relocation of the poor would continue.

Placing out, an idea borrowed from Europe, found its own niche in American society. The emigration of children, as well as that of some adults, required a cooperative effort between the society and receiving communities, between agents and local committees, and between the Aid Society and other eastern institutions. The program's success depended on responsible placement, but the stories of relocation are as individual as those placed. While one woman remembered that as a child she was "just tickled to have parents," another placed-out child would have only memories of hardship, growing up "in the fields and homes of people who would feed and shelter him for a day's work."[52] All may not have achieved the American dream in their new homes, but Brace would have argued that at least they had been given the opportunity.

To judge the success of placing out is not easy. The Aid Society had no rigid criteria, since its purposes were bound to ideals of self-help and self-improvement, impossible qualities to measure. When agents presented glowing reports or thankful letters from receiving families or the placed out, these seemed to serve as proof enough that the system worked. Perhaps success for the Aid Society was just the sheer number resettled. On the receiving side, it could be argued that the system was successful, for there were few complaints from families, employers, or local communities. In the scheme of things, it was just assumed that there was a happy outcome for those placed out, despite examples to the contrary. The general view, then, was that the program offered benefits to all concerned, and other charities began to add the program to their own plans for the care and redemption of the poor.

CHAPTER 3

Others "Think of a Home Over There"

A large number of fatherless boys and girls are leaving the cities of New York and Boston by the aid of missionary societies, and coming West to look for homes.—Aurora Daily Beacon, *April 20, 1857*

*A*LTHOUGH the Aid Society's early attempts at placing out and western relocation were apparent successes in terms of positive responses from rural communities and eastern charities, the numbers actually removed from street life, tenements, and institutions had no noticeable impact in draining the city of its destitute. In fact, if that had been the only reason to begin placing out, the system was a dismal failure. The population of city poor and dependent was not reduced to any visible degree. The alternatives that placing out offered and the need for labor in expanding farm communities did, however, prove attractive to other charitable institutions, and the idea took hold. Other societies, individuals, and institutions began to follow the plan set down by Brace.

These other placing-out attempts were diverse and sometimes short-lived, as they were done in reaction to a specific crisis or done to place a particular group, and they were prone to deviate in some ways from the Aid Society's established practices. Nonetheless, those who placed children did agree on the basic values of what childhood should be and concurred that a change in environment was best if those standards were to be met. These institutions and charities were intent on removing children of the poor from the urban world, relieving cities of the great burden of care and institutionalization. Additionally, there were organizations that resettled girls and women exclusively, following the Aid Society's basic principles and practical format for placement. These organizations shared in the belief of nobility in country life and the need to tap the rural demand for labor as a solution for urban problems.

The extent to which organizations or individuals were successful in placing out, as well as their periods of operation and the numbers relocated, are not always easy to determine. References to some placing out activities are spotty, if not outright vague. There are also the institutions that reported and solicited financial support for placing-out programs when, in fact, their activities were in-city or in-state placements; some resembling foster-care programs rather than permanent new-home placements. This creates confusion as to the institutions that transported children and adults across state lines. Within the system of placing out there were a few organizations, such as the New York Home for the Friendless, the Boston Children's Mission, and Boston's New England Home for Little Wanderers, that engaged in sending their charges to out-of-state homes, but this was done on a more limited scale than the work of the Aid Society. Often the placements were sporadic, such as those by the Home for the Friendless, which transported, under the direction of the Reverend G.A.R. Rogers, fifty-three children and six adults to Illinois in 1856, and then seemed to redirect efforts to communities more to the east. Fewer children and teen-agers were relocated by these organizations, and more often their efforts targeted placement communities far less afield than those of the Aid Society, giving them a lower profile within the broader picture of the system.[1]

Some placing-out activities have been identified through news-paper stories and secondary sources. At their best, the primary references provide eyewitness reports; at their worst, they are re-prints of press releases or circulars from the organization in question. Where secondary sources exist, there is a tendency to group activities by more than one organization into a generalization of one or two lines. Despite these drawbacks, there is evidence that several organizations were involved in placing out, sometimes visiting the same towns in which the Children's Aid Society deposited children. Some of the organizations working directly with the Children's Aid Society already have been mentioned, but there were others, as well as charities that chose to enact their own programs, independently of the Aid Society.

One of the first to practice placing out was the Boston Children's Mission, which based its programs on the image of the poor as expressed by the Unitarian minister Joseph Tuckerman. To Tuckerman, who began serving Boston's lower classes in 1826, the city's poor was not one distinct class; rather there were the worthy caught in situations beyond their control, as well as those who had no redeeming qualities and could not be changed. For rehabilitation and salvation, the minister advocated removal of the worthy "from the scenes and associates of the iniquity." Following this simple outline, the mission first placed children in Boston homes and with rural families within the state of Massachusetts. This sort of activity was not new. It was, in fact, more in keeping with the already established practice of placing children in homes by indenture. With its first placements in 1850, the mission did provide, however, groundwork for the placing-out system as it came to be, and three years later, when the New York Children's Aid Society made its first placements, it was following the lead of the mission. This is understandable when the connection between the mission's president, John E. Williams, and Brace is remembered. Brace not only knew Williams as a contemporary who shared his interest in placing out, but Brace had been an officer of the Boston mission prior to the founding of the New York Children's Aid Society. Later, Williams left Boston to join Brace in his work.[2]

In its first annual report the Boston Children's Mission stated as its purpose the "rescue from vice and degradation the morally exposed children of this city." A missionary was employed to establish day and Sunday schools, and funding for the endeavor came, in part, from the "free-will gifts" of more fortunate children in church congregations around the city. Thus, "the movement originated in the heart of childhood," and the formal name for the mission—Children's Mission to the Children of the Destitute—had real meaning. In terms of the broader societal expectations for childhood, the activity was viewed as innocent children lending a Christian hand to other innocents less fortunate than they.[3]

In its first year of placements, 1850, the Boston Children's Mission saw "seventy boys and girls . . . provided with places, in and out of the city; many of them to learn trades." Three of this first group were noted as being adopted, but those reported as learning trades were probably indentured. Evidently, the mission used both avenues in future placements, deviating from Brace's aversion to indenture as an option. The mission did not ignore the New York Children's Aid Society program for western emigration, however. After the New York Children's Aid Society proved emigration feasible, mission officers decided in 1857 that Boston's poor "might be greatly benefited by being removed to one or more of the Western States." In April of that year, 46 youngsters boarded a train for Chicago. The Children's Mission had been in contact with three ministers in northeastern Illinois communities, who located rural homes for the children before their arrival. Accompanying the children were the mission's city missionary, Joseph E. Barry, and Pastor Perez Mason, who was paid $57.36 to help with the children on the train. The children were quickly placed in homes, thanks to the local clergy. Some children were indentured "with farmers or mechanics"; the remainder were adopted as members of their new families. Barry, flushed with the excitement of this outing, returned to Boston with applications for 30 more children.[4]

Mission supervisors considered the program a success. The total amount expended on the entire enterprise was only $333.09, and ladies from several church congregations had been involved in the project, providing through their sewing circles new clothing for the travelers. A second expedition was sent out in June, going to Michigan, and 85 children were found homes in the New England states—these were not elaborated on in the annual report. Thus, by the end of the year, 150 children and teen-agers had been sent to out-of-state homes. Some were orphans, but the majority had left Boston with the approval of their parents. These children, and the placed out that followed, were visited by Barry or other appointed emissaries of the mission, and as with the practice of the New York Children's Aid Society, correspondence played an integral role in keeping track of children in their new homes. Missionary Barry saw his work as providing a new life for children, but a minister co-worker recognized the realistic implications: "An insatiable demand [exists] for labor throughout the West; and yet boys and girls all about us [are] going to ruin for want of anything to do!"[5]

The need for labor was accepted as part of the program, but the mission received at least one suggestion that deviated from the general scheme. In 1857 a gentleman offered to serve as a placing agent if the mission would support a "colonization of children." The man, in slave-state Missouri, reasoned that if enough children were sent out to serve as laborers, there would be no need for owners to keep their slave property. Thus, slavery might cease to be a point of contention in the region.[6] This proposal evidently was not acted on, but it suggests a direction that the placing-out system could have taken. Colonies of children used in place of slave labor could have become an option if those practicing the system had seen such an arrangement as beneficial. The idea, while it may have corresponded to the need for labor, did not project the desired results of children being saved from horrendous conditions to enjoy the benefits of childhood prescribed by American society. It is equally unlikely that northern states, with their strong abolitionist groups, would have considered such replacement labor as acceptable.

Ignoring the suggestion from Missouri, the Boston Children's Mission continued its emigration work. In 1858, Illinois and Michigan received seventy-seven children, the New England states took in ninety-eight, "ten or twelve" boys were sent to Connecticut, and there was one rather unlikely placement of a woman and her child in Kansas Territory. Although this last placement may have been a matter of helping a destitute woman reach family or friends, it represents the occasional work of the mission and other institutions in aiding the resettlement of adults. By the end of its second year of out-of-state placements, the mission was satisfied with its decision to undertake western relocation. The mission's program was reportedly "treated with great kindness" by the railroads, and correspondence showed its great benefit to the children. One child reported, "I prefer to stay upon the broad prairies," and a girl, once accustomed to Boston dance halls, wrote that all who were "idling away their time" in the city should come west. Encouraged by the rightness of the practice, the mission would continue this work until the turn of the century, sending children to the West but concentrating on placements in the Mid-Atlantic states and New England.[7]

One of the earliest attempts to duplicate the Aid Society's system began not in an eastern city but on the Illinois-Indiana state line. In Vermilion County, Illinois, in 1855, the Reverend Enoch Kingsbury, a Presbyterian missionary in Illinois since 1819, took it upon himself to bring New York orphans to Indiana and Illinois. There is no indication that Kingsbury had any connection to the New York Children's Aid Society, but he may have been inspired by that organization since he headed east about five months after the

Aid Society delivered its first groups to Illinois. Kingsbury formed a local organization, the Vermilion County Aid Society, to carry out the logistics of sheltering the children before placement and of locating prospective homes where the children could "become useful to themselves and to the world."[8]

Kingsbury traveled to New York on at least three occasions, returning with what he termed "cargoes" of children. Where these children came from, whether off the streets or from an institution, was never explained in the local press. It may be safe to assume, based on Kingsbury's later activities, that at least some of the children had been inmates of the New York Juvenile Asylum or a like institution. Some of Kingsbury's cargoes were deposited in Indianapolis, with the remainder, at least 150, "furnished with good homes in the vicinity of Danville [Illinois]." It is unclear if Kingsbury's work took place in only 1855 and 1856 or if he and other home missionaries were the persons responsible for also bringing other "worthy orphans," 25 to 50 at a time, to the Illinois towns of Springfield and Danville.[9]

Equally unclear are the obligations set down by Kingsbury for receiving families or employers. One account of the minister's activities flatly stated that the children were legally indentured, but another only implied such an arrangement, stating that receiving adults were under written obligation to treat the children well. Another obligation required that the children all be brought together on the Fourth of July for an anniversary celebration. This may have been intended to reunite separated brothers and sisters for one day a year.[10]

In the broader spectrum this requirement is not unusual. Incidents of placed-out children seeing or recognizing each other were not uncommon. Letters to the Children's Aid Society and reminiscences by those who were placed out indicate that there was contact among the children and teen-agers, whether they were siblings or they simply had traveled together. The placed out did not exist in a vacuum. They lived in rural areas or small towns where people knew each other's histories and where those who had arrived together knew of the others' whereabouts. In 1860 one boy recorded his encounters with other placed out children in his Illinois community: "I saw W—— there [at the county fair], so we spent the day together. . . . I saw Austin about a week ago: he is well." More recently, a man resettled at the age of nine recalled some of the forty-two children that arrived with him in Arkansas: "Albert and Violet Bailey were brother and sister. Albert went with a farmer named Wilkerson. Albert died young. Violet went to a very nice home. . . . One boy named Jack has the adopted name Dennis."[11]

Kingsbury's work received praise in the local press, with suggestions that the program be carried out "on a much larger scale." The local community had a sense of doing good works while it also gained needed labor. Undoubtedly, Kingsbury's activities reflected a Christian impulse, but good works and economics came together and not long after his placement of urban children, Kingsbury became president of a local booster-business group dedicated to furthering the area's economic development.[12]

News reports after 1856 make no mention of Kingsbury personally traveling east for the purpose of relocating children, and it seems that the local aid society ceased to exist. The short-lived placement work by a home missionary in a western state became just a small chapter in the history of placing out. Kingsbury, nonetheless, kept "his hand in" with the system. In 1860 a Vermilion County newspaper identified Kingsbury as the contact person for those farmers who wished to apply for children being placed by the New York Juvenile Asylum; another mentioned agent was John R. Johnson of State Line City, present-day Illiana, Illinois.[13]

The New York Juvenile Asylum was one of many youth asylums organized in the mid-1800s to house and educate youngsters who were not yet part of the criminal world but whose behavior or family life might lead them in that direction. Juvenile asylums were not the same as orphan asylums and by the 1870s such institutions were more often referred to as industrial or reform schools. No matter the name, the purpose was the same. The New York Juvenile Asylum, incorporated in 1851 under the auspices of the New York Association for Improving the Condition of the Poor, saw itself as "a reformatory and disciplinary institution." Those sent to the asylum were labeled as city vagrants, delinquents, and "vicious children"—although "vicious" might mean anything from engaging in petty crimes to being beyond a parent's influence. Whatever the reason for placement, those sent to juvenile asylums were labeled "juvenile offenders," but observers of the times cautioned the public to remember that many juveniles had been placed in such institutions by their parents and that "the taint of crime [was] fixed upon some of the inmates unnecessarily." The New York Juvenile Asylum recognized this, but its job was to provide the "moral and educational means" by which "industrious habits could be formed." A way in which to achieve this was placing out, and the asylum soon adopted Brace's formula. Railroads were used for transport, local contacts were responsible for screenings, and the destinations were usually to rural areas, with the intent that farm families would take in the insitution's charges. Some of those placed out were noted as adults, but they were probably still in their late teens or early twenties. The Juvenile Asylum had both male and female charges, but its greatest interest for resettlement was the young men. This correlates with the Aid Society's emphasis, but the asylum differed in the manner of placement. From the time it was founded the Juvenile Asylum had indentured some of its charges to rural New York homes, and thus it continued to use indenture when it sent the youthful urban poor to the western states. Indenture was one way in which the population of the institution could be maintained at a manageable level, and the practice supported the asylum's stated purpose of "building character" and teaching the lessons of "order and obedience."[14]

New York Juvenile Asylum indentures in Illinois serve as an example of the organization's out-of-state placements. As with other states, indenture in Illinois was possible when the area was still a territory. The legalities of indenture were part of the early territorial laws and became more formalized with succeeding state statutes. Indenture in Illinois, as well as in other midwestern states, generally meant that a child was going into the home of a farm family, and indenture papers reflected this by noting that the person being bound out was to learn the "art of farming," the "art of animal husbandry," or the "domestic arts of housewivery." An early New York Juvenile Asylum placement account from 1856 noted this farm link to its program. The asylum sent 75 children and 25 adults to Illinois, via the Erie Railroad, to "become agriculturists or engage in other useful employments." In a more general vein, the same story observed, "The number of children and youths annually sent out from that city [New York] to the Western states, through the agency of philanthropic institutions is becoming quite large." By 1868, the numbers sent out to the country and indentured by the Juvenile Asylum totaled 2,886, and into the turn of the century the practice continued.[15]

The evidence of Juvenile Asylum indentures in Illinois provides a look at the practice in general. As was the custom of local indentures, the Juvenile Asylum used preprinted forms in which all one had to do was fill in the blanks for the child's name and age— "as nearly as can be ascertained"—the name of the employer, the date of indenture, and the number of years that the contract was in effect. Although the standard number of years of an indenture was seven, the amount of time varied, based on the apprentice's age at the time. In most states, a girl legally reached the status of adult at age eighteen, boys when they turned twenty-one. Although there were occasions where an adult might bind himself out, contracts for indenture of minors terminated at the age of majority. It was customary for the contract to detail the employer's obligations of providing "sufficient food, lodging, and apparel," as well as a basic education and moral direction. At the end of the indenture, employers were expected to provide the apprentice with a Bible, suitable clothing, and sometimes a specified amount of money. In these basic requirements, indentures, whether by the Juvenile Asylum, county courts, or other institutions, showed little variance.[16]

Juvenile Asylum visits to Illinois further illustrate the dispersion of western emigration. All sections of the state received visits from asylum agents. Chicago and its outlying rural districts received children and some adults as early as 1856, and by 1859 there were placements in east-central Illinois, with indentures in Champaign County. One of those indentured was nine-year-old James Robertson who, although taken in by a judge with a fine household, ran away four years later to join the Union army. A year after Robertson's placement, forty boys, between the ages of eight and fifteen, arrived in Vermilion County, and a total of twelve boys were indentured in August and December of 1860 in centrally located Fayette County. Of these latter placements, the average age was nine years old, with the youngest seven, the oldest fifteen. All were indentured to "learn the art of farming." Later placements in southern and northwestern Illinois brought those areas their share of asylum children. In August and September of 1885, for example, there were arriving "companies," with about fifteen children per group, in McLeansboro, a county-seat town in southeastern Illinois. And, in 1888 broadsides distributed in northwestern Rockford advertised "indenture free of charge" to any who would take asylum children coming to that town; they were described as "being mostly of respectable parentage" and "desirable children [who were] worthy of good homes."[17]

The New York Association for Improving the Condition of the Poor oversaw the Juvenile Asylum and was itself interested in an expanded program of immigrant relocation. The association, organized in 1843 and incorporated in 1848, funded numerous activities and served as a sort of clearinghouse for poor relief. Association "visitors" were assigned to city districts and were expected to aid the poor by finding established charities that would assist them, locating medical aid, and providing emergency "outdoor relief" from the association. This relief comprised food, fuel, and other necessities, but never money. These visitors also identified children who were victims of parental mistreatment or without any means of support. These children were sent to the Juvenile Asylum and then, whenever possible, placed out. The AICP was greatly interested in moving the poor out of the city. Not content that the Juvenile Asylum was already sending some to the country, the association wished to send large groups of adults and families west. Clearly, the AICP's directors shared with Brace a fear of what a growing destitute class could do to American society, and by 1858 the organization directly focused on "relief for our overburdened city of pauperism, by migrations to the country." Robert M. Hartley, who had early shared Brace's interest in placing out, reported, however, that the plan, "though a very popular idea . . . found serious practical difficulties in the way, that had not been anticipated by its advocates." Chief among these difficulties was the fact that newly arrived immigrants, most of them Irish Catholics and the AICP's primary candidates for emigration, did not wish to "encounter the trials and difficulties of life in the West." Apparently, these immigrants did not share the vaulted views of rural life held by so many easterners. Additionally, the Catholic community, particularly parish priests, denounced the proposal as Protestant nativism. The AICP continued its arguments for emigration and asked the city's Commissioners of Public Charities and Correction to investigate the possibility. The immigrants, however, could not be forced out of the city, and the association had to be content with those willing to be relocated and those indentured out by the Juvenile Asylum.[18]

It may be argued that the AICP, Brace, and other reformers cloaked their fears of the lower classes, especially the foreign element, in the guise of charity. Certainly by standards of the late twentieth century their attitudes smack of bigotry and intimidation, but the times in which they lived must be considered, not to excuse, but to explain a viewpoint that allowed heartfelt concern for the worthy poor to coexist with apprehensions for what immigrants and a growing American-born class of poor might bring. This was the time of the anti-immigrant, anti-Catholic Know-Nothing party, a period of America for Americans sentiment, and a time when educated men and women still spoke of Native Americans as "savages" and debated the question of blacks as a subhuman species. If Hartley, Brace, and their contemporaries are today to be interpreted as racists, that label must be applied to much of society. Just as city missionaries labored among the immigrants, missionaries among the Indians attempted to impose the white work ethic and standards of conduct, and those sympathetic to the plight of blacks, including the strongest abolitionists, often viewed that group as children who could not progress without white guidance. These attitudes did not diminish real compassion. In fact, for the times, men like Brace and Hartley were viewed as forward thinking. They, at least, were willing to tackle the needs of the destitute and downtrodden, despite rhetoric that today seems to curse the very people they were sworn to help.

Whether inspiring platitudes or dire warnings, the rhetoric of placing out laid the foundation for this form of emigration, and during the 1850s the program took root. At the same time, the country faced a severe economic upheaval, culminating in the panic of 1857. In the western states, agriculture and small businesses felt the crunch, but the brunt of the panic was in the eastern United States, with its commercial and industrial centers. There were over five thousand bankruptcies. Manufacturing houses closed, resulting in unemployment, adverse times for small businesses, and increased demands for charity and public aid. Philadelphia had an estimated thirty thousand unemployed, and New York City had at least forty thousand.

While the panic displaced workers, the marvels of the Industrial Revolution also had their impact on the working class. Advancements in mechanization brought an end to much hand labor. Sweatshops abounded, but home workers found it more and more difficult to eke out a living. Labor and production became consolidated in large mills and factories, and by 1850 the top 1 percent of the population in northeastern cities held almost half the property.[19]

Displacement and abandonment of home industries were particularly noticeable in garment and shoe manufacturing, with their high number of female workers. Although the sewing machine was hailed as the invention that might have been "considered one of the benefactors of the age . . . [constituting] a new era in the history of women, "[20] female workers who had once made their living with hand sewing or fine needlework were no longer needed in the mass production of apparel or fabric. These women had to either join the numbers going into mills and factories or look for another means of making a living.

In 1857 it was estimated that at least two thousand women and girls worked in Philadelphia's shoe industry. Of these laborers, almost none worked full-time because of the introduction of stitching machines. Women already at the low scale of income saw their salaries of about one hundred dollars a year drop to half that amount in the panic of 1857. Many women were reduced to no earnings in a trade that had once given them meager support. The certainty of the workers' predicament and the availability of women who needed work was summed up by a Philadelphia writer who assured prospective investors that female laborers had "no practical concern with the ten-hour system, or the factory system, or even the solar system." Added to these women were those society considered educated and accomplished but who had been reduced in circumstances. These genteel poor, "mentally and morally cultivated," needed employment but were often viewed as feeble, their intellectual development having sapped their physical strength. They were, however, "anxious for some honorable means of earning a livelihood."[21]

The plight of eastern women, either out of work or marginally employed, was known in the western states. Newspapers in Illinois and Indiana, for example, carried stories of food riots in eastern cities, destitution created by the economic panic, and the general conditions of workers in the new mechanical age. Westerners were aware that their call for more female labor came at a time when that source was in dire straits. The general conditions of women in eastern industries, prompted by the emergency of 1857, induced a special effort to find work for women and girls in the West. The New York Children's Aid Society set up a special office to place out seamstresses and trade girls, since in that city the curtailment in clothing production and retailing most affected this segment of the female work force.[22] More instrumental, however, in the relocation of women workers was the Philadelphia Women's Industrial Aid Association and the Woman's Protective Emigration Society of New York.

The Philadelphia association, organized in 1857, had the objective of finding "homes in the West or elsewhere for women of good character." It operated rather like a modern-day employment agency. Women wishing to be relocated were required to provide references, and the Aid Association advertised its available supply of workers. Contacting newspaper editors in the western states, the Aid Association identified the points at which "females are most needed, " and circulars were distributed for further advertisement. Potential employers were expected to pay a fee to the association. This in turn was taken out of the new employee's pay. Circulars advertising the Aid Association's intentions were distributed, and there is evidence that women were sent to employment in the central Illinois towns of Urbana, Decatur, and Springfield.[23]

Whether more active or more successful in its advertising, another organization for placement of women, the Woman's Protective Emigration Society of New York, received much more notice. As early as January 1857, Emigration Society agent Vere Foster had scouted prospective locations in Indiana and was in Bloomington, Illinois. Foster was looking for proper "situations in the country for women of good character, who [had] been thrown out of employment." Successful with newspaper advertisements that asked, "Who Wants Domestics, Seamstresses?," he found places for seventy women and telegraphed New York to dispatch eighty more. The system of appointing local contacts was used to screen would-be employers and to house the women until they were placed.[24]

The placement of women seemingly continued unabated until the spring of 1858. There were continuing reports of arrivals and immediate employment, but the demand for female labor could not be met. The groups sent out by the Emigration Society were large, ranging from fifty to eighty women per group, and the ages spanned from sixteen to forty. Also noted in the local press was the arrival in these groups of "married women, with children, mostly under two years of age." There is no evidence that any were indentured, and since these women were expected to repay to the Emigration Society the cost of their transport, they probably were hired with the understanding that they could leave if they wished.[25]

Time and again the women's good, moral character was stressed. They were presented as honest but "helpless females . . . left without the means of support in New York City." No taint of prostitution, alcoholism, or loose living was attached to these women, despite the fact that besides domestic and garment work, prostitution was a chief occupation of urban, working-class women. They were victims of an industrial society, and both the placing agencies and the receiving communities emphasized their goodness while combining charitable works with the obvious demand for labor: "Our citizens will have an opportunity of obtaining necessary assistance, and at the same time accomplish much good." Those who employed these "worthy poor" were recognized for the "blessed thing" they did in guarding the women from "misery, sin, vise, and suffering." Interestingly, there was never any mention of these women becoming wives of potential employers or of a demand for the "mail order bride," as alluded to in some western themes of frontier settlement.[26]

High moral platitudes aside, these placements, as those of children, brought with them individual dramas and stories. In Bloomington, Illinois, the newspaper editor gleefully reported the discomfiture of a local man who had gone seeking from the newly arrived a servant for his family, only to be confronted by the wife he had deserted five years before in New York. The bigamist was reported to have "made better time from the Western Depot than [John] Colter did on the banks of the Yellowstone, when five hundred Blackfeet Indians were after his scalp." Tragedy replaced comedy when a sixteen-year-old arrival was raped by her new employer. The story was circulated widely and the whole of central Illinois seemed to be up in arms, demanding that Agent Foster redouble efforts in screening prospective employers.[27] While Foster was somehow held responsible for the incident, there was also an inward rage. These women had been brought west to be saved; rural life represented all that was good. Yet, in a local community an outrage had occurred, one that many would have liked to believe possible only in the wicked eastern cities.

Newspaper accounts of arrivals indicate that the Emigration Society ended its western work in the spring of 1858. The last newspaper report of these placements, dated April 2, 1858, noted that 8 girls had arrived for employment in Bloomington. By the end of 1857, Foster had deposited about 700 women in Illinois and Indiana, and by the time of the April announcement, the number

1. The graphic realities of
street life for children of the
urban poor prompted the
New York Children's Aid
Society and other charities
to undertake placing out as
a form of child rescue. (The
Jacob A. Riis Collection,
no.122, Museum of the City
of New York)

RESCUED.

HOMELESS.

OFF FOR THE WEST.

THE YOUNG FARMER.

ADOPTED.

2 (left). In 1873 the popular magazine *Harper's* provided for its reading audience "Work of the Children's Aid Society," illustrating the evolution of children from street waifs to new members of "western" families. (*Harper's New Monthly Magazine*, August 1873)

3 (above). In 1869, *Leslie's Illustrated* carried this drawing of boys from London's Home and Refuge for Destitute Children on their way to Wakefield, Kansas, where they would find homes and work with British immigrant families. (*Frank Leslie's Illustrated Newspaper*, December 25, 1869)

4. Expanding rail lines were the key to success for any plan to send children to western, rural homes and communities. This photograph from the turn of the century has been identified as an orphan train on the Atchison, Topeka & Santa Fe Railroad line; location and date unknown. (Santa Fe Collection, Kansas State Historical Society)

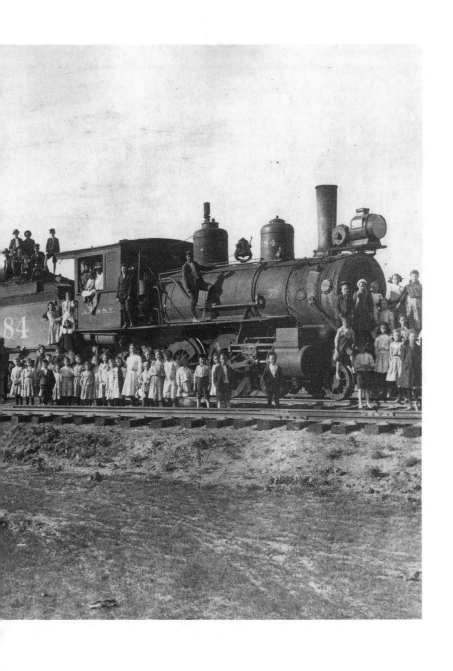

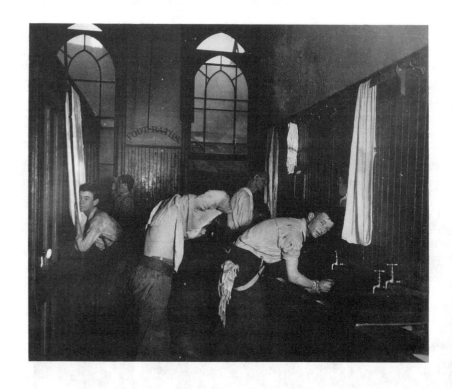

5 (above). One of the Aid Society's best known city programs was its lodging houses for boys and girls; many who took refuge there were later placed out by the society. Pictured is a scene, entitled "Washing Up," from the Duane Street lodging house for newspaperboys. (The Jacob A. Riis Collection, no.164 Museum of the City of New York)

6 (right). Broadsides and newspapers announced impending arrivals from the New York Children's Aid Society. This advertisement appeared in a Troy, Missouri, newspaper. (State Historical Society of Missouri)

WANTED

HOMES for CHILDREN

A company of homeless children from the East will arrive at

TROY, MO., ON FRIDAY, FEB. 25th, 1910

These children are of various ages and of both sexes, having been thrown friendless upon the world. They come under the auspices of the Childern's Aid Society of New York. They are well disciplined, having come from the various orphanages. The citizens of this community are asked to assist the agent in finding good homes for them. Persons taking these children must be recommended by the local committee. They must treat the children in every way as a member of the family, sending them to school, church, Sabbath school and properly clothe them until they are 17 years old. The following well-known citizens have agreed to act as local committee to aid the agents in securing homes:

O. H. AVERY E. B. WOOLFOLK H. F. CHILDERS
WM. YOUNG G. W. COLBERT

Applications must be made to, and endorsed by, the local committee.

An address will be made by the agent. Come and see the children and hear the address. Distribution will take place at the

Opera House, Friday,
Feb. 25, at 1:30 p. m.

B. W. TICE and MISS A. L. HILL, Agents, 105 E. 22nd St., New York City. Rev. J. W. SWAN, University Place, Nebraska, Western Agent.

7 (above). In 1909 a New York Children's Aid Society group was photographed on its arrival in Lebanon, Missouri; the adults are society agents. (Kirk Pearce Collection, Lebanon, Missouri)

8 (right). Among the organizations to practice placing out was the New York Juvenile Asylum. This broadside announces a group arrival in Rockford, Illinois. (Courtesy of the Illinois State Historical Library)

ASYLUM CHILDREN!

A Company of Children, mostly Boys, from the New York Juvenile Asylum, will arrive in

ROCKFORD, at the Hotel Holland,

THURSDAY MORNING, SEPT. 6, 1888,

And Remain Until Evening. They are from 7 to 15 Years of age.

Homes are wanted for these children with farmers, where they will receive kind treatment and enjoy fair advantages. They have been in the asylum from one to two years, and have received instruction and training preparatory to a term of apprenticeship, and being mostly of respectable parentage, they are desirable children and worthy of good homes.

They may be taken at first upon trial for four weeks, and afterwards, if all parties are satisfied, under indentures,—girls until 18, and boys until 21 years of age.

The indenture provides for four months schooling each year, until the child has advanced through compound interest, and at the expiration of the term of apprenticeship, two new suits of clothes, and the payment to the girls of fifty, and to the boys of one hundred and fifty dollars.

All expenses for transportation will be assumed by the Asylum, and the children will be placed on trial and indentured free of charge.

Those who desire to take children on trial are requested to meet them at the hotel at the time above specified.

E. WRIGHT, Agent.

PLEASE EXTEND THIS INFORMATION.

9 (left). Children housed at the New York Foundling Hospital and those placed in New York City foster homes by the charity were brought together for a Christmas party in 1872; *Leslie's Illustrated* portrayed the event as "Santa Claus Among the Foundlings." The hospital, a Catholic charity, also sent children to out-of-state homes. (*Frank Leslie's Illustrated Newspaper,* January 20, 1872)

10 (above). This scene from about 1900, entitled "Mealtime," at the New York Foundling Hospital conveyed the message that no matter how well managed an institution might be, the best place for children was in a home. (The Byron Collection, Museum of the City of New York)

11 (above). When children from the New England Home for Little Wanderers arrived in Goshen, Indiana, in 1888 they were photographed at a local studio. The adults are agents for the New England Home; it was that institution's practice to send at least four agents with each group placed out. (Orphan Train Heritage Society, Inc.)

12 (right). The founder and long-time leader of the New York Children's Aid Society, Charles Loring Brace was among the chief advocates of placing out and as such, he and the society received the most criticism when the plan came under fire. (Charles Loring Brice, IV)

Ever sincerely yours

C. L. Brace

13. Despite debates and
complaints, placing out
continued into the
twentieth century. These
boys, charges of the New
York Children's Aid
Society, were photographed
in New York City before
beginning a journey that
would take them to Texas
in 1912. (Orphan Train
Heritage Society, Inc.)

placed in Illinois alone was at least 620 women, girls, and a few toddlers. That Illinois had received such a deluge of placements may have been a result of the familarity of the society's founder, Eliza Woodson Farnham, with that state, for she had once lived in central Illinois and had authored a book based on her "frontier" experiences there.[28]

Farnham's work in the placement of women was an outgrowth of her philanthrophic activities in New York. Organizing with other women, she had many charitable interests and was a member of the American Female Guardian Society and the Women's Prison Association. Farnham's goal was to aid poor, destitute, and marginally employed women to become self-sufficient. Proclaiming that a woman should "be able to support herself through life," Farnham was active in women-oriented organizations that attempted to find employment for women in eastern industries. Farnham's work in sending women west was an extension of previous activities. Considering her work, she probably was aware of the English transportation program for women, but she used the placing-out system as it had been designed by Brace. There is no indication that Farnham credited Brace or the Children's Aid Society with her own program's function, but she shared Brace's view of self-help and of the rural West as "purifying, enobling, and elevating."[29]

The panic of 1857 seems to have been the only major economic upheaval of the nineteenth century to create a concerted effort to place out eastern girls and women. The Civil War, affecting the very fabric of American society, served to provide another, but surprisingly to a much lesser degree for women than for children in terms of placing out. The war has been credited with creating a class of destitute women, many of whom turned to prostitution or headed west or did both, and with influencing attitudes about what proper women could and could not do, as evidenced in society's changing view of women as career nurses. The war had little influence, however, on creating a mass western movement of women via placing out. In fact, when an emigration of women, such as that inaugurated by Asa Mercer in 1864 and 1865 to send over one thousand war widows and orphans to Washington Territory, took place, the plan was viewed as novel. In contrast, reports of child placements were almost matter-of-fact in attitude. Although the women who went to Washington were intended by Mercer to become brides on a female-starved frontier, the plan had the trappings of earlier placing-out programs for women. Mercer arranged for their transportation—in this case by ship—and employment, although what work awaited them other than becoming wives was not made clear. Mercer, like others who engaged in placing out, had official support. The governor of Washington Territory gave his stamp of approval with a letter of introduction: "Mr. Mercer will . . . work in the noble & good cause of aiding young women of respectability, to better their condition in life, by securing good homes, in a new and exceedingly healthy, & productive country."[30]

Women and occasionally couples were a part of the placing-out system, but the relocation of children remained the primary focus. Another New York institution to attempt placing out in the 1850s was Five Points Mission, the testing ground in which Charles Loring Brace had worked as a city missionary. In one of the city's toughest areas, which saw first Irish and then Italian immigrants, Five Points Mission was established in 1852 in an old brewery building and was sponsored by the Ladies' Home Missionary Society of the Methodist Episcopal Church. The mission's purpose, stated in lofty prose by its women supervisors, was "to raise the fallen and to save the lost." The need for some form of charity in the Five Points section, near the East River but within sight of Broadway, was acute: "The streets . . . are generally narrow and crooked. The gutters and roadway are lined with filth, and from the dark, dingy houses comes up the most sickening stench. Every house is packed to its utmost capacity. In some are simply the poor, in others are those whose reputations make the policemen careful in entering them."[31]

While the mission carried out charitable programs within the confines of its district—the mission became so well known that Abraham Lincoln was given a tour in 1860—there was an interest in placing out. This no doubt resulted from Brace's earlier connection with that charity and certain knowledge of the Aid Society's successes in finding homes for children in the West.[32]

When Five Points Mission began its association with placing out, Aid Society agent the Reverend W. C. Van Meter served double duty. He placed out children sponsored by the Aid Society and those from the mission. The situation was confusing at best, for Aid Society children were placed in homes with no legal agreements, whereas the Five Points children were indentured. That Van Meter worked for both institutions was underscored in an 1857 announcement: "It is well known that the Children's Aid Society and the Five Points Mission of New York City collect the vagrant children of the city, and with the leave of their parents, send them to the west."[33] Since Brace objected to indenture, it is unlikely that he gave wholehearted sanction to the Five Points program, and it may have been that Van Meter simply served as an agent for both charities without the two principals having any working arrangement.

Van Meter had been placing children for the Aid Society since at least 1855, and his efforts had been applauded by local western communities that believed "the bringing of these children to the West, [would] benefit all parties concerned." For whatever reasons, the Five Points placements did not attract the same positive press or results experienced by the Aid Society or other placing-out institutions. Instead they proved prophetic of criticisms to come. When Van Meter traveled in 1857 to a southern Illinois town in the section known as "Little Egypt," he was fined one hundred dollars "for bringing paupers into the town." The local citizens were incensed further when it was learned that not all of the children were true orphans. This incident may have provided additional proof to Congregational and Presbyterian ministers and missionaries that the area was uncharitable, and there is no evidence that Van Meter wandered into the region again. The minister moved to central Illinois, supposedly a more congenial area. There, however, almost a year after the earlier incident, Van Meter was taken to task. In this case, it was not an angry citizenry, but a cynical newspaper editor who questioned the methods, if not the impulses, that directed the system. Van Meter had arrived in Springfield, Illinois, with "30-40 children from Five Points Mission" with the intention of indenturing them.[34] Learning this, the editor took note and drew sharp parallels between the placing-out system and slavery, the great question of the times:

> *There are a great many good Christian families about Springfield and Jacksonville [Illinois] that are wealthy and do not wish their sons and daughters to do manual labor—are not partial to colored servants—are very religious: could not bear the thoughts of slavery. Oh, mercy, no! not for a moment, that find it very convenient to open their hearts to the poor creatures of the Five Points and give them so good a home—How benevolent! And yet the whole truth told, it is to fill the office of servants they want them. The unfortunate poor who, are doomed to that species of* family equality, *in those fashionable circles of society are not half respected and beloved as the black man and his children. . . . If some Missionary Agent had taken that many little negroes from the plantations of Louisiana to Springfield or Jacksonville, and should have prepared to do the very thing with them that everybody knows will be done directly or indirectly with these poor children from New York, our good abolitionist friends, with the editor of the Morgan Journal [Jacksonville, Illinois, newspaper]*

at the head, would all have fainted at the horrid thought. (Emphasis in original.) [35]

The equating of placing out to slavery was not the kind of publicity Brace or the system in general could afford. No mention of placements by Five Points Mission could be found in the Illinois press after that editorial appeared in April 1858. If the Aid Society had been working with the Five Points Mission, that association was evidently ended. In fact, the mission may be the only example of charitable institutions to fail to generate positive press and community relations and to fare poorly in implementing a placing-out program. In fact, among its own city missionaries there was dissension as to the propriety of the practice, and one very vocal skeptic, analyzing Five Points' programs, announced in a popular journal:

> *Neither does the plan of separating children and others from their families and scattering them through the country furnish the adequate remedy. It may save the individuals removed; it will not regenerate the mass that remains. The place—the community—is the same as it was before, and the vacuum produced by the removal is immediately supplied from abroad. Instead of healing the waters, we are merely dipping them out drop by drop, while the pond is still kept full and overflowing from the streams that so constantly pour into it.* [36]

Clearly, the mission was at odds with itself, and it moved away from placing out to western communities, giving emphasis to programs that directly influenced the Five Points district.

Brace and the Aid Society did not, however, abandon their contact with the district. A new cooperative relationship simply was developed with another Five Points charity, the Five Points House of Industry. This institution, established in 1853 by the Reverend Lewis M. Pease, was in a building across the street from

Five Points Mission. Pease had helped found Five Points Mission and had been a city missionary there when Brace had first come to the mission. Over time, however, Pease had found the mission's lady supervisors less than receptive to his ideas of charity—another indication that the mission suffered discord. In reaction, Pease founded the House of Industry, whose purpose was much the same as that of the Five Points Mission. Families in the neighborhood were given some forms of charitable relief, children received daily classes in trades or domestic service, and a number of children were taken in as residents of the institution. The House of Industry then attempted to place these children into foster homes or with those who would take a child as a paid laborer. In this final endeavor, Pease turned to the New York Children's Aid Society and his friend Brace. The House of Industry did not initiate its own placing-out program with agents and western contacts but relied on the Aid Society for placement of children. This working relationship was evidently successful, for it continued into the twentieth century. Recorded among placements in the early 1900s was a family of three children, sent to Iowa in 1904, and four siblings relocated to Nebraska in 1914. All had been residents of the Five Points House of Industry before their release to the Aid Society.[37]

Within this realignment of associations among Five Points charities and the Aid Society, Van Meter did not fade into the background. In 1861 he too set up a mission in the Five Points neighborhood. In 1864 this mission was incorporated under state law as the Howard Mission and Home for Little Wanderers. The charity provided food, fuel, and clothing to families; operated a day nursery for working mothers; and sought work for the unemployed. The chief focus of Van Meter's work was, however, children, whom he divided into three categories: those who came to the mission for food and clothing but who lived with their parents; those who were given over to the mission to be placed out in new homes; and those who needed temporary shelter but "whom we [the mission] are not authorized to send to homes." Clearly, Van Meter was still involved in the placing-out system. He had learned from his earlier experiences as an agent, and now used those lessons to expand the number of charities that chose western placement of children as an alternative to poverty and institutionalization. After its first ten years of existence, the mission could report, "Hundreds of these [mission children] have been provided with good homes." It should be noted, however, that many of these placements remained in New York State.[38]

The success of the Howard Mission, in turn, spawned another organization to engage in placing out, Boston's New England Home for Little Wanderers. In 1865, the Howard Mission school principal, the Reverend Russell G. Toles, went to Boston to help that city's ministers organize the Association for the Relief of Little Wanderers. Under this group's direction the Boston charity, sometimes known as the Baldwin Place Home for Little Wanderers, was created as a refuge for children of the immigrant poor and for those who had been orphaned or left destitute by the Civil War. Toles then left Howard Mission in New York and took on the role of first superintendent of Boston's newest charity. A man of great energy, Toles was determined to make the home a success, and prior to its official opening, he publicly gave out a list of needs: "The *Home* will soon be open [with] 100 children . . . ready to enter. . . . We shall want shoes . . . clothing . . . bedding . . . coal and meat and bread. We expect to beg for *Little Wanderers* and it will do any man good to give." From the first, the home took in children from not only Boston but from surrounding states, and there was no discrimination on the basis of age, sex, religion, or race. The majority were American-born, but home charges also included black, American Indian, Portuguese, Swedish, and British children. Those that could be placed in private homes were given over to families to be legally adopted or "treated as a member of the family": indenture was not approved, and the home stressed that children were not to be used as servants or hired help. The need for the home, as well as its acceptance and success, can be seen in the numbers of children received in the first five years of operation. Between 1865 and 1870, at least twenty-five hundred children entered the charity's care, with a number placed beyond the boundaries of Massachusetts. In fact, soon after the charity opened, children were being found new homes, perhaps thinking of the hymn often sung by the home's youth choir—"Oh, think of a home over there." By September 1865 three companies had gone west, and for the next forty years, from one to four companies of children were placed out each year.[39]

The manner in which placements were made by the New England Home for Little Wanderers did not differ dramatically from the practices of other agencies. Nevertheless, the association's reports and its monthly, the *Little Wanderers' Advocate,* convey the sense that the charity was not simply playing a follow-the-leader role in child placement. There were definite ideas about correct procedures. First, the home staff targeted "a large town or small city of 8,000 or 12,000 people, with good schools and churches, and a good farming country around it." Ministers and prominent citizens were asked if they would aid in finding placement homes. When the answer came in the affirmative, groups of children were organized with as many as four adults in charge; one of these agents would precede the group to the town, arrange for local ministers to be involved, reserve rooms in the local hotel (usually hotels gave free lodging to the children), and see that handbills and posters were printed. Interestingly, reports of these emigrations stressed the large amounts of food taken along for the train trip and the fact that the children had hotel accommodations until they were placed with families that had applied for and been accepted as worthy. Of his experience in Adrian, Michigan, one minister reported that fifteen children had been placed, but determining the suitability of homes had been difficult: "Others would apply and examine the children about as a man would a horse or ox. 'How much can I make out of this boy?' . . . seemed to be the idea. My answer was, 'Nay, if it is simply a matter of profit and loss, you must apply elsewhere. These children have souls to save as well as work to do.'" This attitude, it should be noted, contrasted sharply with Aid Society advertisements that often highlighted the farm labor potential of its charges. In fact, by 1890 the home was making it clear to all concerned that its placed out were to be "treated as *sons* and *daughters*" (emphasis in original), and that legal adoption was highly encouraged.[40]

Like agents of other placing-out organizations, those who brought children west for the home also made visitations. Of his duties, the Reverend Edward C. Winslow wrote: "The first company I pioneered went to Rochester, Indiana. After finishing my arrangements there, I went to Warsaw, fifty miles away, and visited a company placed there a year ago. I found all doing well but two, who had to be changed." By 1866, the home had placed children in Michigan, Ohio, Maine, New Hampshire, Vermont, Connecticut, Illinois, Rhode Island, California, New York, New Jersey, Iowa, and two had gone to Canada. By 1906, however, when the home ended emigration, placing out had become more regional: "Applications have come to us from 25 States and Territories for children. The call for children far exceeds the supply, therefore we have declined the distant calls and placed them as near home as possible." These near-home placements included nearby states and Canada.[41]

The number of charities that sprang up during the 1850s and 1860s presents an almost dizzying array of attempts to deal with the urban poor. It also emphasizes the increasing bent for ministers, missionaries, and churches to sponsor their own programs of charity, rather than to consolidate beneath an umbrella of cooperation or one large charitable institution. As these societies of good works multiplied, they borrowed procedures and ideas from one another, and as can be seen with the examples from Five Points and Boston, placing out became a standard response to the problems of the poor.

Until the latter portion of the nineteenth century, this formula for child relocation was Protestant based. The idea, however, did not escape the notice of Catholic clergy, who felt somewhat embattled on two fronts. On the one hand, they felt threatened by the perceived attempts of Protestant missionaries to convert newly arrived Catholic immigrants; on the other, many parishes did not offer the kinds of charitable programs available from Protestant or secular institutions.

This situation was not limited to New York City. In Boston, the Catholic community boycotted the Unitarian-backed Boston Children's Mission when priests viewed the charity as an intruder, and cautioned parishioners against any contact. For the Children's Mission this meant a drop in its Sunday school enrollment, from over one hundred to about thirty students. The mission protested that no attempts at conversion were made; it had tried to teach only "the simplest moral and religious lessons." Such arguments were to no avail and the Catholic population followed the advice of its spiritual leaders.[42]

Besides fears of Protestant conversion, the urban Catholic communities also had to face the reality that some children of that faith were being placed in rural, Protestant homes by non-Catholic organizations. In reaction to this dilemma and the need for organized charity to its poor, the Catholic Protectory of New York was organized. The protectory deserves mention, not for its successes within the system of placing out but for what its presence created. This organization, founded in 1863 as a direct response to the work of the Aid Society, vigorously protested the placement of Catholic children in the West. Sure that the Aid Society was anti-Catholic and intent on converting Catholic immigrants, the Catholic Protectory stepped in to provide the night schools and other immigrant aid services offered by the Aid Society. Although the protectory was not immediately successful, by the 1870s it had established immigrant services and schools, as well as four orphan asylums for Catholic children and the Society for the Protection of Destitute Roman Catholic Children. Less successful were the protectory's attempts to establish a large-scale plan for child placement. It had been intended that a program to indenture or provide foster care for orphaned Italian children within their city neighborhoods would lead the way to placements outside the city. A limited number of in-city homes made this program nearly impossible, and for the protectory any attempts at placing out in the West were unrealistic. The protectory's contributions within the area of placing out were in the form of its vocal protests and attempts to offer an alternative within the Catholic community, thereby encouraging others to consider using the Aid Society's program. In the case of placing out, it was another Catholic institution that was to become successful.[43]

The New York Foundling Hospital, established by the Sisters of Charity of St. Vincent de Paul in 1869, took up placing out with such success that their program became an equal of the Aid Society. Chartered by the State of New York in 1870, the hospital, under the direction of Sister Irene Fitzgibbon, had the authority "to receive and keep under its care, charge, custody and management children of the age of two years and under, found in the city of New York, abandoned or deserted or left with [the hospital] and to keep such children during their infancy."[44]

The need for such an institution was apparent. Infant mortality in New York's tenement sections was a topic of general concern. Although some commentators believed that child deaths increased during sweltering summer months, when the stench of refuse and the lack of sanitary conditions were most obvious, harsh winters in unheated, damp dwellings had as much effect on the health of infants and children. The physical environment took its toll, and the crushing despair of the tenements took more. Infanticide and the abandonment of infants and toddlers was an everyday occurrence. By the turn of the century, an average of four abandoned babies a day were turned over to charitable institutions by New York's Bellevue Hospital, and the mortality rate was appalling for abandoned infants placed in the care of women inmates in almshouses, a common practice. There were, of course, alternatives to public institutions. One of these was the privately funded Nursery and Child's Hospital, which received rave reviews in the popular press. *Frank Leslie's Illustrated Newspaper* found much to recommend in the private hospital, but, interestingly, could give the public foundling hospital on Randall's Island credit only for upgrading the appearance of its buildings—evidently physical improvement did not correspond to better inmate care. *Leslie's* praise for the Nursery and Child's Hospital was deserved, for although it selectively denied admittance to some children, the hospital could boast of a mortality rate of only 15 percent. With this number the Foundling Hospital compared favorably, which is rather astonishing since it took in children in all conditions of health, as well as from all ethnic and racial backgrounds. Its rate of about 19 percent was considered "remarkedly low for a Foundling Hospital" especially when compared to the 60 to 76 percent death rate at the facility on Randall's Island.[45]

Experience showed that babies and small children kept together in institutions created an environment for high mortality figures; the easy spread of infectious diseases and the inability to give each child concentrated care, including that of wet nurses, were the chief contributors to institutional infant mortality. Added to these factors was the state of infants when admitted. Many were premature and at-risk babies, suffering from exposure, malnutrition, and dehydration. During the reporting period of 1872–73, as an illustration, the Foundling Hospital noted that of the infants and toddlers taken in during that year, 470 were still alive. There had been 599 deaths, however; the leading cause, contributing to 364 mortalities, was "intestinal" problems. These had many origins but most were brought on by the lack of a wet nurse and the inadequate artificial feeding options common for the time, such as home brews of cow or goat milk (often contaminated), grain, and water. To counteract the institutional atmosphere and increase the probability of infant survival, the Foundling Hospital encouraged mothers, many of whom were unwed, to care for their newborns at the hospital. Through this effort, the hospital was credited with reducing infant deaths, as well as drastically decreasing the "horrible crime of infanticide."[46]

To care for the abandoned children and those voluntarily given up by their parents, the hospital also enacted a home-care program, placing many of its charges in private city or country homes. The success of this plan was evident within two years, for between 1870 and 1872, the hospital's in-home placements numbered 907. This program was an early form of America's foster-care system, which had its roots in the French custom, among the middle and upper classes, of putting babies out to country wet nurses. Many approved of this custom for America, including the Massachusetts Board of State Charities and Charles Loring Brace, who asked, "Why will our benevolent ladies and gentlemen keep up the old monastic idea of the necessity of herding these unfortunate children in one building?" In agreement was at least one doctor in the growing field of pediatric care who argued that foundlings should be kept out of large institutions and placed in private homes, in the country whenever possible. The Sisters of Charity and the Foundling Hospital could not abandon completely the institutional setting, but they had no intention to house hundreds of infants and toddlers who could otherwise be placed with families. A natural step, therefore, from in-city and in-state foster care was placing out as formulated by the New York Children's Aid Society.[47]

The hospital, through the Sisters of Charity, carried out its own emigration program beginning in the 1870s. The hospital's work reached full maturity under the direction of Sister Teresa Vincent, administrator for the institution beginning in 1896. Placing out by this Catholic charity was almost identical to Brace's program. Like the Aid Society, the Sisters of Charity preferred that children not be legally adopted or indentured. There are, however, numerous placing-out accounts that indicate adoption did take place, and more regularly than if the child had been placed by the Aid Society. There are also accounts of indentures that occurred after placement.[48]

The Sisters of Charity targeted homes in Catholic communities, and the area priest most often served as the local arrangements person. Prior to placements in a new area, priests were approached by letter to determine if their areas would welcome children. "Parish priests throughout the country were notified of these orphan children and those families interested were to select a child." If a community was agreeable to receiving these children, the placements began. It seems that once a promising region was discovered, the Sisters returned again and again with their charges. Besides working with local priests, the Sisters of Charity of New York had a network of contacts with members of their order throughout the United States. By 1906, the order numbered about five hundred in the western states, with Sisters of Charity "academies and hospitals in Kansas, Nebraska, Colorado, New Mexico, Wyoming, and Montana." In fact, the Sisters of Charity as early as 1867 had established an orphanage in Galveston, Texas, after a yellow-fever epidemic decimated the population; later, Texas was to receive children from New York's Foundling Hospital.[49]

The method of placement indicates a well-orchestrated program, based on the guidelines of the Aid Society, but with variations. The local arrangements person chose the receiving families before the children left New York. Each family was given a number or a name that corresponded to that sewn into the child's clothing or worn on a tag. A girl placed in Tulsa, Oklahoma, in 1912, remembered that her tag bore a number corresponding to that held by her new parents. When she was taken from the train, her number was matched to that of the receiving couple and she was quickly placed into the care of her new family. Among other placing-out accounts is that of a woman who later recalled the tags worn by the children on her train and that hers read "Mr. and Mrs. Rudolph Kramer." This Nebraska couple met the trainload of children in Stuart, and retrieved their new daughter, who regarded her new farm home as "good" and her parents as "lovely" people. Thus, under the Foundling Hospital's system of placement, children and new parents were matched soon after the children reached their destination.[50] There was no great meeting with a selection process and little chance for a child to be left untaken. One eyewitness to a Sister of Charity placement in Hays, Kansas, in 1902, recalled: "The children were attended by nurses and must have ranged from 2 to 4 or 5 years of age. The people were lined up all around the station and the nurses brought the little ones out. All of them had tags on their clothes with the name of the person who was to adopt them and the nurses passed them out to the people who called for them."[51]

Foundling Hospital arrivals in the receiving communities, like those of the Aid Society, were noted in the local press, generally without any comment except for a statement of facts:

> *A Missouri Pacific train brought twenty foundlings from New York City [through Kansas City]. They were forwarded to Ellis, Hays City, and Victoria, Kansas. They were accompanied by an agent of the New York Foundling and Orphan Asylum and by a nurse. . . . The eldest of the twenty was six and the youngest two. Some of them have the records of their parentage. . . . The pet . . . was so little that she could scarcely have passed her second year. She goes to Victoria to be adopted by a well-to-do merchant.*[52]

The towns mentioned in this story, all situated along the Union Pacific Railroad line, were not exclusively Catholic, but each had sizeable Catholic populations. In Hays, a Father Emmeram was identified as the contact person, who "set about organizing an adoption program in the county," visiting families and preaching sermons to encourage the reception of Foundling Hospital children. Another priest in the county at the time noted, "Many of the families . . . already had 8, 10, or 12 of their own [but] people were kind and many made room for another mouth when they had difficulty taking care of their own."[53]

Schoenchen, another Kansas town that received Foundling Hospital children, was overwhelmingly Catholic in character, and for one girl placed there, life was unbearable. Arriving in Schoenchen in 1910 at the age of six, Teresa was given over to a childhood of hardships and beatings. Placed in a German-speaking family and knowing no German, she was considered a difficult child, and was eventually placed by the family in a Kansas orphanage. The root of the problem was an assumption made at the Foundling Hospital. Teresa, with a Germanic surname, was assumed to be German-Catholic, when in fact she was of German-Jewish descent. Her placement was doomed from the beginning. Although the Sisters of Charity, like the Aid Society, boasted of regular visitations to the placed out and did remove at least two other children from Schoenchen homes, the rescue never came for Teresa, who left the orphanage and by sheer determination gained a college education later in life.[54]

Another story, one that underscores the tenuous position of all placed-out children, was of the settlement of a boy in Glen Ullin, North Dakota, in 1912. Given up to the Foundling Hospital by a mother who could not care for him, Giovanni, renamed John, was placed with a Catholic family. He was never adopted and when his new "father" died, his North Dakota mother informed the Foundling Hospital that John could stay only if he made no claims to her late husband's estate and, as she put it, "behaves himself."[55]

Kansas and North Dakota were just two of the states visited by the Sisters of Charity as they carried out their placement program. States and territories visited by the Aid Society, such as Nebraska, Missouri, Illinois, Texas, and Oklahoma Territory, also took in wards of the Foundling Hospital via the work of the Sisters. The numbers sent from the hospital, however, were much larger per group than those of the Aid Society's groups of approximately 30 little wanderers. The size of each Foundling Hospital group created an image of trainloads of children, "baby trains," on the way to far-off destinations. One placed-out child who was taken to Manchester, Oklahoma, in 1911, later recalled, "[I was] with 200 other children and none of us knew where we were going or what was going to become of us." In 1910 a press story noted, "A whole carload of babies not one of whom was over three years old, passed through Chicago today on a 2,500 mile trip. . . . They were billed to Houston and San Antonio, Texas, where each will be adopted by a southern family." Still larger numbers were reportedly sent to Louisiana, where a prominent Catholic population provided receptive homes for the New York babies. In 1909 one of the largest transports of children was reported in Loreauville, Louisiana. There were 300 young children passengers on one train: this single number dwarfs the Aid Society's Louisiana placements which in 1893 totaled only 28 in forty years.[56]

While public and private institutions of the east brought city children into western and southern locales, an aberration of the placing-out system was forming in the states that accepted the eastern poor. These states, agricultural and rural, were developing their own cities, receiving immigrants, and by the late nineteenth century were facing many of the same problems experienced by metropolitan centers of the East.

Placing out's original purpose had been to remove children from the streets and asylums of eastern cities and send them to rural areas, primarily in the West. The boundaries of the West, however, were ever changing. Chicago, with a population of 29,963 in 1850, boomed, and by 1860 the city had 112,172 residents, the majority foreign-born. The once-isolated frontier trading post became an urban center with the problems previously associated with only eastern cities. Chicago, a railroad hub and gateway for children from the east, had its own growing class of urban poor, and the story was the same for other former frontier towns, such as Cincinnati, which in 1860 ranked ahead of Chicago in population.[57]

By the 1870s the phase of frontier settlement and economic development had passed for the states of the old Northwest Territory and the labor of those years had produced thriving centers of commerce and industry. These achievements had a substantial impact on placing out. Western urban centers and their environs had their own children of poverty and their own public and private institutions to care for them. Indianapolis, often cited as a point of eastern placing out, had by 1870 three caretaking institutions for local children: the Orphan's Home, established in 1849 as an alternative to children being sent to the county poor farm with adults; the German Protestant Orphan Asylum, established in 1867 and sanctioned to indenture its charges; and the Colored Orphan Asylum, established in 1870. Likewise, Cleveland, Ohio, had by 1896 eleven institutions for the care of poor and orphaned children. These included the Jewish Orphan Asylum, a home for foundlings, and the Children's Fresh Air Camp. The complaint of Indianapolis's German Protestant Orphan's Asylum was a common one among charitable institutions: "In the growth of our city [there is an] increasing demand" for charity among the poor.[58]

For solutions to the problem of charity, the West looked to the East as it had for guidance in forming territorial and state laws. Now "western" institutions and aid societies borrowed the plan of placing out, sending their resident poor farther west. By 1893 orphanages in Cleveland, as well as the Children's Home of Cincinnati, were sending at least 200 children a year to Indiana. Meanwhile, the state of Ohio still accepted the eastern poor and had by 1893 received 4,418 placements alone from the New York Children's Aid Society. Indiana, in turn, became a receiving ground on two levels; children continued to arrive from the New York Children's Aid Society as well as from the New England Home for Little Wanderers. At the same time, children transported from Ohio arrived in Indiana homes. Among those sent to Indiana by the Children's Home of Cincinnati were Stella May Zimmerman and her sister, Myra Edna. They, and perhaps three brothers, boarded a train on October 16, 1894, and were sent to new homes in the west-central Indiana county of Montgomery, which by the 1880s boasted three rail lines. This experience was not an unusual one for charges of the Children's Home of Cincinnati. That charity, established in 1864 under the sponsorship of Quakers, had by 1870 placed out 460 children. Some placements were in-state, but into the twentieth century this charity used placing out as designed by Brace, transporting children across state lines.[59]

At the same time Indiana homes took in children from the East and from Ohio, young wards of Indiana institutions were sent farther west. In 1893 it was reported that Indiana was sending at least 75 of its resident children, per year, to homes in "western" states. As the Children's Aid Society of Indiana rhapsodized, these children were being given new opportunities in Nebraska, "that state of vast possibilities." In the judgment of those responsible for the care of the orphaned and indigent, "the children [were] better if moved several hundred miles from their former residence." In addition, adoptive or foster parents preferred to have the child "cut loose from its relatives and former associates."[60]

Illinois, like Indiana, continued to receive the eastern poor, but by the end of the century it too sent its own children out of state.

One organization, the Children's Home Society of Chicago, sent its charges to homes west of the Mississippi, and by 1893 it could boast that 2,990 children had been provided with homes. One of the receiving states was again Nebraska. That Nebraska had by 1890 its own institutionalized population of about 1,000 in the state's industrial school and the Home for the Friendless did not dissuade the Children's Home Society of Chicago from its attempts at western placements. Overseen by the Reverend M.B.V. Van Arsdale out of an office on LaSalle Street, the Chicago organization was clearly in the child-placement business. Advertisements described available children—"Very promising, 2 years old, blonde, fine looking, healthy, American [boy]"—and a general statement of policy was provided: "All Children received under the care of this Association are of SPECIAL PROMISE in intelligence and health, and are in age from one month to twelve years, and are sent FREE to those receiving them, on ninety days trial, UNLESS a special contract is otherwise made."[61]

As did other states, Illinois had public and private institutions that placed children, either by indenture or adoption, within the state. When a private Illinois organization, the White Hall Orphan's Home Society, boasted that it did not "ship children . . . out of state," but had made placements in over sixty Illinois counties,[62] the society was not necessarily condemning out-of-state placement. Rather, it was recognizing placing out as a viable option that it had chosen not to take.

Whether unintentional or overtly encouraged, the placing-out program developed by Brace and the Children's Aid Society spawned a system of resettlement for the urban poor that grew in dimension and form. Placing out, as a solution to urban ills and as a means of salvaging the lives of children, had the support of laymen, reformers, and professionals in social and missionary work. The system was touted as the best way in which to care for the destitute and orphaned, and supporters contended that proof of these children being wanted was evidenced when "the effort to place children of the poor in country families revealed a spirit of humanity and kindness, throughout the rural districts."[63] The same also could be argued for those communities that accepted girls and women in special times of crisis.

Charity played its part, as did the supply and demand of labor. The system, however, took on a new meaning and reflected the changing landscape of rural America when western, not eastern, institutions chose to adopt the system. This adaptation was to portend changes and controversy yet to come as America grappled with the question of what to with the children of the poor.

CHAPTER 4

A Plan Embattled

Don't let us say they [Aid Society administrators] have done wrong, but point out where they may rectify their methods and do more good.—W. J. Baxter of Michigan, 1883, quoted in Miriam Z. Langsam, Children West: A History of the New York Childrens Aid Society, 1853–1890

*B*Y THE LATTER portion of the nineteenth century, placing out was considered by many charitable institutions and urban reformers as a workable means to provide child care and salvation, both spiritually and materially. Despite its acceptance and the number of organizations to adopt the system, placing out nonetheless was coming under scrutiny, and many observers were reaching conclusions that were less than favorable to the practice. Over time numerous criticisms arose, resulting in a growing tide of voices demanding that the system be ended. For the destitute the immediacy of their own trials obliterated any knowledge of an increasing controversy over relocation. Likewise, it is doubtful that the majority of employers or families receiving the placed out were aware that within the developing social work profession and in the community of correctional and charitable organizations there was a mounting concern over the system of emigration.

Certainly, there had been isolated complaints and accusations from the beginning. Most of those, however, did not target the entire system. Aggrieved employers complained when their new-found "laborers" simply left to seek their fortunes elsewhere. Sometimes an isolated community protest, such as Five Points Mission's unfortunate indenture experiences in Illinois, drew public comment. Generally, however, placing out brought no major protests from the public.

This was particularly true at the local level, where the placed out and the receiving community came face to face. Childless couples suddenly had a family, farmers and merchants had an extra hand, overworked housewifes had "help," and the community shared in a feeling of providing a positive alternative to the lives these children might possibly have led. Those taking children may not have articulated such motives. Certainly, among the recorded reasons for taking in a child there is diversity and a straightforwardness that offer little insight to personal reasons for taking a child. Generalities most often serve. One woman said that she chose a child because his last name had the same pronunciation as her maiden name. Another, when asked her reasons, could only reply, "That's the $64,000 question. I just liked his personality." And, from a placement account in Sabetha, Kansas, came the story: "Big, good natured Jake Aberle wanted a boy. He has no children. He didn't care much what boy he got—they all looked good to him. So, when he walked out with his boy, he drew his chest out, every whit as proud as if it were his own child. Jake Aberle wanted a boy for what it would contribute to his home life, and the committee was as glad when he was supplied." Although Jake "didn't care much," some families were particular. Provided with a toddler from the Foundling Hospital, a Nebraska man was enthusiastic: "Beats the stork all hollow. . . . We asked for a boy of 18 months with brown hair and blue eyes and the bill was filled to the last specification." This planned arrival was in sharp contrast to those who found them-

selves caught up in the moment and took children on a "whim."
More than one placing-out account mentions adults who did not
know about the placements beforehand but while in town stopped
by for a look, only to take a child home with them: "The Darnells
didn't know about it until a druggist told them. They went over and
Howard came up and hugged Mr. Darnell's legs. He said no at first,
but came back and said he wanted the little fat boy."[1]

Evidently, there was little questioning of the program that
brought these children to their communities, and testimony to the
system's local acceptance can be found in the number of places that
received groups of children time and again, never complaining that
more eastern poor were entering the area. Notably, in the recorded
remembrances of those placed out there is no mention of negative
reactions from the communities in which they came to live. When
one placed-out boy recalled that most farmers took children because of a need for labor, he also added, "Most of the town people were very good people and were proud of the children they
adopted." Another of the placed out, sent to Benton County,
Arkansas, agreed, using his personal experience as an example: "I
went to school, church and had as good a life as anyone around me.
There seemed to not be anything different about my being an
orphan."[2] It would seem that the placed out were accepted as they
went to school, attended church, and shared in community activities of picnics and fairs, as well as the calamities of natural
disasters and uncertain farm economies.

Within the philanthropic world, however, the system and its
possible abuses were being considered, with serious consequences
for all engaging in the practice. As a result, the burden of proving
emigration's merits forced the Aid Society, as champion of the
system, to marshal its supporters. By the 1870s the Aid Society, as
the symbol of placing out, faced a rising tide of criticism. Complaints were based on incidents that had occurred in the placing-
out process, and the questions came from peer organizations and

the boards of state charities. The first crisis point for the Aid Society came in 1874 at the National Prison Reform Conference. At that meeting a delegate complained that for "the past twelve or fifteen years car loads of criminal juveniles, . . . vagabonds, and gutter snipes" had been sent west, specifically to Wisconsin. The next year, at a Conference of Charities and Correction, Wisconsin, along with eight other states, joined against the system. The complaints were general but tended towards a concern over the character of the destitute. Generalizations became pointed accusations in 1876 at the National Prison Congress, when representatives from three states—Michigan, Illinois, and Indiana—again took placing out to task. An almost immediate result of this confrontation was a major reduction in the number of children placed in complaining states.[3]

The formal complaint made at the 1876 Prison Congress accused the Aid Society of knowingly sending delinquents and undesirables west, with the express purpose of ridding New York of this element. Consequently, these homeless were now "crowding the Western prisons and reformatories." The theme continued at the 1879 meeting of the American Social Science Association. This time the accusations came from the superintendent of the Michigan State Public School for Dependent Children, Lyman P. Alden. Interestingly, these complaints reflected the ongoing discussion within American society as to the innate qualities of the children of the poor. Despite arguments to the contrary, there was a continuing suspicion that these children were made "different" by circumstances of birth and environment. Brace, of course, did not agree, and the Aid Society by its own accounts had taken children and teen-agers from prisons and almshouses, where many had been sent for committing "petty" crimes. The Aid Society steadfastly denied the possibility that repeat offenses had occurred once these youngsters had been salvaged by their new environment. To prove all charges false, the society set out to investigate. The result of an in-house study, conducted by society agent Charles R. Fry, reported that of the thousands sent to Illinois and Michigan, none were incarcerated. The same could not be said for Indiana, however. In that state, Fry found five of the Society's placed out in reformatories—one girl was in the Girls' Reformatory and Women's State Prison, and four boys were in the Indiana State Reform School.[4]

This report, no matter how painstakingly compiled, must be considered with a degree of skepticism. Undoubtedly, the complaining parties had exaggerated the circumstances, but the Aid Society could not have done a comprehensive study. It had no idea where many of its placed-out charges had gone, and there is no evidence that Fry, in visiting jails or reformatories, determined inmate life-histories or identified the placed out who may have taken on new names. In fact, it was impossible for him to check these identities when he visited the Illinois State Penitentiary, for, as he noted, "The rules forbid conversation with the prisoners."[5] Thus, Fry could not gain a full accounting of those place out and later jailed. Opponents to the system used just this line of reasoning to ignore the society's findings and continue a campaign against the system.

The Aid Society's lack of information on those it had relocated was itself a point of contention, and one which the midwestern representatives argued. Children, particularly the older ones, did not always stay where they had been placed, and their potential for antisocial, criminal behavior was of concern to local and state officials. Most of these wanderers were boys who simply picked up and moved on. State officials argued that farmers or receiving families felt that they had lost their "help," that they had been deceived and their charitable impulses had been abused. The Aid Society was judged to have perpetuated a scheme, and it appeared to be an incompetent or uncaring organization intent on dumping the "eastern refuse" in middle America.

With these concerns in mind, another receiving state took action in 1884. Acknowledging an "absence of any prolonged and general protest against work [of the Aid Society]," the secretary of the Board of Corrections and Charities of Minnesota nonetheless investigated the Aid Society and concluded, "From our experience, we are positive in the opinion that children above age of twelve years not be sent West." It is impossible to determine if the Aid Society abided by this age limitation in Minnesota, but the state continued to receive children. By 1893 it was reported that 2,448 Aid Society children had been placed in the state. The criticism may have had some impact, however. An agent reported in 1898, "Our agreement to bring back to New York any child who may be found to be undesirable, opens the way for us everywhere, excepting in Minnesota." Placements in that state did not end, however. Beginning in the 1890s the Aid Society simply circumvented official protests. Rather than transport the children to towns for a general selection process among the local citizens, the Aid Society instead used the Children's Home Society of St. Paul to house at least some of the relocated children. The St. Paul institution then found homes for these children as well as for its own resident charges. Presumably fewer questions would be asked if an in-state agency handled the placements, and it is possible that Minnesota families never knew that children they took in had originated in an eastern state. This practice of institutional placements also may have been carried out in other states, although there is little conclusive evidence. One placing-out account from Kansas, however, does suggest this option after that state passed laws restricting out-of-state placements. In 1916, at least one girl was placed by the Aid Society in the state's Methodist Deaconess Home. From there, she was sent to a Kansas family.[6]

The Aid Society's internal investigations and a continuing public relations effort gave high visibility to the organization's positive works and moral intentions. It was imperative that the society not be perceived as abandoning these placements once they were made. The society emphasized the visitations made by agents and the consistency of these visits: "[The] Society's system for visiting children is very complete. In Nebraska, Kansas, and Missouri are permanent Resident Agents, who have oversight of their respective districts. . . . The Society also employs four agents of long experience whose duties are to place the children and subsequently visit them."[7]

Equally important to the Aid Society was that those placed out not be labeled as con artists looking on unsuspecting farmers or rural communities as a soft home, or worse, as a new territory for crime and vice. Public disclaimers were combined with reassuring statements in Aid Society annual reports. In the report for 1885, for example, it was acknowledged that some of the older boys had been the source of problems, and reporting agents openly discussed the teen-agers' tendency to move about. According to the society, it was a standard, and acceptable, situation for some to leave new homes or employers: "Some [older boys] were placed . . . near Milford [Virginia]. They were larger boys, and few remained in their places. A number worked their way to Richmond, and others returned to the city [New York]."[8] Agents accepted this as the status quo and in their reports attempted to emphasize the positive:

In reference to the dissatisfaction sometimes created by our large boys, I have spoken in former reports, but during this round of visiting, and a most careful investigation, it can be said that only one is really doing badly. This boy is still in Kansas, but has been roving from town to town, and a week ago passed through Marysville [Kansas] with a traveling show. Some four or five others . . . became discontented from the start and have made their way back to New York; but that is the worst that can be said of them, and their short excursion can have worked no special harm either to themselves or the community.[9]

To counteract the bad-boy image, the Aid Society in its publications and those of supporters pointed to the successes. The runaway, the juvenile delinquent, was in the minority when compared with the placed out who became respected citizens in their new surroundings. It was noted in the society's standard public relations stories that, of those placed out, there were "ministers, wealthy businessmen and farmers, doctors, lawyers and teachers." Featured prominently in the society's 1915 annual report, for example, was one such success story, that of John H. White, whose picture appeared above the caption "One of Our Orphan Boys Placed in a Home in the Middle West Thirty Years Ago, at the age of Ten Years." White, who supposedly had been left as an infant on the steps of a New York charity, was placed out to a home in Clifton, Kansas, where he became a printer's devil for the *Clifton Review*. Newspaper work became his career, and by 1902 he was manager of the Victor, Colorado, *Daily Record* where he, incidently, became a mentor to fledgling reporter Lowell Thomas. By the time of the Aid Society's story, White had expanded his interests to a political life, having been elected to the Colorado General Assembly. He was a perfect example of the placed out making a respectable mark on the world. The Aid Society could cite other public servants as well. "A mayor of a city," state legislators, and two governors, according to the society, had seen their fortunes rise when as children they had been sent west. Society stories did not always divulge names, but the mayor was Henry L. Jost, who served in Kansas City, Missouri, from 1912 to 1916. The state and territorial governors who had received new homes under the placing out program were Andrew H. Burke and John Green Brady.[10]

Andrew Burke, governor of North Dakota from 1870 to 1873, had been placed out in 1859, at the age of nine, to an Indiana family. Burke's experience may not have been an entirely happy one, since he left that home to enlist at the age of twelve as a drummer in the Seventy-fifth Indiana Volunteer Infantry. He did return to Indiana after the Civil War and worked at a series of jobs, including one with an Evansville newspaper, before finally making his way to North Dakota. He evidently did not regret his placing-out experience, for he later expressed to the Aid Society feelings of gratitude and he encouraged others to come west under the society's program.[11]

The second placed-out child to later achieve a governorship was John Green Brady who, like Burke, went to Indiana in 1859. Unlike Burke, however, this placed-out child found a home with a prominent family that gave him every advantage. Taken in by Judge John Green, Brady was given a well-rounded education, graduating from Yale in 1874 and from the Union Theological Seminary in 1877. Perhaps influenced by the missionary spirit of the man who had championed placing out, Brady too became a missionary, and in 1878 received an appointment from the Presbyterian Board of Home Mission to Alaska. Brady's work extended beyond his missionary duties and his establishment of an Indian industrial school in Sitka. He was interested in and took part in many projects to develop the territory, and because of his good efforts was named territorial governor in 1897.[12]

Testimonials of support for the system, such as that offered by Governor Burke, were a boon to the Aid Society, and these were published as proof of its good works. Brace had many instances upon which he could draw, and these were used with great regularity as the society came under fire. Letters from successes presented the positive aspects of the system. A young man placed out in Indiana and attending Yale in 1871 wrote, "I shall ever acknowledge with gratitude that the Children's Aid Society has been the instrument of my elevation," and a young man wrote from Michigan that his employer had given him eighty acres; "Once a New York pauper, [he was] now a Western farmer."[13]

The everyday lives of the placed out and the apparent ease with which so many adjusted from city to country life also gave support to the society's work. One boy on the raw Nebraska frontier reported, "The people are all newly settled here, so it is a little inconvenient; but we are all happy." Meanwhile, children and teenagers who had once sold papers or collected rags for pennies on city streets were quick to translate agricultural products to dollars and cents. With pride one boy noted, "Our crops are good. . . . The prices of corn range from $35 to $50 cash." Another of the placed out boasted, "We have a cream separator. Cream out here [Republican City, Nebraska] is 38 c," and from Texas came the report that twenty-four dollars had been earned for work that brought in seven hundred pounds of cotton. A girl sent to Grand Island, Nebraska, carefully enumerated for the Aid Society her new family's assets: "We have got as high as sixty-five eggs a day. There only eighteen cents a doz. . . . Mama is making butter this winter. . . . She got as high as 50 cents a lb."[14] Clearly, for many, the fortunes of the family were the fortunes of the placed out, and many of those resettled were happy to link their fates to those of their new families and a farm economy.

Despite the accolades from those who had remained in their new homes and acclimated themselves to a rural environment, many of the placed out refused to stay where they had been sent. The return of the placed out to their home cities and a disinclination to remain in their new homes were a puzzlement, if not a continuing problem. Indeed, the Aid Society felt that a return to the city was life threatening. City missionaries had seen children abused by employers, parents, and relatives. There was a general belief that those who freely returned or were lured to leave their new homes would be used by unscrupulous adults in criminal schemes, worked to death as child laborers, or returned to institutions. This concern led the society to advise against continued contact with known relatives or friends left behind. The removal had to be a clean one. Continued contact, it was believed, simply made acceptance of new surroundings more difficult.

No matter the realistic or protective nature of the society's guidelines, the separation of children from family and friends was a point of contention, and one that Brace did not understand. He railed against parents who objected to public asylums and to city officials that allowed Aid Society placement of their charges. From Brace's point of view, the parents' "attachment to the city, their ignorance or bigotry, and their affection for their children, [would] always, prevent them from making use of such a benefication to any large degree."[15] Clearly, it was beyond Brace's comprehension why any caring parent would not want his or her child removed to a kinder surrounding than an institution or tenement slum.

Along these lines of concern for parental approval of placement, consternation was expressed when an issue was made over the resettlement of nonorphans. Neither the New York Children's Aid Society nor other placing institutions had ever made a secret of the fact that many of the children had at least one living parent; the society and other placing institutions did, however, gloss over the possibility that (in many instances) the living parent was an unwed mother. The stigma of illegitimacy was strong, and instead of dwelling on circumstance of birth the Aid Society filled its reports with references to children who had been given over to the society by parents who saw a better life for their children in the country or who had given up their children because they could not provide for them. Illustrative were children sent to Yates Center, Kansas, in 1895. These included Rachel G——, "father . . . unknown and mother unable to care for her"; Joseph W——, whose mother was dead and father was "unable to support him owing to ill-health"; and Richard S——, who was "surrendered by his mother, who was unable to do anything for him." Certainly, the society reports did not evade the question of nonorphan placement. Of the 19 who went to Yates Center in 1895, the society noted in life history details (some, however, vague) that 12 had at least one living parent. On a broader scale, the Aid Society's report of 1893 noted that the total number of placed-out children to that time was 84,318; of that number, 39,406, or 47 percent, had one or both parents living.[16]

The Aid Society and other placing-out institutions might argue that parents had turned over guardianship to an institution or volunteered their children for relocation, but the accusations of wrenching children from parents, some illiterate or foreign-speaking and thus unable to understand the implications of their agreements, continued. The accusations were sometimes true, but it was a complex situation. Ignored in these arguments was the fact that parents or family members with guardianship used placing out as a solution to their own immediate problems of economic and family turmoil. Additionally, it is doubtful that the Aid Society or any other institution knowingly participated in what was some-times portrayed as child stealing or a policy just one step above white slavery. In the case of the Aid Society placing children from other institutions, the society was at the mercy of those institutions' honesty and policies. When the Aid Society placed children from public institutions or private orphanages, it did so with the belief that the organization held guardianship of the child. It was the responsibility of that institution, not the Aid Society, to know the child's status—orphan, half-orphan, deserted, released by parents. Certainly, it would seem that the Aid Society dealt only with credible institutions.

There were, however, misunderstandings and mismanagement. When one man returned to the Salvation Army Brooklyn Nursery and Infants Hospital to retrieve his daughter, he was told that she had "been put out on a farm in Kansas" by the Aid Society. All other information was denied him. She was in a good home and legally adopted. Few parents sought, or could afford, legal avenues for retrieving their children, but one family in 1872 did sue the Brooklyn Children's Aid Society and the New York Children's Aid Society for sending an eighteen-year-old son west. The societies were acquitted since it was apparent that the boy had used placing out as his way of running away from home. The incident pointed out, however, the working relationships between the Aid Society and other organizations, as well as an inherent weakness of a system that could be too casual in checking parental guardianship.[17]

Although the Aid Society during the system's later years cautioned children against contacting known relatives, there were numerous instances of children corresponding or even visiting with family or friends after being placed out. Arthur Turner, sent to Vermont in 1853, not only traveled to New York on at least two occasions to visit his mother but at age fifteen arranged for her to return with him to Vermont. Others of the placed out were traced by family members who showed up to reclaim them. In another Vermont example, a child was located by his mother about ten months after his placement with a family that insisted the child had "no desire to return to New York City." The boy, however, readily returned with his mother. The results of these contacts were as varied as the individuals involved. When parents arrived in McLeansboro, Illinois, in 1886 to return their daughter to New York, she flatly refused to leave her new family, but in 1902 when a brother traveled to Columbus, Kansas, for his sister, she returned with him to the east. One nine-year-old, sent to a Nebraska home only to be returned three years later on demand by her New York father, wistfully remembered: "I recall I had a nice room, good meals, taking lunch out to the men out in the fields . . . going to quilting parties, also County Fairs. . . . For three short years, I had love."[18]

Episodes of family contact sometimes were reported to the Aid Society by the receiving family or the child in question, and such incidents received space in the annual reports—when the outcome supported the Society's contention that the placed out preferred their new homes to life in the city. In the Aid Society's report of 1861, a letter from Illinois reported: "She [the child] has spoken of her visit from [her stepfather], he came determined to take her away, but she was just as much determined not to go, and avoided any private interview. He said her mother was very sick, and nothing probably would save her life but a visit from B——; this might be true, but she has been too much accustomed to his deception to rely upon it."[19]

Despite such examples of children wishing to stay where they were, the system was accused of snatching them from "the arms of their families" and of tearing them from the only homes they had known, however ragged. Equally ignored were the children who received adequate care and education in orphan asylums and who acclimated themselves to an institutional environment. For many the asylum was not a place from which to escape, but a place in which to live. One woman, placed out in Missouri at the age of eight, recalled that she and her twin sister were happy with their life in a Brooklyn, New York, orphanage: "On every Saturday we went to the Brooklyn Bridge for a walk or to Coney Island. We then went home and had our usual meal, ginger snaps and milk. On Sundays we went to Trinity Church for services." When the girls were selected to go west, the woman later recalled, "Both of us [were] crying for we didn't want to leave."[20]

For charities and social workers who argued the benefits of home over institutional life, such reactions were impossible to understand. For those who criticized placing out, these instances were proof that asylum care was productive and not the pit of unhappiness some portrayed it to be. Additionally, the return by the placed out to city life could be offered as proof that the relocated had been forcibly removed. Even among those who chose to stay in their new homes, it was argued, many would leave if they had the means. For some of the placed out, particularly those who had been sent to farmers as paid laborers, this was true. They saw their experience as just a phase of life that enabled them to earn a living not possible in the city. Perhaps they would remain in their new communities, perhaps not. One teen-ager resettled in Pawnee County, Nebraska, as a paid farm employee clearly intended to return east when he and a friend, another placed-out boy, had saved their money and reached the age of twenty-one. The possibility of good prospects on the farm could not dissuade some from returning to city life. Generally, it was said, the Aid Society and other placing-out institutions ignored the basic desire for the familiar, for "home." Although they did not understand it, the ladies of Five Points Mission acknowledged this desire, for they early noted, "In a vast majority of instances they [the children] cling to their own homes with a tenacity which is truly astonishing when we consider their wretchedness." The contention that children felt the wrench of separation is borne out by an eyewitness account of a placement in Burlington, Kansas, in 1895: "It was a pathetic scene to see the boys separated. Coming from a great city to a country town to be given away to strangers was too much for some of them to stand and they broke down and cried."[21]

Along with the accusations that children were being unceremoniously taken from parents or families, there was the suspicion that they were being sold into bondage. Such stories provided sensationalized fodder for the critics. When a girl sent to Muncie, Indiana, made her way to Indianapolis, reporting that chloroform had been used to force her removal from New York, the press attempted to play up the story. Meanwhile, children that had arrived with the girl and the local citizenry just shrugged and declared the girl to be "a little out of her head." State boards of charity or individuals may have chosen to believe charges of kidnapping and forced removal, but not the communities that received children. In addition, many critics may have misinterpreted the acceptance of employer donations to the society as payment for a child. This, however, did not dispel the notion that children were being bought and sold. Such accusations gained a degree of credibility only when a representative of a once-slave state alluded to children being used as forced labor. This was true of the complaint by J. H. Mills of North Carolina who, at the 1883 Conference of

Charities and Correction, protested the no-questions-asked Aid Society placements in his state. According to Mills, society agents placed boys with men who took them only to avoid paying for cotton-field labor: "Their slaves being set free, these men needing labor take these boys and treat them as slaves."[22]

Placing-out institutions also were accused of renaming the children, making it difficult, if not impossible, for a child to be traced by its natural parents or relatives. There was never any doubt that the names of some children were changed, but this was not done by the Aid Society, the Sisters of Charity, or any other placing organization. Receiving families, particularly if they legally adopted the child, gave him or her a new name. The Aid Society recognized that such situations occurred and did not seem uncomfortable with reporting them: "You remember Mary S—— [in an Illinois home]. Her name is [now] Jennie P," and "Having a William and a John before he [Johnny] came here [Pennsylvania], we have given him the name of Frederick; he is generally called Freddy." In fact, those who asserted that children's names were changed may have confused placing-out organizations with some institutions that practiced confidentiality. A Boston orphanage in 1853, for example, explained that names of its charges were concealed because, if made known, "they would prove injurious to the adopters and the adopted, and serve in a measure to paralyze our efforts." The children were to know no other parents but those who gave them their name and who had "their moral and religious training in hand." The same line of reasoning continued into the twentieth century, and was used, as an illustration, by the Sisters of Our Lady of Charity and Refuge who ran the Good Shepherd Home in Dallas, Texas. Pleading for funds in 1921, the Sisters noted that when girls arrived, they were given a "class" name, with no one knowing their family names but the mother superior and the sister who received them into the home. This was for "the protection of the girls and their families."[23]

Another point of criticism, and surely one Brace would not have dreamed possible, was that of religious prejudice. Brace, as a Christian, had intended that the system would provide good homes with moral, religious influences. The children of poverty, he believed, had little experience with Christian education. If they were to be saved physically and spiritually, they had to be removed to a more wholesome environment. Brace had long argued that his "enterprise" was based on "the broadest and simplest principles of morality and religion," and these had for so long provided a foundation for placing out that any question of specific doctrine taught a child was argued to be irrelevant. The same disclaimer had been made by the Boston Children's Mission for its Sunday school efforts, but to no avail. The important point, argued Protestant charities, was that a chance for Christian education was made available. Social reformer Homer Folks saw things differently and complained about the lack of consideration given to a child's religious background. Interestingly, Folks agreed in principle that home care was best for children, and when he began work in 1890 with the Children's Aid Society of Pennsylvania, he immediately enacted an in-state placement program. The difference, Folks would contend between his procedures and those of the Aid Society, was that homes were meticulously checked and visited, with children placed in homes of like faith. The debate was taken up by Jacob Riis, author of *How the Other Half Lives* and supporter of placing out. Riis argued that the Aid Society and its agents disclaimed any knowledge of a child's religious heritage. It simply was believed that the religious preferences of the receiving family would be conveyed to the child. That these homes were most often Protestant was not addressed.[24]

Although Protestant charities asserted that they tried to place Catholic or Jewish children in homes of those faiths, the sincerity of these efforts was questioned. Brace's Protestant background and the involvement of Protestant ministers during the placing out years certainly predisposed the Aid Society and other non-Catholic organizations to place children in Protestant homes. Possibly Brace gave no thought to the placement of Jewish and Catholic children with Protestant families, and the Aid Society did send these children west. Brace's mind-set was firmly Protestant, excluding the possibility of matching religious heritage. Since there was no conscious attempt to match ethnic heritage, there was no considered effort to match religious backgrounds. The overriding concern was removing children from the city. It could be argued that attempts to locate Catholic or Jewish communities would have taken more time, which there was very little of in the rush to remove children from their debilitating environments. The idea of such placements could have been dismissed on several grounds, but there are many indications that prejudice for Protestant denominations played a role. Brace, like other theologians of his time, distrusted and disliked Catholic doctrine and Jewish sects. When Brace openly expressed a prejudice against some immigrant groups it was because he saw them as "superstitious" Catholics or the "refuse of ill-formed [East European] civilizations." Not surprisingly, one faction to question the Aid Society's work was the Catholic community, through such organizations as the Catholic Protectory of New York. The Aid Society attempted to stem the tide of accusations by noting children who had been placed in Catholic homes: "Michael H—— is in a good home with a Catholic farmer. . . . Michael had been a most troublesome boy, and his foster parents have exercised extraordinary patience with him." The Catholic community could not be deterred so easily, however, and criticisms persisted. Interestingly, in this debate the Sisters of Charity program was not accused by the Catholic Church or Protestant reformers of disregarding religious preference. That program was clearly defined. Foundling Hospital children, usually with their proof of baptism in the Roman Catholic Church, went to Catholic homes; theoretically they were going to families of like faith, and thus the Catholic program did not violate the religious preference of the child or his natural parents.[25]

Catholic attempts at placing out were not immune, however, to criticism, and in one well-publicized episode with religious and racist overtones took the full brunt of a national outcry. The incident began in 1904 when the Sisters of Charity decided to expand its placing-out activities to Arizona Territory. Letters went to parish priests, asking if local families would take children from the Foundling Hospital. A response came from the parish that included Clifton and Morenci, two copper mining towns with divergent populations—Catholic Mexican workers, Catholic Anglos, and Protestant Anglos.

By this time the system operated by the Sisters was well in place. By 1904 the Foundling Hospital was resettling from 450 to 475 children per year. The placement of children in Arizona was expected to be routine, although it was an unknown area for the Sisters. For the trip west there were 57 children between the ages of two and five; 3 Sisters; 4 nurses; and the agent, George W. Swayne. Along the route of travel, 17 children were placed in Missouri and Arkansas, leaving 40 children for new homes in Arizona.

The events that followed brought out the worst in accusations, some of them previously used against the Aid Society, and led to a national scandal that underscored nativist prejudices. Misunderstandings had led the Sisters of Charity to believe that the children, all of white European background, would be placed in Spanish—not Mexican—homes. They also were unaware of the local prejudices that existed between Anglos and Mexicans in the two mining towns, and within Arizona Territory in general. When the destination was reached and the children were taken by their new parents, there was a white reaction that fell just short of a lynch mob. The situation became so explosive that Agent Swayne prudently left on one of the first trains out of town.

The children were forcibly removed from their new homes by a number of Anglo men, and nineteen of the children were taken into the homes of Anglo families who refused to give them up to the Sisters. Eventually, the Arizona Supreme Court was involved and rendered a decision that the Anglos were justified in removing the children. The remaining children were escorted back to New York and resettled in areas better known and more hospitable to the Sisters.

For those living in the Southwest, the episode proved a too-close look at its prejudices. The children had not been excluded from their intended homes on the basis of religion, but because of race; white children could not be cared for by Mexican families. Meanwhile, some in the national press luridly proclaimed, "Babies Sold Like Sheep," and made the accusation, "This notorious institution [Foundling Hospital] has for years been shipping children in car-loads all over the country, and they are given away and sold like cattle." Such headlines caught national attention, but other reports attempted to play down provocative details. The *New York Times* simply noted that "the action of the good sisters was undoubtedly taken in entire good faith" and then took on yellow journalism's use of the subject by suggesting, "Of course, nobody is deeply interested in the fact of a foundling or it would not be a foundling." The Sisters of Charity continued work in placing out, but the Arizona debacle had allowed a national chorus of criticisms. That many of the printed stories were untrue gave little relief to the image of charitable works.[26]

A changing and growing society created a confusion of signals about what was to be done with the lower classes. Placing-out agents reported a continuing demand for children in the West when, at the same time, official representatives and reformers were becoming more skeptical of placing out. There were champions for both sides of the argument. Some, such as Folks and state boards of charity, decried the system. Matched against them were such people as Horatio Alger—who for a time took a room in a newsboys' lodging house and incorporated real-life acquaintances there into his fictional characters[27]—Jacob Riis, financial supporters, agents of the Aid Society, as well as a considerable number of Catholics interested in their own program.

An Aid Society agent to speak in support was Francis H. White, whose career evolved from placing-out agent to sociologist. Although White was biased towards the Aid Society, his arguments echoed those of others: "When one endeavors to reform, to make radical changes in a human life, he undertakes a serious task that may weigh heavily upon his soul [but] . . . the placing out of dependent children is by far the most economical, the most humane, and the most successful way of caring for them." The allies of placing out agreed that there had been mistakes and that the system was not perfect in its outcome for each person, but they argued that the system could not be condemned outright when it did such good and provided such positive experiences for those involved. As Reverend Russell Toles of the New England Home for Little Wanderers explained, the work was a mission and those who carried it out were accountable foremost to God: ". . . to manage a public institution in such a manner as to please even all its friends would require someone more than human. We do not expect to do this. But in the fear of God, we mean to care for these little wanderers."[28]

Since some placing organizations did not indenture, forcing children to remain in their new surroundings, numerous circumstances were created under which the system could be questioned. It may be that criticisms and the circumstances of runaways or parents and children seeking each other were, in part, reasons that younger children were more often placed out during the latter years of the system. When placing out first began, sturdy workers were part of the advertised benefits to the receiving families. By the end of the century, placing-out organizations made much less of the benefits of labor, shifting emphasis to the need for good homes. In fact, potential families were warned: "Homes are desired for those children in town and country, but they must be good homes where influences are of the best and under no circumstances will a child be placed with people who wish chore boys or kitchen drudges." In reality, using them for farm labor was still a common reason for taking in these children, and admonitions to the contrary were often ignored. Into the twentieth century, farmers sought the eastern poor as a source of extra help, despite placing out institutions' new emphasis on younger children and adoption. And there were still some among the placed out who experienced hardship, overwork, and abuse. Sent to Missouri, one of the placed out recalled that after her third year of school, she was kept home to spend her youth as the family's full-time cook and housekeeper: "My foster mother was so cruel—oh, she was a crackerjack. They wanted one of the sons to get me pregnant so I'd stay home and work. How could they do that?" Another remembered no sign of affection or interaction with his new parents; for his labor there was room and board, nothing more: "They never touched me or said they loved me, and they didn't want me to call them Mom and Dad. Think what that does to you. They weren't mean, they were cold. . . . When I was 15 or 16 I decided I'd live in a garbage can before I'd stay there any longer." And, for a boy sent to Kansas, arduous farm work was interspersed with beatings and threats of more physical violence if he did not pretend all was well when the Aid Society agent came to call. Eventually, he was removed from that home, but rather than being returned to New York as the Aid Society promised, he was sent to another Kansas town. In 1924 he wrote a sister, also placed out in Kansas: "I found a good home at last, but it took three years of hell before I got here."[29]

As the system progressed into the twentieth century, groups of the placed out contained more toddlers, and the older children were usually less than twelve or thirteen years of age. Official records for age levels for each year are lacking, but review and comparison of newspaper advertisements and arrivals of children, as well as the ages of those placed out early in the twentieth century indicate a drop in the ages of those sent out of the eastern cities. The drop in ages began to appear in the 1890s and was quite apparent by 1920.

The Foundling Hospital had always placed younger children, but the Aid Society too began to make a concentrated effort in the relocation of those below the age of six. This suggests several changes in the placing-out system and in the thinking of those responsible for it. By the turn of the century, American society recognized the adolescent and the maturation problems of that time in life, and this age group along with older teen-agers was deemphasized in placements. At the same time, placing-out organizations focused on families, rather than employers and single men and women, as candidates for taking in children. Additionally, many families wanted younger children, not the older adolescent. The "large boys" and older girls may have brought so many problems that placement of teen-agers and young adults was restrained to lessen possible recriminations from the general public. Brace recognized the problems and, echoing his disenchantment with salvaging adults, pronounced that girls—he made no mention of boys—over the age of fourteen were "hopeless."[30] A shift had occurred in the philosophy of the Aid Society and other institutions.

Younger children were in demand. They were less likely to remember their previous homes and had not, theoretically, had the time to develop deep attachments to persons or places they had known. This is borne out by the memoirs and reminiscences of many of the placed out who had no memory of homes other than the ones in which they were placed or the rail trip that brought them to those homes. "But I remember way back, a faint recollection only, of sitting on luggage at a station"; the station was in Iowa and provided the only memory for one woman of her placing-out journey.[31]

If one considers the situation from a purely economical standpoint, the younger child might need care and nurturing for an extended period of time, but he or she was far less likely to run off after a few weeks, months, or a year. But there were other reasons for families to seek the younger child, the toddler, or preadolescent. Childless couples or those who had lost a child through death wished to take into their homes younger children. This quest for a child to replace one lost was not unusual, and in some cases those taken into homes knew the role they were to play: "My [new] mother had twin girls that were stillborn, and I guess I was supposed to make up for them." By the early decades of the twentieth century, adoption in general created such a demand for infants and toddlers, especially infant girls, that commentators on the American scene woefully announced, "Not Enough Babies to Go Around."[32] Meanwhile, the sense of doing good works and providing a moral, healthy environment were still strong incentives for families to take in older youngsters, although these were usually not over the age of twelve.

Despite the apparent increase in legal adoptions during the latter years of the system, implicit in debates over placing out was the question of the legal status of those removed from the cities. If placing-out institutions did not demand indenture, adoption, or agreements with families to serve as foster care parents, who accepted legal responsibility for a minor? Certainly, there were those who were indentured and had the contracts as proof of their status within the home. There were those who had been legally adopted, giving them the benefits of family name and rights of inheritance. It is apparent now, as then, however, that many of the placed out, and perhaps the majority, existed in a kind of no man's land of legal status. The institution to release the child for resettlement may have verbalized the rights of "prior" guardianship, but most orphanages or asylums that worked with placing-out organizations, expressed little interest in the outcome. For those placed out and not indentured or legally adopted, it was a state of limbo. It is clear in placing-out accounts that many, unsure of their place, assigned themselves a status. Many twentieth-century accounts state that the child was adopted into the family or treated as one of the family's own, but being treated as part of the family and having a record of adoption are quite separate things. It is probable that many receiving families were uneducated or unaware of the niceties of the law and therefore never considered or understood either option. When Peter Manachisa, for example, was placed by the Sisters of Charity in a Louisiana home, his new parents signed indenture, not adoption, papers; Peter was given his new family's name and he later learned that his parents, of limited education, had believed they were adopting him.[33] For a growing number of reformers and officials of state boards of charity and institutions, the rather cavalier attitude of placing agencies in ignoring the legal implications of status may have represented just another reason for the system's abolition.

During the last twenty years of the nineteenth century, critics and supporters continued to wage their arguments, with neither giving ground. To prove its case the Aid Society launched additional internal investigations in 1881 and in 1883. The former, again conducted by Agent Fry, was intended to trace persons placed out twenty years before. Evidently, the society hoped to prove that these early placements, now men and women, had prospered and gained from their experience. The names of forty-five who had been placed out were drawn at random; the only common denominator was that all had traveled by the Michigan Central Railroad to their new homes. Fry searched for six weeks and located thirty-four of those on his list. What he found were ordinary people going about their everyday business; only one had ended up on the wrong side of the law, having stolen from his employer. In the 1883 investigation,

Agents Fry and Schlegel checked placements in Wisconsin, while a study of boys placed in Minnesota and Kansas was conducted by Agents J. Mathews and E. Trott. Their findings were about the same as those of the 1881 investigation. None of those traced had become "successful, prominent" citizens, but none had become burdens to their new communities.[34]

How the Aid Society and Americans in general judged personal success was, of course, arbitrary. Certainly, many of the placed out considered their interests and options for work a triumph in themselves. "Ordinary" citizens in their new environment, the placed out often echoed the Aid Society's study results. One young man reported in 1920 that he had worked in a garage for some time before taking up farming—a common occupation in his Nebraska community. Another wrote that he was farming but had found time to join a literary society where he planned to present an essay on "brush-making, which I learned in N. Y." As a model citizen, he was comfortable with sharing a part of his former life. From a girl in Stromsburg, Nebraska, the proud news came that a "scholarship to any college in the State of Nebraska 'free'" had been received; education now opened doors to any possibility of careers.[35] While not the prominent community or state leaders the Aid Society wished to find, these men and women had become exactly what the society said it hoped for—successful in the society's ideals of self-help and self-improvement.

Since placing-out opponents took a jaundiced view of in-house studies and the selected letters published in Aid Society reports, Hastings Hornell Hart, later director of the Department of Child Help for the Russell Sage Foundation, decided in 1884 to conduct an outside investigation. Highly respected as a leader in progressive child care and with no connection to the Aid Society, Hart and his findings could not be disavowed on the basis of partisanship. Minnesota was chosen as the study area, and the results were mixed, from the Aid Society's point of view. In the society's favor was

vindication from accusations that it deliberately sent juvenile delinquents to the West. Hart found that although some ended badly,
the society was not at fault. Additionally, it was reported that when
cases of child abuse occurred, the society acted responsibly. Interestingly, Hart also discovered that many reports of abuse were the
product of community gossip based on jealousies or feuds; if one
did not like a neighbor, one could just whisper of mistreatment of
his New York worker. The failing of the society, the report decided,
was in the initial procedure for placing children—a basic component of the system. Hart personally witnessed placements in No-
bles and Watonwan counties, and was appalled at the lack of
judgment shown by the local committees, the noninvestigation of
employers and families, and the rather hurried attitude of the agent
in charge. In fact, he found that local committees were afraid to
oppose applicants for children; they feared making enemies within
their home communities.[36]

Whether this investigation brought converts to placing out or
successfully answered critics is debatable, but for many professionals the Hart inquiry was impressive and had a major impact. In
1899, partially because of Hart's report, the Conference of Charities
and Correction, which had seen such acrimonious debate over the
system in the past, gave placing out its official approval.[37] Undoubtedly, this professional support allowed the system to continue
into the twentieth century.

The Aid Society did not rest on any professional endorsements,
however, and into the twentieth century it continued to present
reports and studies to support its contention of careful and continuing investigation into the fate of those placed out. The 1924 report
of Agent Anna Laura Hill, "All Children Placed Since 1911 in
Family Homes in or Near McPherson, Kansas," was just one of
many, and important for today is its comparison against her 1911
account of McPherson placements, providing a microscopic view
of the system. Both the 1911 and 1924 reports contained the usual

glowing language used by agents. In 1911 the children, according to Hill, were placed in neat, comfortable homes, "all very high class," and by 1924 these same placed out were noted as attending college or with promising careers or with families of their own. John McKellar, placed out at the age of ten with the family of a McPherson furniture dealer, had by 1924 found work with the Rock Island Railroad and had "a nice suburban home for which he was able to pay cash." John's brother, Gilbert, placed out at the age of five, was by 1924 a college student with a part-time job in a newspaper office. The other stories were almost identical in that they displayed positive experiences for the placed out. When the first of many Aid Society children were taken to McPherson in 1911, eighteen made up the group. By 1924, four of those had died—one as a soldier in World War I, the others by causes not given. One of the eighteen was by 1924 considered to be a "failure." Placed out at the age of seven and described as "a bright boy but of a very peculiar disposition," he had returned to New York. Interestingly, another also had returned east, but this young man who had been placed with "one of the oldest and most respected families in the town" was not determined by Hill to be a failure—perhaps because he had returned to an older sister in New York and had found gainful employment at a state hospital. Also representative of the placing-out program were the numbers of brothers and sisters who traveled together to new homes. Among the 1911 group of eighteen there were three sets of siblings: the Mandt children, Charles, Violet, Timothy, and Milton; the Koedel children, Alma, Ida, and Henry; and the McKellar brothers, John and Gilbert. Except for Charles and Violet, who were four and eight years old at the time, none of the siblings were placed together in the same homes. Hill noted in 1911 that all of the brothers and sisters were "near" one another; Hill was correct if closeness was defined in broad geographic terms, but one has to wonder how often Alma and Ida Koedel, for example, had contact with their brother, taken by a family that lived some fifteen miles away. The point was not the proximity of placements, after all, but showing that the children had been successfully placed. Both the 1911 and 1924 reports supported this view, and the 1924 review, additionally, conformed to earlier studies in that, of a specific group, one could find a minority that had not met expectations but the majority were leading constructive lives as a result of their western placement.[38]

Despite reports, in-house studies, and the Hart investigation, debates did not subside. Accusations of juvenile delinquency among the placed out and other criticisms of the system from some states came at a time when those areas were beginning to wrestle with the problems long known in eastern cities. The midwest and plains states remained heavily rural with economies tied to agriculture, but there were growing industries centered on livestock, farm implements, grain, and supplying goods to a rural population. Manufacturing, livestock yards, and heavy industry created new jobs and a need for cheap labor, much of which was supplied by an influx of new immigrants. Western urban centers boomed and suffered the same problems of their eastern counterparts. Certainly, there had been a poor, destitute, and orphaned class in the western states since the days of early settlement. As early as 1815, Pennsylvania and Ohio noted a "growing relief problem in Western communities," and the Benevolent Society of Cincinnati, "overwhelmed" with requests for aid, campaigned for construction of a poorhouse. Such problems were more localized on the western frontier, however. Traditional responses, such as indenture, aid from churches or ladies aid societies, as well as local poor laws and the building of asylums or poor farms, usually dealt with area problems. Whether enacting poor laws carried from the eastern states or establishing institutions for the poor, western communities were in effect replicating the accepted forms of relief and care for the poor. By 1855, for example, Chicago noted a "growing number of juvenile offenders," and by 1858 the city had its own Home of the Friendless, founded to find jobs and homes for destitute women and children.[39] The general urbanization of the west, on the other hand, presented new demands that could not be met with simple solutions.

In Chicago, as well as other western cities, it was apparent by the last decades of the nineteenth century that stronger directions were needed. By the 1870s the once "western" states were in the throes of developing structured institutions and programs. Within this context, one historian has offered an important explanation for receiving states' complaints against placing out. As these states attempted to erect institutions for the poor, destitute, and orphaned in the population, the theory of the home as the best environment was viewed by many to undermine the very institutions that state governments were trying to establish and finance. Michigan's Lyman P. Alden flatly refused to believe that home care was preferable to institutional life. He complained of the system, but he had a vested interest in gaining support for the proinstitution viewpoint.[40] This analysis addresses the motives of many who decried placing out, particularly when it is noted that the critics were often superintendents or directors of institutions or state boards of charity. This point is of major importance and underlies the heated controversy concerning institutional versus home-centered care. Within this discussion, it must be remembered that western institutions did not always strictly adhere to institutional programs; these charities, too, indentured, offered children for adoption, and used placing out to send their charges across state boundaries. Developing institutions and their managers, however, felt a threat from anyone who argued the home-placement route as preferable, and it is possible that they viewed placing-out organizations as competition, vying for the same placement homes. Since Brace and the Aid Society were vocal leaders for placing out beyond the confines of the city, they became visible targets.

Into the twentieth century, home-care advocates were assailed, but they persisted in arguing for alternatives to institutions. Perhaps Brace's son Charles best stated the pro-home case when he replied in 1910 to a *New York Times* letter that praised institutions:

> *Orphan asylums are necessary and beneficial in much the same way the hospitals are. By all means let us take into institutions the fatherless and motherless and those whose home life is degrading and can lead only to disaster; but, as in the case of the hospital patient, let us discharge them when convalescence is reasonably advanced and not develop chronic invalidism. There are few more pitiful specimens of humanity than the youth who has spent his childhood in an institution and who is at last forced out into a world of which he knows nothing by actual experience, unfitted for usefulness and doomed to failure.*[41]

Thus, differing points of view on institutionalization continued into the twentieth century. Reformers may have called for action and enlightened treatment of the poor, but often what constituted the best methods could not be agreed on. Beginning in the 1870s governmental bodies, states, and individuals worked at cross purposes, having no defined agreements as to the best means for poor relief. There was an accepted custom for treatment of the poor, and classifications of the worthy and unworthy were standard. The decade was, however, one of transition in thought on institutionalized care and its reform.

Actually increasing the opportunities for placing out was New York State's 1875 Children's Law, which made it obligatory for all children over two years of age to be removed from poorhouses and almshouses. Only infants and toddlers could remain to be cared for by their mothers or other women inmates. One form of child institutionalization was banned, but the children's needs remained, allowing placing out to continue as an alternative to their care. Meanwhile, a serious look was being given to child migration. On the Eastern Seaboard, Franklin Sanborn, of the Massachusetts Board of State Charities, argued that states were responsible for their own destitute and should not extradite the problem. In agreement was Ohio's state board of charities member W. J. Scott and the Indiana Board of Charities, which, upon its creation in 1889, complained that the state was "a dumping ground for dependents from other states." Legislation was sought immediately to regulate "the importation of dependent children." Concurring was the board of the small White Hall Orphan's Home Society in Illinois, which proclaimed: "We think New York is amply able and should care for her own paupers, and not thrust them on Illinois." Ironically, the states represented by these individuals or boards placed out their own resident children. Further, it was argued that if every accusation leveled at the Aid Society, and by implication other placing-out organizations, was true, then "a social vice [was] fostered."[42] States began to examine closely procedures and to mandate statutes for the resettlement of out-of-state children.

Michigan took a major step in 1895 when it required institutions to place a bond with county probate judges for each child resettled. Four years later Indiana, Illinois, and Minnesota passed statutes that forbade the placement of children with mental deficiencies and certain diseases, and required more stringent standards for placement homes. Missouri followed suit in 1901 with a similar state law. In that same year, Nebraska allowed that any person, corporation, or association holding legal guardianship of a child by "written" approval could place that child up for adoption. On the one hand this would seem to give a free reign to those wishing to place children, but in fact the statute's language was restrictive in that it demanded legal proof of guardianship and it specified adoption—not foster care or home placement without legal documentation. Such state laws were inclusive of both in-state and out-of-state institutions that practiced home placement of children, but the implications were much more serious for the work of organizations that wished to place nonresident children.[43]

That state statutes included a passage on mental and physical problems was perhaps a result of another charge against placing out. While critics focused on the possibilty of a criminal element being loosed on western states, there was some concern that mentally and physically handicapped children had been transported. If such was the case, then states faced the possibility of caring for these placed out at some point in their lifetimes. Thus, a drain on the resources of state institutions would be created. Although the Aid Society did not address directly relocation of the handicapped, there is evidence that both physically and mentally handicapped children were transported. John H. White, the newspaperman, most certainly suffered from a birth defect that caused a severe limp, and a girl sent to Kansas later recalled her fear that she would not be placed because of "physical deformities"—a congenital hip defect forced her to walk with a limp and a webbed stump on her right hand took the place where the first two fingers should have been. How many of these children with special problems and needs were resettled is impossible to ascertain. One Aid Society case file noted a boy with epilepsy who was returned almost immediately from his placement home in Massachusetts,[44] and Brace himself noted one placement example from Ohio of a child with low mental abilities. The point he was attempting to make in publishing this letter from the receiving family, however, was the importance of good Christian charity:

> *I feel that, considering her mental deficiencies, she [Carrie] has made as much progress in learning as could be expected. . . . I am often asked by my friends, who think the child is little more than half-witted, why I do not "send her back, and get a brighter one." My answer is, that she is just the one who needs the care and kindness which Providence has put it into my power to bestow.*[45]

One of the first states to legislate comprehensive restrictions on placing out was Kansas. In April 1901 the state legislature mandated that the State Board of Charities had authority to scrutinize all organizations or institutions placing children. With that legislation in hand, the board immediately ruled that no homeless children could be brought into Kansas without a certificate of good character and a five thousand dollar guaranty bond. When New York Foundling Hospital personnel arrived in Kansas eight months later to place twenty children, the state's governor, William Stanley, ordered the State Board of Charities to investigate: "We cannot afford to have the state made a dumping ground for the dependent children of other states, especially New York."[46]

Stanley's order and the 1901 law brought reaction from Foundling Hospital agent George Swayne. Writing to Stanley, the agent stressed that he and the Foundling Hospital were willing to do whatever was necessary in furnishing bonds. Swayne followed up the initial letter with another, including a circular that outlined the work of the Sisters of Charity. In this second letter, Swayne explained that thirty-three thousand children had been placed out in "Western States" through the Sisters' program, and he responded to the governor's concern that Kansas was being made "a dumping ground": "We do not dump our children but see that they get good homes and we keep records & look after them until they are twenty one." Swayne also took aim against the New York Children's Aid Society, blaming that organization for the legislation under which the Foundling Hospital now had to work in Kansas: "Our children must not be confused with other children that range in age from 10 to 14 years that have been dumped upon the Western States by other New York institutions."[47]

Swayne's concern over the 1901 Kansas law was echoed within the state. The Reverend Christian Krehbiel, superintendent of the Mennonite Orphans' and Children's Aid Society and overseer of the Halstead Indian Industrial School for Cheyenne and Arapaho children, questioned the law's meaning for the Mennonite-supported charities in Kansas. Certainly, Indian children had been taken across state and territorial lines for much of the nineteenth century to be housed and educated in government and church-sponsored boarding schools, missions, and orphanages such as the one at Halstead. This had been done with little legislative notice, and Krehbiel must have wondered at the consequences of the new state statutes. Although the Indian children brought into Kansas from Oklahoma Territory were not placed out in Kansas homes, they were housed in a private Kansas institution. Therefore, Krehbiel wondered if "this law would also apply to children, who were sent for before the passing of the law, but who have not yet come?" The reply to the minister is not extant. Additionally, surviving state records, for either the Kansas State Board of Charities or the secretary of state, which would have received registrations for out-of-state institutions, show no registrations or payments of guaranty bonds by any institution in or outside of Kansas.[48]

In attempting to deal with an area new to them, Kansas lawmakers had not considered all of the implications of the 1901 law, as pointed out in Krehbiel's query. Evidently, lawmakers also had overlooked the need for a coherent approach to enacting legislation. Out-of-state placements continued and seemingly were checked only when the governor called for an investigation. Such was the case in 1902 when the president of the State Charities and Corrections Board of Trustees was ordered by Governor Stanley to again study the Foundling Hospital and reports that it had distributed "a carload of orphans." The answer was in the affirmative; ten children had been placed in Wichita-area homes. The response to Stanley confirming these placements also presents some puzzling bits of information. The investigator noted that the Foundling Hospital was "under bond of $10,000 to comply with our statutes in reference to sending into the state diseased or deformed children and remove from the state at their own expense, any children who shall, within a term of five years, become a public charge." The report also noted that the State of Kansas had given the organization a license to operate because "the state [was] not being done any injustice through receiving orphans placed within its borders by this sisterhood [Sisters of Charity]." Evidently, Agent Swayne, who had brought the children to Wichita, had been successful in persuading, if not the governor, the governor's board on charities to allow the Foundling Hospital continued placements, paying not the five-thousand-dollar guaranty bond required by law but a sum double that.[49] The lack of records today and the report made in 1902 certainly indicate discrepancies that, if nothing else, underscore divergent thoughts concerning out-of-state placements. The governor's actions suggest a desire to end the practice, while the state's board of charities evidently sanctioned the operation, monitoring only when told to do so.

Perhaps because of the murky area in which state officials found themselves, the state legislature in 1903 attempted to clarify and expand its earlier legislation. The new law dealt with requirements for adoption and built on the earlier placing-out legislation: "No probate court was to permit the adoption of any minor child sent into the state through the auspices of any association incorporated in any other state until all requirements governing adoption had been met, including the requirement set down in 1901 regarding a guarantee that the child was healthy in mind and body and not [of] 'vicious character.' "[50] The focus of this legislation was out-of-state organizations and their activities, although the board of charities was still responsible for overseeing all institutions, public and private, within Kansas.

Investigations and debates continued in other states. In 1915 the Illinois State Legislature launched a joint committee investigation of placing out. The findings damned the practice as "unwarranted, illegal, and uncharitable," and likened the system to slavery. The committee's report condemned the placement of eastern children in the state and the placement of Illinois' resident children in other states and foreign countries (these were not detailed). In effect, it reported that placing out was nothing more than "commercialized childhood," with the "controlling factor" the need for child labor.[51]

What had begun as a system to supply farmers, mechanics, and homemakers with the workers they needed, and to remove the poor from unimaginable conditions, had evolved into a social pariah. Proponents and opponents could debate the system's merits, but somewhere the once-heralded system had lost. Despite professionals' support, the arguments for Christian duty, and the desire to create a positive childhood for the orphaned and destitute, state boards of charities and state legislatures, along with noted reformers and social workers, condemned and demanded an end to placing out as created by the New York Children's Aid Society.

The reevaluation of placing out and the calls to abolish the system were outgrowths of a changing America. The system itself was caught in the intellectual debate of what comprised the best form of child care, the home or the asylum. As importantly, however, placing out was a point of contention between western states' growing urbanization and eastern cities that had long contended with poor relief and successive waves of immigration. Bringing together these concerns was Josiah Strong, who in 1886 published *Our Country: Its Possible Future and Its Present Crisis*. The impact of this volume on American thought was, according to the chief librarian of Congress, as intense as that of *Uncle Tom's Cabin*. For his readers, Strong "had gauged correctly the mind and mood of Protestant America." What he articulated for thousands of Americans, particularly those in the midwestern and plains states, was a fear of new immigrants and the cultures they brought with them. Strong asked what impact these would have on "formative" institutions: "We may well ask—and with special reference to the West— whether this in-sweeping immigration is to foreignize us, or we are to Americanize it?" Clearly, an underlyinng theme in Strong's arguments was caution against the Catholic immigrants, but one sees echoes of state complaints against the dumping of "eastern refuse" in western states. "During the last ten years we have suffered a peaceful invasion by an army more than four times as vast as the estimated number of Goths and Vandals that swept over Southern Europe and overwhelmed Rome."[52] Strong's comparison was not lost on those who decried placing out. They could argue that an invasion of children had taken place; children who were not wanted or needed in the urbanized West.

For the regions of the country that had received the eastern poor, placing out became just another example of the east foisting itself upon the rest of the country, particularly the western states. In this regard the question of placing out had less to do with the needs of children than the conflict between west and east. Under such a combination of forces, the placing-out system was viewed as flawed, and when new, so-called enlightened ideas for social welfare were added to the struggle, the system was doomed. Despite its champions and its continuation into the twentieth century, the days were coming to a close for this plan of relocation.

CHAPTER 5

The Close of an Era

The results—so far as we could ascertain them—were remarkable, and, unless we reflect on the wonderful influences possible from a Christian home upon a child unused to kindness, they would almost seem incredible.—Charles Loring Brace, The Dangerous Classes of New York and Twenty Years' Work among Them

*I*N 1988, Mary Mixon, who had been placed out at the age of three in San Antonio, Texas, wrote, "I am interested in whatever this [placing out] is about."[1] A participant in the relocation of thousands of children, she, like many others, has a unique history without a framework for understanding. The end of placing out did not come about before at least two hundred thousand infants, children, and teen-agers, as well as thousands of women and hundreds of men and couples, had been relocated by several organizations. The exact numbers resettled cannot be established with certainty. Agencies often blurred their reports of numbers resettled between in-state and out-of-state placements. Some kept little accounting, and short-lived programs maintained few, if any, records. There is also the probability that all placing-out institutions have not been identified, particularly the smaller, private organizations that limited their programs to specific regions. The number of two hundred thousand is an estimate based on figures reported in accounts of the system.

For many descendents of the placed out and the population of placed out still living, the unknowns of the system create a circumstance by which they have no knowledge of their place in America's social history or of past family histories and the whereabouts of relatives. This is a fact of late twentieth-century America. For the general public who find interest in the subject, popular accounts of the system and firsthand stories from those who were placed out outline a patchwork of ideas and images that present a part of the whole, but not the broad overviews necessary to consider placing out in any larger context.

A prevailing misconception of the system is that all of those placed out were orphans. Most were not, having at least one parent living. Countless children were handed over by parents who could not care for them, and thousands of others had been institutionalized as "half-orphans" or because of destitution before they emigrated to new homes. In addition, many of the placed out had volunteered for emigration, they maintained contact with relatives, and they even spent time with their families. Therefore, the representation of placing out as an orphan-oriented system is misleading, overlooking the family ties that thousands maintained with their natural parents and siblings.

Within the placing-out story there are also the girls and women transported by associations organized especially for them. There were also many adults, particularly couples, who were relocated. In 1860, for example, the Reverend James McLaughlin noted that, along with the thirty children escorted to Jacksonville, Illinois, there was a New York couple and their infant; the man and woman were "both North of Ireland protestants, sober, industrious, and trustworthy." The placement of families received little public attention within the overall placing-out plan, but it was a function of the system. In 1886, "a company of families, mumbering about a hundred souls," was reported on its way to Iowa, and in 1901 the Aid Society noted that during the year, couples and their children, the total over five hundred persons, had been relocated to western areas where work was waiting.[2]

Today, myths and realities of the system mingle to create for many a romantic notion of placing out. As writers in mid-nineteenth-century America presented melodramatic stories about orphans receiving their rewards, some today would like to portray the placed out as orphans gaining a new life in a new land, rising as Alger would have had them do. There is also the cultural belief that the placed out were grateful for their luck at being given a new home "out in the country." Judging from formal institutional reports, testimonials to the system, and the reminiscences of those placed out, this was true for many. There were those, however, who made their way back to the eastern cities or the new urban centers of the west. These placed out would not be tied to a rural life. Adjustment did not always come easy, and for some the familiar, however squalid, was preferable to the unknown.

Perhaps one of the most prevalent misunderstandings, encouraged by Brace and others, remains in the geographic distribution of placements. Much of Brace's writings and nineteenth-century literature in general promoted the idea that placing out relocated the poor only to the "West," (actually the country's midwest). Although thousands were sent to the old Northwest Territory and to the Central Plains—the West as Brace and others interpreted the location—placing out also sent children and teen-agers farther west, to the Pacific Coast, as well as to New England and the Mid-Atlantic States, and to the deep South and the Southwest. The Sisters of Charity engaged in southern and southwestern placements, and other eastern organizations concentrated on Mid-Atlantic and New England homes. The Children's Aid Society, too, relocated children to these regions, but a large number among those labeled as placed out by the Aid Society remained in New York State or went to nearby states. A very few also were sent out of the country. When the Aid Society in 1893 gave a comprehensive accounting of its placements, the largest number, 38,719, had remained in New York State; 4,149 were attributed to New Jersey; 384 had gone to Canada; 63 to Europe; and 1 to South America.[3] In these instances, the placed out were sent to rural areas, but not to "inspiring western life."

There is the temptation to present the system and those it placed as curiosities, representative of a subculture within society's view of children and their treatment. While it is true that society grappled with the worthiness of the lower classes and their ability to be redeemed, the prevailing sentiments for childhood allowed that the children of the poor could be nurtured and saved to enjoy a life of good. The temptation to portray the system as a melodramatic story devalues the experience and its place in the cultural history of America. Placing out is much more than an account of children sent to faraway homes and separated from poverty-stricken families or removed from streets and orphan asylums. The system itself tells much about what America was like, what care existed for the poor, and what Americans believed about social welfare and themselves during the nineteenth and early twentieth centuries.

The country was in transition, and as it changed in its industrial and rural landscapes and its population faced new challenges, there were numerous experimentations with differing lifestyles and social structures. The strategies for survival and the rules for living that had served in the Old World or on the Eastern Seaboard when the country was young were not always effective as the population moved west. Although the mainstream of America attempted to transplant on the expanding frontier the institutions and culture that it knew, there was a belief that frontier life could not always depend on the established forms for guidance. This was a major thesis of Frederick Jackson Turner, a view now under revision but one which reflects a mind-set of the nineteenth century. Long before Turner, writer Henry H. Riley presented the same idea in his *Puddleford, and Its People* (1854). The story revolved around a frontier community where the customs of eastern society did not solve all the problems in the new settlement. The citizens had to create new solutions, many of which were ridiculous but which pointed out to readers that frontier life sometimes demanded alternative thinking. New possibilities were reflected too in the thoughts of Hubert Howe Bancroft who wrote of California settlement in the 1870s: "We lack the associations running back for generations—the old homestead, the grandfather and grandmother and uncles and aunts and cousins. There's nothing around us hallowed by an indistinct past. There's nothing older than ourselves, all that we see has grown up under our eyes." Concurring with this theme was a Kansas settler who wrote: "I had not met any people since I came east to compare with my friends in the West. We didn't speak the same language. Like a flash it came to me—in the West we were doing things, we were creating, building up a great commonwealth." How that new world, that "great commonwealth," was created, many believed, did not depend on the old ways, and the children of poverty were accepted, for they too would have the "opportunity of becoming useful citizens of the great country."[4]

Experimentations in what today would be termed "alternative lifestyles" were plentiful in the nineteenth century. Some were reactions to increased industrialization, but all reflected the newness of a land in which social structures were in transition. Democratic philosophies allowed people to believe that there was freedom to attempt variations of life patterns and social organizations known in the Old World. The numerous communal and socialistic communities that sprang up during the nineteenth century provide one example of the alternatives suggested for coping with a new and sometimes frightening environment. Placing out, it can be argued, was another such social option for combating a changing world.

Although the idea of placing out was European in origin, the acceptance of the system in America and the attendant emotions and justifications, if not needs, for the system, made the emigration program much more than an exercise in relocation. Its social and moral overtones, the arguments for and against, and the eventual end of the system allow a look at an America that demanded industrialization, encouraged emigration and westward expansion, and at the same time struggled with their consequences.

Placing out was a hardy program. It survived wars and economic upheavals, criticisms and accusations, and even the death of its chief advocate. When the system, as established by the New York Children's Aid Society, ended, however, it did so for many reasons. The arguments and attitudes against placing out certainly aided the system's demise, and when the criticisms are compared with the earlier arguments for placing out, a barometer is provided for studying changes in American thought regarding social programs for the poor. The end of placing out provides a window through which we can view the changing nature and role of America's concept of social services and responsibility.

Placing out was based on a simple premise. Cities were over-flowing with destitute and orphaned children, as well as men and women, who faced life on the streets, paltry jobs when they could be found, or banishment to institutions. Rural America, perceived as the cradle of wholesome values, was expanding and needed all the laborers available. The symbiotic relationship of supply and demand may not have been acted upon, however, if it were not for three important factors in American life: a changing societal atti-tude about what children and childhood were; a revivalist spirit that swept the country in mid-century and revitalized itself periodically in the twentieth century; and the basic advance of transportation—the railroad.

The question then is what brought placing out to a close. The system ceased at the end of the 1920s when the two major active institutions, the New York Children's Aid Society and the New York Foundling Hospital through the Sisters of Charity, abandoned their programs. The Foundling Hospital halted placing out in 1927, when the number of in-state foster homes proved sufficient for its needs. The Aid Society for all intents and purposes closed its emigration department in 1929, although one writer has maintained that the society's board of trustees in 1930 agreed to some placing-out activities within the state of New York and in New Jersey and Connecticut. By that time, however, the Aid Society largely had redirected its efforts, increasing its city programs for neighborhood playgrounds, fighting malnutrition, and expanding its fresh-air programs. That the society had abandoned placing out and intended to focus its efforts on the enhancement of child-care services within the city is apparent in its 1930 annual report. No mention was made of past placing out or of current foster-care needs. Instead, the society concentrated on raising over $3 million to support buildings for boys and girls clubs, one in Harlem and one on Hester Street; additional summer camps; and twelve playgrounds in neighborhoods where children had no recreational areas but the streets.[5] There is no indication that the Crash of 1929 and the resulting economic collapse had any influence on the end of placing out. The Aid Society, as well as the Sisters of Charity, had made the decision to abandon the system before the economic crisis occurred.

Many factors brought about this close of an era in child transportation. Of course, a number of reasons for the system's end can be found in the allegations against placing out, some of which were valid. There were children placed in poor home environments. Some accepting families and employers simply wanted unpaid labor and ignored the admonitions to provide good home care. There were instances of children being separated tragically from their biological parents and from brothers and sisters, and there were some placed out who became burdens to their new communities. These circumstances, however, were the excuses, not the reasons, used to condemn the system and contribute to its end. The denial of the system's positive aspects, such as saving children from abject poverty or sterile institutional life, was a direct reaction to the urbanization of the west. Juvenile delinquency, wayward children, and destitution did not recognize state lines, and by the time midwestern states began to complain, they too were facing the monumental problems known for almost a century in the east.

Reflecting the problems of poverty and the rise of western urban centers was American fiction. The Chicago depicted in Theodore Dreiser's *Sister Carrie* (1900) was not a quaint frontier town. Instead, it contained the elements of poverty, materialism, and lack of human emotion usually reserved for descriptions of eastern cities. Echoing Dreiser's view of the new cities of the west was Ole Edvart Rölvaag's *Giants in the Earth* (1927), which underscored the acknowledged separation of midwestern urban and rural cultures: "Unknown to themselves [city dwellers], they are leading an unnatural life, cut off from the kindly and wholesome influence of nature, surrounded by vulgarity and ugliness, with no traditions, no loyalties, no culture, and no religion."[6] Hence, what nineteenth-century Americans said they believed about city life continued to be a part of twentieth-century thinking. The honest farmer was still a romantic notion, whereas cities, no matter their geographic location, remained places that would steal the soul.

To preserve the sense of pure rural life there was a collective move to keep eastern "refuse" out of the West—perhaps the reasoning was so simplistic as to assume that if the eastern urban population was contained, the problems of western poverty would disappear. More implicit, however, was the western sense of being exploited by eastern interests. States that had once not only accepted the urban poor but demanded that they be transported west as a labor force and that had themselves placed out resident children attempted to end the practice. State statues were passed to control charitable institutions and to prohibit the transportation of children across state boundaries. Placing out could not endure when states continued to publicly complain of the system or pass legislation that prohibited the placement of out-of-state children or made emigration so difficult that it was easier for a placing organizaton to find another alternative.

One historian of placing out has speculated that the system ended when child-labor laws and progressive home-care programs within urban areas were developed. Certainly, changes in home care and new alternatives to institutionalization influenced the end of the system. With foster care, financial support to dependent mothers, day care, tenement reform, and other in-city options, it was less necessary for families to give up the care of their children to institutions or for the orphaned to become wards of the city or state. The kindergarten movement played its part by providing early childhood education and a suitable care environment for children. An adjunct to kindergartens were day-care centers, first established in eastern cities by charitable organizations including the New York Children's Aid Society. Soon these programs, like the kindergarten movement, were adopted farther west. A program in Omaha, Nebraska, is one illustration. That city had its first day-care center in 1887, and the state of Nebraska, as well as many others, offered "outdoor relief." This form of charity had been practiced during the Colonial period, fell out of favor in the nineteenth century when public officials decided that it encouraged indolence, and was revitalized at the turn of the century as a progressive option. Outdoor relief provided destitute mothers with baskets of groceries and allowances for such things as coal and children's clothing. This relief was welcome but limited. It did not pay a family's rent or always provide a margin of support that would allow parents to keep their children at home rather than turning them over to institutional care. Nevertheless, it was a practice that at least recognized in theory, if not always in reality, the importance of maintaining the family unit. By 1908 and the White House Conference on Dependent Children, which stressed that whenever possible, aid should be given to mothers in order to keep children at home, such programs received more attention. This mandate had evolved by the 1920s into county and city governments administering aid-to-mothers programs under state law. Illinois, Pennsylvania, New York, Ohio, Massachusetts, and Michigan had such legislative statues, enacted to keep children with their families. Correspondingly, agencies that targeted family needs saw themselves as addressing "the job of making the family an asset and not a liability to society, economically and socially."[7]

This is not to say that every charity agreed that its work was family salvation and rehabilitation. Many still engaged in the single-minded goal of child rescue and did not support the multipurpose programs that attempted to reach the entire family. Organizations such as the American Humane Association, founded in 1885, clung to the argument for child protection over all else, echoing the philosophy of Brace and many of his contemporaries who had seen children, not adults, as salvageable. Whereas some charities continued to rely on this deep-rooted orientation for saving children, many began to support family programs that allowed children to remain with or near their parents.[8] This expressed a change in thought. Child care could now involve the whole family, not the child as a separate entity. This may suggest that by the turn of the century the lower classes had been imbued with the Victorian standards of the perfect home, but more likely it reflects the standards of social workers who had grown up under those expectations and applied their middle-class values of family life to programs for the urban poor. Thus, the child was not to be removed from his environment unless abuse or life-threatening circumstances demanded it. Home still could be argued as the best environment for children, but it was not home as Brace and other mid-nineteenth-century reformers had envisioned it—a place away from the child's original environment.

A leader in social-service thought was, of course, Hull-House, founded in Chicago by Jane Addams in 1889. The settlement-house concept, with its emphasis on family, community improvement, education and day care, among its many activities, made Hull-House a standard to be studied and emulated. Acknowledgment of the importance of programs that included the entire community and its residents was apparent in many applications. In 1915 the National Conference of Charities and Correction discussed as its meeting topic, "The Family and the Community," and by 1925 a number of cities had opted for neighborhood programs. Among these urban areas was Milwaukee, Wisconsin, which used its department of health to institute a system of day care and boarding homes. This allowed working mothers or those ill and unable to care for their children an alternative to institutionalized care. Parents were not forced to relinquish guardianship, and the children were cared for within their home neighborhoods, near their parents.[9]

In the east, institutional solutions were being reevaluated. Expanded foster care and rural in-state care centers received more focus. The Sisters of Charity expanded efforts to establish foster care nearer children's home neighborhoods. Meanwhile, the New England Home for Little Wanderers in the early 1900s focused on children with emotional or educational problems. Farther west, the Children's Home of Cincinnati established as early as 1867 a rural farm school and by 1912 gave more emphasis to a rural environment by housing some children at a country center rather than in the Home's city building. This reflected a decided change in how institutions and private charities viewed their work. Large, dormitory-style institutional settings were giving way to cottage housing, foster-care homes, or specialized schools. That many of the institutional shelters were placed in a rural environment indicates a continued belief in the benefits of country life and fresh air. These programs for care and housing were alternatives to placing out and slowly replaced that system while it continued to operate. By the turn of the century the Children's Home of Cincinnati was more involved in foster care than in placements across state lines. The same was true of the Boston Children's Mission. By 1900 it had removed itself from out-of-state placements to emphasize foster and child health care in the city, and by 1925 it had added a rural housing complex for children.[10]

An important factor in placing out's demise can be found in the way governmental units began to define their role in social services and in the forms of child-related legislation passed. Although it is debatable how much direct influence child-labor laws may have had on the termination of placing out, the discussion of such laws certainly included a system that relied on the demand for child labor. Reformers, including Charles Loring Brace, had demanded for years protective laws that would eliminate child labor in some industries and restrict working hours in others. By the early 1900s states and territories were enacting statutes that addressed the problem. Oklahoma, for example, in 1907 prohibited employment of children under sixteen in occupations that were "injurious to health or morals" or hazardous to "life or limb," and Kansas in 1909 passed a similar bill specifically aimed at child labor in mines and industries. Although these laws were often circumvented by both parents and employers, these attempts to limit and protect children were important first steps.[11]

In 1912 the first national Children's Bureau was created and put under the the direction of one-time Hull-House worker Julia C. Lathrop. Her experience was invaluable, and by 1916 the bureau had lobbied successfully for federal enactment of a child-labor law aimed at industrial and commercial enterprises. Although applauded, the bill had severe limitations: "Congress has not abolished child labor [but] how far does it reach? Only 150,000 children will be affected. The other 1,850,000 children are left untouched. No federal law can reach them." Among the unaffected were "truck-garden conscripts" such as the children who labored in Nebraska's sugar-beet industry, domestic farm workers, and hired hands.[12]

That the bill barely scratched the surface in policing child labor was an argument used by those who wished to enact a national child-labor amendment to the Constitution. Debate was heated, with many decrying the idea as an infringement of state's rights. More to the point was concern over how a general amendment would affect "family" labor such as farm and domestic workers and farm children working with their parents. In this area the Grange and the American Farm Bureau Federation stood solidly with those who opposed the amendment; the farm home and its economic survival could not be ensured if a child's work on the farm was regulated. The merits of such an amendment were discussed into the 1930s without it becoming a reality, and it was not until 1938 and the National Industrial Recovery Act and the Fair Labor Standards Act that the country could say that it had brought about some effective measure of comprehensive child-labor legislation. In the final analysis, the failure of those early attempts to enact a national child-labor law is perhaps of less importance than the questions and concerns its proposal created.[13]

As many recognized, child-labor legislation as a rule had little or no impact on farm labor, since few considered farm work performed by children to be in the same category with sweatshop labor, factories where children were often chained to their machines, mine work, or employment in unsavory establishments such as saloons and houses of prostitution. The most visible forms of life-threatening and demoralizing occupations received the greatest outcry from reformers. For the placing-out system, the passage of child-labor laws was of little consequence. If placing out was affected by legislation related to a child's workday, compulsory school-attendance statutes, which did include farm children, more likely had an impact. In many agricultural states these laws were specifically designed to force farm families to see that their children received an education beyond a few weeks squeezed between seasonal work.[14] For those who had accepted placed-out children as a way to gain additional farm workers, compulsory-attendance legislation, which became more stringent in the twentieth century, meant that there would be little advantage in using child labor if those workers were forced by the state to be in school for a number of hours each day for six to eight months out of the year.

Perhaps what most influenced the end to placing out was the professionalization of social work and the recognition of sociology as a field of study. In 1883 there were no chairs in sociology in American universities and few courses were offered in the field. By 1896 this had changed drastically, partly as a result of the organization of the Academy of Political and Social Sciences in 1890 and the beginning in 1895 of its publication, the *American Journal of Sociology*. Structured, academic training for a career in social work became an option, and by the early 1900s young men and women interested in the expanding profession were told, "Charitable, philanthropic, and other social-welfare institutions have been greatly multiplied, while their work has been put on a scientific basis. The modern method of securing employees in such places is that of calling persons especially trained and fitted to do the work required." While many still learned about social work through firsthand experience in the field, graduation from a training school was becoming the norm. An impetus to such schools was World War I, during which universities and colleges trained men and women as Red Cross and other war service workers. Training in wartime led to education in peacetime, and by 1923 there were sixteen university programs allied with the Association of Training Schools for Professional Social Work. Members of this association included the respected programs of Johns Hopkins University, the University of Chicago, and the University of Minnesota. The University of Indiana, University of Oklahoma, University of Wisconsin, and Harvard were nonmember schools, but each offered "more or less complete professional courses" in social work. Added to these were numerous university programs that provided special institutes for asylum attendants, prison guards, and probation officers. Supporting the new curricula was an abundance of social-work and sociological literature, ranging from specific problems—"What Shall Philadelphia Do With Its Paupers?"—to practical advice on organizing and administering a charity.[15]

People who regarded themselves as trained professionals, either graduates of specialized programs or those who gained experience through their work at such places as Hull-House, questioned what had been accepted as the proper way to deal with the poor and indigent. Nineteenth-century standards were giving way to new ideas. When the Reverend Frederic Knight took over in 1907 as superintendent of the New England Home for Little Wanderers, for example, he brought with him the new, scientific approaches and by 1920 there were twenty-four professional social workers, a pediatrician, and one psychologist on staff. Recognizing the changes within the world of social welfare, Jane Addams noted, "[by 1909,] we had already discovered that our intellectual interests, our convictions and activities were becoming parts of larger movements and that research into social conditions was gradually being developed in the universities and by the great foundations." Of these, she identified the Russell Sage Foundation as a prime mover.[16] In 1925 the directors of the Boston Children's Mission bore witness to this sense of being a part of a greater scheme:

While this thorough work with the individual, work which shows tangible results, is of first importance, we must keep ever in mind

the whole community and see that we fill a need not otherwise
met and dove-tail our work into the larger plan, of which the
Children's Mission is only a part. We have our place, therefore, in
the Boston Council of Social Agencies, in the various conferences
and committees with statewide and national scope and also in the
Child Welfare League of America, which is raising standards of
work throughout the country.[17]

With this professionalization and intellectual articulation of
social services, a basic component of placing out—Christian charity—suffered. Sociology was a science, not a missionary effort.
Ministers and church-sponsored charities refused to accept this
premise, but sociologists and social workers were quick to separate
themselves from the long-held ideals of denominational charities.
Religious workers and social work professionals viewed each other
with suspicion and feuded over which produced the most positive
results for those in need. For the academically trained social
worker, denominational programs exhibited "sentimental inepti-
tude." For their part, church-sponsored charities as a whole continued to view sociological field work as "technique" and to invoke
the nineteenth-century belief that no good could come unless
religion played a role in the lives of the less fortunate. Evangelical
women, for example, continued to rely on religious instruction as a
way to redeem the "erring" woman who sought help in charitable
lodging houses and maternity homes. It was believed that such
educational benefits would return the "fallen" to "the glory of their
womanhood"; a view declared by social workers, both male and
female, as "unimaginative" and "backward." In fact, women who
had served as kindly "visitors" to the poor were dismissed by the
new professionals as pretentious busybodies better left to their club
meetings and church bazaars. To bridge this chasm, at least one
social-work journal, *The Family*, attempted to openly discuss varying points of view. While it presented a forum for polite debate, it is

unlikely that either side was swayed in the fundamental point of contention—religious works replaced with scientific theories of human behavior and response. This split between the secular and religious views of charitable work directly affected placing out since those institutions involved in the program were funded by or closely tied to denominational support. Within the new world of social work, any religious connections to poor relief, in this instance placing out, were open to question.[18]

It was becoming clear by the 1920s that those preparing for the ministery could not assume that they were automatically social workers; training for that work was becoming more often the realm of secular universities. As a result, sociology did influence a number of ministers and laymen, particularly those who were part of the social gospel movement of the late nineteenth and early twentieth centuries. This movement, encompassing numerous causes, such as temperance, labor laws, and reforms in government, had as its chief focus programs for the benefit of the poor. The approach, however, included the new lessons of sociology. When the Reverend Charles M. Sheldon, a Congregational minister, for example, set out to discover the needs of blacks in Topeka, Kansas, he attempted to apply simple sociological techniques. A systematic enumeration of the black population was made. Sheldon then concluded that the black settlement was made up of three "distinct classes," a typical classification system used by sociologists to evaluate a population base. Then, from this data, Sheldon determined the social services most needed.[19] He already knew that there was tremendous want in the black community, but he had no intention of committing charitable contributions or the time of his church until a sociological study had been made. Among those who would have approved of Sheldon's scientific approach was the Reverend Worth M. Tippy, considered by his peers as a progressive activist in the social gospel movement and who took to task those not informed in the new ways of good deeds:

It should be remembered that but a brief while ago most social work, as well as education, was in the hands of the church. . . . It has been aggressive in civic and moral reforms, in the care of immigrants, . . . and, moved by humanitarian zeal . . . one church or another has entered upon almost every form of social experiment, sometimes in undignified ways and frequently to the confusion of constructive undertakings. . . . If a church undertakes case work, it must be scientific as well as cooperative.[20]

The need for such strategies was argued for in every facet of social welfare, including the nineteenth-century bastion of child care, the institutional orphan asylum. One of those to take on the asylums was Dr. Rex Rudolph Reeder, a well-known leader in child welfare and a colleague of Homer Folks in World War I relief efforts for refugees, specifically children. As the superintendent of the Orphan Asylum Society of New York, Reeder in 1900 began a reorganization of that orphanage, revamping the institution into a cottage setting. Convinced that the orphan asylum was "not a real childhood home" and that only a minority of children needed any institutional care, Reeder, in 1925, argued for the scientific approach.[21]

For more than a century in this country they [orphan asylums] were unmolested . . . while the great current of change and progress swept by unobserved. . . . They were usually sponsored by the most benevolent and deeply religious people in the community. . . . That they are now drawn within the scope of social investigation as to methods, results, [and reason for being] is entirely due to an awakening of social consciousness and the application of scientific procedure of all ways and means employed in child welfare work.[22]

The advocacy for training and the scientific method were cited as appropriate to the professionalization of all social work and charities. On a practical level, however, there was a more pressing concern. From the end of the Civil War into the twentieth century there was a virtual explosion in the number of charities, aid associations, orphanages, and institutions. When a 1918 study showed that in just one Iowa town of five thousand residents, there were 189 voluntary groups and organized associations providing some form of aid, few professionals expressed surpise. In this Iowa location, churches, Sunday schools, women's groups, lodges, children's clubs, and established welfare agencies all had their projects, from providing food baskets to running a lodging house for the unemployed. The same proliferation of charities, public and private, organized and temporary, could be found in any city or state. Needless to say, there was a rise in organized institutions—and an increase in their populations. Institutions for all types of children multiplied, and between 1890 and 1923 the number of children under sixteen years of age in some type of institution grew from 60,981 to 204,888. This growth resulted from an increase in destitute urban populations and a new emphasis on careful, scientific care of the insane, the incarcerated, and those with perceived handicaps such as epilepsy and blindness. Some institutions were the outgrowth of the Civil War. States had their homes for war orphans and widows, and by 1876 there were twenty such places in the United States, with more added by the end of the century. Economic crises also created a greater general need for aid, both in the cities and the countryside: there was a "close connection" between the industrial depressions experienced in the 1870s and 1890s and the "unprecedented growth of new societies and a revival [of others] in places where earlier gains had been lost." To meet an increasing demand for relief, some states actually fueled an already uncontrollable situation by allowing easy incorporation of private charities. Nebraska, as an illustration, allowed that "three or more persons who may desire to become incorporated for any charitable purpose" could simply record articles of agreement with the secretary of state. Obviously, the hope was that private charities would take on more of the burden, allowing state governments to use their funds elsewhere.[23]

Adding to the numbers of social agencies and aid societies, were the foundations of philanthropists who had their own special interests. Some gave to existing charities. Many others, however, established their own aid-giving organizations, which had no church affiliation, to assure that specific problems in society were addressed. With this "plethora of agencies," both public and private, the complaints most often heard were those of duplication of effort, lack of standard policies, and no governing authority. To gain some control, states began to establish state boards of charity. These were to lobby for protective laws that directly affected those for whom the boards were advocates, and they were to administer and monitor all institutions, public and private, that fashioned themselves as charitable organizations. Massachusetts, New York, and Ohio had established in the 1860s the first state boards of charity, and by 1923, only three states—Mississippi, Nevada, and Utah—had not followed with their own state overseeing bodies. These agencies, of course, did not appear full blown. There were rocky beginnings, illustrating confusion over responsibilities and philosophies. The first state board in Nebraska, for example, was the private Women's Board of Associate Charities. Established in 1889 and dedicated to the "holy cause" of building up "public institutions that should do honor to the state," the board was ineffectual and one might argue, out of date. Its administration of the Nebraska Industrial School demonstrated minimal health care for inmates and the only instruction seemed to be in sewing. High moral platitudes to "rescue the fallen" did not produce the needed results and by 1894 Nebraska replaced the private sector with a public agency. The call had been for control and standardization, and through trial and error, state boards over time provided this. Supporting state efforts were national, state, and city organizations that set guidelines for professional ethics, programs, and adherence to state mandates. One of the most important was the Charity Organization Society, which, beginning in 1877, attempted to serve as a clearinghouse agency to create order out of chaos.[24]

Professionalization of social work affected charitable institutions in how they went about their business, and it largely influenced how states met their obligations. The onslaught of national charitable and prison conferences, beginning in the nineteenth century, indicated a need for communication between states on how each dealt with problems of the poor, as well as thought for the treatment of special segments of the population, such as the insane and the incarcerated. On the local level there was also a movement to form protective leagues and regulatory commissions charged with policing responsibilities in specific locales. In Cleveland, Ohio, reforms were called for in the city's orphan asylums, which by 1925 housed five thousand children, 91 percent of whom had one parent living. The intent was to remove the children from institutions and into adoptive homes and foster care. In Chicago, that city's Joint Service Bureau, beginning in 1918, took on persons or organizations that advertised themselves as "baby boarders." Supposedly these agencies were home-care facilities similar to those established in Milwaukee, but in fact they were brokers in black-market adoptions.[25] Such local activism was a signal to charities and those purporting to be such that it was no longer business as usual. Reforms and professional conduct, conforming to criteria set down by governing agencies, were not only expected but demanded.

Before this revolution to organize, standardize, and professionalize charities, private institutions had worked pretty much in their own world. They made the decisions as to what their programs would be and their good intentions gave their actions validity. While state or city statutes and incorporation agreements might designate expectations for public institutions, private charities were free to set their own priorities, generally following accepted custom for aid to the poor. Respectable charities would incorporate themselves under state statutes, but primarily this was to meet the letter of the law, not with the intent of following strictures set down for public institutions. Since few states in the mid-1800s had boards of charity, there were limited avenues for official review of policies and practices. Later, when those boards came into being, they more often were interested in the operation of state asylums, hospitals, and penitentiaries. Until late in the nineteenth century there were few defined boundaries for private charities. There may have been loose cooperative agreements and communication among those involved in these charities, but there was not the formal network of social-work professionals or standardization of policies that later came to be.

Within this changing world, Brace's strong fight to maintain the option of placing out is perhaps more understandable. When he began, few rules, except custom, existed for care of the poor. One simply knew that it had to be done, and among Brace and his supporters, it was believed that a humanitarian, noninstitutional solution had been found. Although Brace had in many ways contributed to a growing field of social work, he often found its new constraints and criticisms confusing. The man, however, was as complex as the events surrounding him. Brace advocated change in the way state and public institutions were run, and would have agreed with twentieth-century reformers who expected superintendents and workers in public institutions to do more than serve as caretakers and disciplinarians. He probably would have been less receptive, however, to the idea that private organizations, particularly church-sponsored ones, could not continue to operate simply on the lofty desire "to reclaim the fallen, to bring them under good, wholesome Christian influences."[26] By the twentieth century, good intentions were considered insufficient replacements for aid and rehabilitation directed by trained individuals.

The progressive age with its multifaceted bent for reform in everything from how cities and counties cared for the poor to municipal forms of government, had its influence on social obligations to the needy. Jane Addams wrote that from 1909 to the beginning of the First World War, there was a "veritable zeal for social reform throughout the United States." She attributed much of this activity to the Progressive party, which to her "demonstrated what political history has many times made evident, the new parties ultimately write the platforms for all parties."[27]

In this new world of educated social workers and theorists and progressive thought, indenture, one of the long-held social options for placement came under scrutiny and was found lacking. Indenture of children and adults was deeply rooted in American life. It routinely served as a means of reducing the inmate populations of institutions and as a way for parents to provide their children with board and the means of learning a trade. By the end of the nineteenth century, however, there were rumblings. The superintendents of the Soldiers' Orphans' Home in Atchison, Kansas, had seen heated debate when state approval was given for indenture, and they were not unique in suffering, as one writer put it, the "wrath of the parents and relatives of [indentured] children, and of the politicians who are, or think they are interested in them." One of those politicians was Governor Arthur Capper of Kansas, who received this viewpoint from a private citizen: "In fact it is my opinion that both boys and girls in this Institution [Soldiers' Orphans' Home] if permitted to remain where they are until they can acquire the training and education in household and other vocations will be able to go out and take employment independently and without being indentured to their employers."[28]

Local complaints supported a growing national concern. In 1927, twelve states—Wisconsin, Illinois, Michigan, Indiana, Kansas, Pennsylvania, Arkansas, Maryland, Rhode Island, Virginia, West Virginia, and Nebraska—still allowed indenture of their institutional charges and of children who had been turned over to county authorities or poor farms. These states were pushed into the national limelight when calls were made for them to abolish the practice for "more intelligient child care services." Pressure increased when the national Children's Bureau published its study of indenture in Wisconsin. That study reflected some of the same criticisms made of placing out, citing children who were "worked virtually as unpaid servants in households and on farms, often deprived of schooling and . . . sometimes cruelly treated." The Children's Bureau demanded abolition of all indenture, calling it "a relic of sixteenth-century England."²⁹ If indenture, a much older practice than placing out, could be cited for its antiquarian principles, then surely placing practices that sometimes included indenture could be called into question.

One of the positive aspects of placing out, although some would argue whether it had any redeeming qualities, was to create a discussion of the best forms of child care. Opponents of the system had something against which to compare other programs. Meanwhile, placing-out supporters found theories of child care within the program worth keeping. Within this dialogue emerged some concensus for what constituted proper care, and ultimately a happy, productive childhood for the less fortunate.

In this discussion some of the philosophies of Charles Loring Brace and his contemporaries of like mind were retained. In fact, almost forty years after his death, Brace still was regarded as a major force in social work, as evidenced by the editors of a social-work journal who wrote in 1929:

The work of child-placing agencies has greatly developed in the seventy-five years since Charles Loring Brace sent his first "emigration party" from New York to Michigan. But he was a great pioneer who had courage and faith, enthusiasm and tireless en-

*ergy. The fact that he was only twenty-eight years old [sic] when
he sent his first group of children west is one of the astonishing
things about his work.* [30]

Brace had argued against institutionalized care of the indigent
and supported the home environment as more appropriate for the
care of children. He had banned indenture as a practice of the New
York Children's Aid Society, and he had stressed the importance
of self-help programs such as industrial training for the poverty
stricken. All of these concepts, while not immediately acted on or
accepted by social agencies or reformers, eventually became the
"enlightened" approach in the twentieth century. The irony of
Brace being taken to task and then having many of his ideas
adopted is apparent in social-welfare literature. Social work and
education journals, as well as hundreds of conference speeches, of
the early twentieth century testify to the tremendous support for
industrial schools. Unlike the questionable education programs
offered in some nineteenth-century asylums and orphanages, these
would train children for a job in life. That the job would be at best
that of a skilled laborer was an improvement over earlier offerings
or the prospect of indenture as the way in which to learn a trade.
Additionally, on the question of institutionalization, Brace's beliefs
were simply echoed when "professionals" concluded, "Home is the
best place in which to place and train a child, . . . there are as many
childless homes, wanting children as there are homeless children
wanting homes." [31]

It also may be suggested that placing out allowed evaluation of
foster care and adoption, both closely intertwined with placing out
in principle. They shared the philosophy that home life was preferable to an institution and sought placement of children in private
homes. Social workers and reformers simply accepted or dismissed
from the placing out system what was useful in defining foster care

and adoption programs, providing standards for twentieth-century practices. Since much of this redefinition of acceptable programs pivoted on what had been criticized in placing out, one important point becomes evident. In the discussion of adoption and foster care, the accusations concerning institutions' religious prejudice played a role. By the twentieth century laws began to contain "religious protection" clauses. Children—even those too young to have any idea of religious preference—were to be placed "as far as practicable" in foster and adoption homes of like faith.[32] On this point and within the general debate over home rather than institutional placement, it can be argued that placing out, through its existence and its eventual end, created a point of reference in formulating child-care policies for the states and within the country at large.

As it was for those who attacked or supported placing out, evaluating the system today is difficult. The concept is both appealing and appalling. When faced with what urban life offered the poor—street life, crime, prostitution, overwhelming deprivations, incarceration, and little hope for escape—the argument must swing to Brace's heartfelt appeals for relocation in rural America. In the world of mid-nineteenth-century America, the choices were few, based on what tradition accepted as help to the poor. One writer has called placing out "one of the most heartening chapters in the social history of America." While that may be an overstatement, in one sense placing out was certainly a hopeful alternative to what awaited urban children of the poor. When, however, the process and the lives it affected are viewed in terms of the long-lasting effects on human emotions and development, the system is less appealing. The image of human "cargoes" (a term used by the Reverend Enoch Kingsbury in the 1850s) or "human freight" (a phrase used by a Kansas newspaper in 1908)[33] is more reminiscent of America's history of slavery than of humanitarian efforts. And the psychological effects, hardly considered when the system began, are apparent in the on-going search by the placed out for family roots and connections.

Today, many of the placed out or their families have a need to know about their past and they share the behavior and feelings of adoptees who wish to locate their biological parents. Noting these impulses was Sister Marie Catherine of the New York Foundling Hospital, who wrote of a Nebraska reunion of the placed out in 1962: "These people . . . had been drawn to this reunion by a common need—to try to fill the void in their hearts created by the absence of knowledge about their identity." This desire and the need to locate family is not a contemporary phenomenon. An 1863 letter from Iroquois County, Illinois, to the Aid Society recorded the poignant plea: "Have you heard anything of C——, or where she is? I have not heard anything of her for the last four years, and I am anxious to know what has become of her." To this may be added an 1894 example offered by Jacob Riis, a placing-out supporter. Riis intended to demonstrate the good that had come to an Indiana minister who had been placed out as a child after his drunken mother had "cast him aside." His search for family, however, was no less wrenching or resolved when he was told: "Your mother was killed in a drunken fight by your father, who was sent to prison."[34]

Certainly, many of the placed out have had an overwhelming desire to search out family roots. This reaction to life's circumstances is offset by the many accounts of those who found the substance of their new lives sufficient so they could accept their past as it was. Thus, analysis of the human dimension in the specific can be as varied as each individual who experienced placing out. One writer has offered the analysis that as a group the placed out exhibit "common traits"—a strong commitment to marriage and family; an absence of divorce; a need to accommodate; and an almost fatalistic approach to life: "Whatever fate gives you, that's what you've got." These observations were made after firsthand interviews with persons placed out in the twentieth century and may have a basis for truth. Placing-out accounts share many common threads, and the experience itself may be said to have created a view of life or behavior patterns that bear similarities.[35]

One also might wonder if the placed out attempted to emulate in adulthood the ministers and missionaries involved in placing out or to replicate childhood institutional experiences. It is apparent that a number of the placed out became clergymen or engaged in careers considered to be public service oriented. There is evidence as well that some returned to institutional life in one form or another. Harry Colwell, for example, who was sent to Kansas, became a teacher, but eventually returned east for a career in social work supervising children's homes, including one in Saco, Maine, and another in Randolph, New York.[36] While generalities point to similar life patterns shaped by placing out, the possibilities are only speculative. No substantive studies have been made to determine if the placing-out experience did indeed produce particular life patterns, forms of behavior, or shared values and if, in the larger picture, it influenced community or family values as the placed out became a part of rural America. In addition, while studies of nineteenth-century women strongly suggest female bonding, even on the frontier, as a result of shared life experiences and societal expectations, there are no studies to indicate that women placed out together felt special kinship or exhibited a feminist attitude other than that generally dictated by society.

Today, as we move closer to the twenty-first century, America retains living reminders of the placing-out system. The two prominent institutions in the system, the New York Children's Aid Society and the New York Foundling Hospital, still exist, as do other institutions that at one time practiced placing out. The personal histories of the placed out and the institutions that carried out the program have left a startling legacy. This legacy has received increased attention as families are searched for and as the placing-out experience takes on some of the aura of folklore and Americana.

Some view the system as a tragic chapter in America's social history; others choose to romanticize the experience. Between the extremes must be the recognition that this was not a malicious design to rob the poor of their homes and families, nor was it intended as a capitalistic conspiracy to exploit a defenseless labor force—although capitalism and the industrial rise of America created an environment in which placing out became a solution to urban problems. Additionally, it must be remembered that it was acceptable, if not essential, for children and teen-agers to serve as farm laborers in an expanding farm economy. On the other hand, resettlement was not a romantic adventure with the placed out receiving their just rewards. Rather, the system was a circumstance of urban reformers reacting to prevailing social thought and conditions while alleviating diverse demands—the need to reduce an indigent population and offer a chance at self-improvement, and the cry for labor on an expanding frontier.

Perhaps the most important point in evaluating the system is that placing out and the people it involved reflect the complexities of American life and growth. The placed out were participants in a program with international roots. As Americans, particularly children and women, were placed out, so too were their European counterparts. The underlying reason was fundamentally the same in all instances. Expansion and development of a country depends on an available labor source. Remedies for solving the problems of poverty are many times limited, particularly when customs and revenues bind society to set forms of action. Charles Loring Brace and those who shared in his vision attempted to break longstanding ideas, and in doing so fostered a form of child care not earlier seen in America. To Brace's mind, Christian duty demanded that the children of the indigent classes be given a chance to not only survive, but to experience childhood as society had defined that phase of life. Brace and his contemporaries feared a growing underclass, but in the name of charity, the worthy children of the poor were not to be excluded from the nurturing lessons of careful discipline, self-worth, and Christian living offered by a warm home environment. In this, American society agreed. The New York Children's Aid Society and the many other organizations that practiced placing out responded to the demand for labor, the charitable impulses of the population, and the opportunities offered by the technology of the age to achieve the goal of resettling the poor.

Placing out came into being and was allowed to exist for specific purposes. Once those no longer served to support the system— once society had evolved in a number of ways in its attitudes towards social service and care for the poverty class—the system was discarded. The Cult of the Child remained a strong force in American thought, but the ways in which children of poverty were to reach that ideal changed. Social reform, new theories in social welfare, and specialized training of those who worked with the poor created other avenues for the uplift and care of children. The new social-welfare theories affected the families of these children. A holistic approach that included the entire family unit came to be the way of things in social welfare. Children had their special problems, but separation from parents as a solution was seen as less inviting. Society still believed in the value of fresh air, but the increase in charities, individuals, and governmental agencies that provided country and fresh air programs made it less important that children find permanent homes in rural areas. These rural regions changed too. Increased populations, legislation that controlled child labor and education, and problems with an expanding poverty class made these areas less receptive to transported children. While American society may have clung to what it believed to be true about children, about rural life, about Christian duty, and about the rewards of hard work and self-determination, it had itself changed in the ways in which those beliefs were expressed.

An important final point of discussion on the demise of the system is the way in which placing-out institutions themselves changed. Criticisms and legislation, labor and compulsory school statues, and professional outcrys all contributed to ending placing out. By the turn of the century, institutions were more likely to engage in formulating in-city and in-state care options, relying heavily on the use of foster care, adoption, or maintaining children in the homes of their parents. In addition, the two organizations most noted for the resettlement of children, the Aid Society and the Foundling Hospital, responded to outside influences, rather than ignoring them. The work of placement organizations was not legislated out of business, although state laws had their impact. Nor were those working for placing-out charities ostracized by professional peers. The practitioners of placing out evidently agreed that the time had come to end the system, to find alternatives. This was a voluntary action, although the Aid Society clung to placing out longer than any other practicing organization. Placing out was abandoned for other home-care programs, for expanded child health care, for battles against malnutrition, and for widening city-reform movements to improve living environments, education, and recreation. Those who had used the "West" as a solution decided to fight the ills of urban life within the city itself.

The reminders of placing out are still with us, and as society still struggles with the problems of the poor and those unable to care for themselves, the legacy of Charles Loring Brace remains evident in an 1855 declaration of purpose of the Children's Aid Society:

> *Our objects have been, the improvement and elevation of the vagrant and poor children of the street, boys and girls; of those engaged in the petty out-door trades; those who beg, or pilfer, or*

pick the streets for a living, and those who are driven by homeless-
ness and poverty to the prison, or who are confined there for petty
crimes.[37]

Many would have agreed with Brace that placing out had provided "improvement and elevation." Thousands had been saved
from unimaginable conditions, and emigration had provided communities on an expanding frontier with laborers at a critical time in
its development. Placing out also brought to childless homes and
caring families children who would receive love, care, and education—the ideals of childhood. There were additionally the homes
and employers who gave the placed out an opportunity to earn
wages for their labor and to learn skills that would give them a
livelihood. On a very personal level, Brace's goal came to have life-
changing meaning and an impact—for better or worse—on the
children of the poor. For American society, his stated purpose came
to mean an acceptance of child emigration for three-quarters of a
century, creating a special chapter in the country's history of expansion, social change, and experiences of its children.

Epilogue

*T*HE ORPHAN as a literary character had its greatest popularity during the nineteenth century, but it has not entirely faded from American fiction. As a device to tell a story, the orphan is still used to provide a certain drama. *An Orphan for Nebraska*, written in 1979 by Charlene Joy Talbot, is a good example of the continuing use of the literary orphan, and here provides an opportunity to compare the real-life experiences of the placed out with those of a fictional character.

At the center of *An Orphan for Nebraska* is eleven-year-old Kevin O'Rourke, an immigrant from Ireland who will eventually find himself on the prairies of Nebraska. Kevin's father, a schoolteacher, has died in Ireland, and Kevin's mother soon follows, falling to "ship's fever" on the passage to America. Kevin is, then, a true orphan, and his only known relative is Uncle Michael, in America. This is the only adult upon whom Kevin believes he can depend, but that hope is short-lived when Kevin arrives in his new country and learns that the uncle is jailed on Blackwell's Island. This leaves Kevin entirely on his own, with the uncle able only to offer advice through prison bars. Thus, a boy who once had a stable family life, an educated father who provided for his family and a mother who gave him love and care at home, is reduced by life's circumstances to no support but what he can gain for himself.

Kevin must make his own way, and in this he is no different from the nineteenth-century characters of Horatio Alger or the true-life children of interest to charities such as the New York Children's Aid Society. Without adult supervision, Kevin is on the streets, but the uncle's advice is followed—begin as the uncle did in America, become a newspaperboy. Having no other opportunities, Kevin takes himself to Newspaper Row and begins to earn a small living on the streets of New York. This, of course, throws him into contact with other street boys, and with his new-found acquaintances he begins to sleep on the streets, visit theaters on the Bowery, and gamble away what little he has earned. If this story had been a product of nineteenth-century literature, Kevin's behavior would be couched in the language of warnings about a good boy about to go wrong—led by his friends into unsavory establishments and small vices and just waiting to go to ruin. Descriptions of such boys and their activities were also a part of the Aid Aociety's literature, with the same conclusions of what would happen if the behavior continued unchallenged. *An Orphan for Nebraska* is much more sanguine; Kevin is simply learning what life on the streets is all about and doing what the other boys do. They are their own community, their own family. They really are good boys who look after each other and offer companionship and support.

Eventually, Kevin and some other newspaperboys, including his new pal Patrick O'Toole, are driven from their sidewalk sleeping spot. One of the boys suggests that they explore a lodging house for newspaperboys. This is one of the places of refuge offered by the Aid Society. Finding the lodging house and its school hospitable, Patrick says, "You know what puzzles me? How come there ain't *more* boys? How come this place ain't overflowing with boys? It's too good to be true, that's why! How come they're doing this for us?" Soon the boys learn about groups going west and conclude that there is no overflow because boys are always being sent from the city. "Why are they sending them away?" "'Cause," comes the answer, "they wants to get them off the streets, and people out West wants boys."

Not too long after this discovery, Kevin is asked if he would like to join one of these groups, one that will go to Nebraska. Patrick has the opportunity too, but he, it turns out, has a mother, whom he does not want to leave. Kevin and Patrick are in the position of deciding for themselves if they want to leave the city. Certainly, there are documented cases of children and teen-agers making that decision, but the evidence suggests that most of the real placed out had no choice in the matter. Kevin, then, is representative of some, but certainly not all, who were relocated to rural life. Torn by a loyalty to his uncle, whom he often visits in prison, Kevin first discusses the decision with his only relative. Uncle Michael encourages the move and promises to join Kevin out west when he is free. Here the story deviates from what many of the placed out actually experienced. Kevin knows in advance that he is going to Nebraska; he even knows the name of the town. He and his uncle plan to keep in touch and to meet again out west; in real life this sort of arrangement would certainly have been frowned on by placing-out institutions since children were expected to break entirely with their past relationships.

Kevin's trip west with an agent, three other boys, and four girls— Kevin, the eleven-year-old that he is, finds the girls a bother— closely parallels evidence provided in placing-out accounts. The book, however, has the group traveling by boat to Albany—a practice that was quickly discontinued by the Aid Society because children were prone to seasickness. Kevin's group is also treated to meals in rail-station restaurants, something for which there is little evidence in reality. He also traveled in an emigrant car with masses of new immigrant settlers, something that was not done unless there was no other way to travel. The author, however, conveys a sense of accuracy for the particular situation recounted. Of Kevin's experience she wrote: "It was noon before the train started and the long ride began. The Irishmen passed around whiskey and sang. German men and women smoked and sang. Babies squalled and were nursed." Compare that passage to an actual Aid Society agent account: "Irishmen passed around bad wiskey and sang bawdy songs; Dutch men and women smoked and sang, and grunted and cursed; babies squalled and nursed, and left no baby duties undone." If anything, the author's research allows for a realistic description of an event that actually occurred.

When the group finally arrives in the fictional Cottonwood City, Nebraska, the children react as one would suppose many of the placed out did. Looking across the town towards the open plains, one of the city kids, used to the congestion of urban life shouts, "That's not a city! There's more of us than there is houses." These fictional characters, like many of their real-life counterparts, were not prepared for what they saw.

Once off the train, Kevin and his group are taken to church services. From there, having been inspected throughout the sermon and hymn-singing, the children are taken to the courthouse for selection. The book generally overlooks the town committee as a screening device, but then, in real life, questions certainly arose over how effective such committees were. Perhaps equally true to realism is the book's scene in which a man bursts into the courthouse and announces that he has "orders for two girls" to go out and live on the "claims." This demand is satisfied, and eventually only Kevin is left. Small for his age and fair skinned, he has been passed over. Some farmers think him too frail; others say that he will burn up under the prairie sun. Clearly, here the emphasis is on gaining a good farmhand. Things look rather hopeless until the town's newspaper publisher, a bachelor, turns up. He is cajoled into taking Kevin as a printer's devil; after all, Kevin has the ability to read and write, something not all of the placed out can claim.

Reluctantly, the publisher agrees, but the arrangement turns into a happy one. Kevin learns his trade, is sent to school, and when spring comes he moves with the publisher out to a homestead claim. Kevin also periodically comes into contact with some of the children with whom he traveled. This idyllic life, however, is threatened when Kevin's uncle appears. Let out of jail for what amounts to good behavior—a concept unheard of in the actual prison system of Blackwell's Island—Uncle Michael has carried out his promise to come to Nebraska. He has also found a job for Kevin as a hand on a railroad crew. Kevin is, of course, torn, but a happy compromise is found. Kevin stays with his publisher protector but keeps in contact with the uncle, who becomes part of the railroad's work force. Kevin has the best of it, with a stable life, a chance for education, and a way to maintain ties to his only family.

While Kevin's story is in many ways typical and reflects the real-life experiences of the placed out, Kevin's situation, like all good fiction, is edged towards success from the beginning. The boys he falls in with on the streets of New York are just high-spirited. They are not mean or bent on leading Kevin into real danger. His uncle is kindly, despite the violence that landed him in jail, and the uncle has the wherewithal to keep his promise to come west. Further, Kevin has two adults to look after his welfare—the uncle and the man who took Kevin in when no one wanted him. Kevin truly has his reward—as did the nineteenth-century orphan—and he can look forward to becoming what the New York Children's Aid Society said it wanted for its placed out—a credit to himself and to his new community.

Unlike the child characters of nineteenth-century literature, Kevin is not surrounded by the rhetoric of innocence, and unlike the pronouncements of the Aid Society outlining the need for child rescue, *An Orphan for Nebraska* ignores the complex social and economic demands that prompted the creation of the placing-out system, and allows Kevin's situation to speak for itself. Kevin is in many ways innocent and he engages in an honest trade on the streets, but his most important quality is adaptability. He learns to hawk newspapers, he adapts to life in the city, and he learns the ways of his new life in the West. He cannot afford to be sentimental so he follows the advice of his friend Patrick and sells what he has of his dead mother's possessions. What is past cannot be dwelt on, and he does not look back. Neither does he, once in Nebraska, look back to his city life. Kevin simply looks forward.

When Kevin encounters prejudice, he seems not to recognize it. Arriving in America, he tells an immigration officer that he has an uncle who lives on Baxter Street. Of course, Kevin has no idea where this is and does not comprehend the meaning of the official's remark, "What can Ireland be like, if Baxter Street and Five Points are an improvement?" And, when Kevin first arrives on Newspaper Row, he is jeeringly called a "Paddy"; the insult must be explained. Perhaps Kevin is no different from the thousands of children who did live in the urban world of the nineteenth century, unknowingly the subject of discussions as to their worthiness and the object of scorn and prejudice. On one level the fictional Kevin is insulated from the ugly world of hate and rascism. Some of the newspaperboys use their fists on each other when there are insults, but Kevin is unaware that a whole force of Americans would like to keep the Irish, particularly if they are Catholic, out of the country. He faces some tough times, but his value as a person is never questioned. He is allowed to be an individual.

An Orphan for Nebraska, like Horatio Alger's books, was written for a juvenile audience. When its story is compared to real-life accounts of the placing-out process and experience, one finds a reliance on research rather than melodramatic, wrenching scenes. Perhaps part of the book's success comes from the clear and unchangeable circumstances of the character. Kevin is a true orphan. There are no parents from whom he is separated; his one relative is kind-hearted, with no schemes of using the boy to personal advantage; and once he is placed out, his course is charted for a rewarding life. There are few entanglements, and the Aid Society as the source of Kevin's relocation remains in the shadowy background—no agents come to call or check his progress, no sermons of lofty purpose obscure Kevin's story. This fictional life portrays real experiences with a high degree of accuracy and a smattering of device that reminds us of the literary orphan's continuing place in literature and the times when life serves to provide the stuff of which fiction is made.

Notes

INTRODUCTION

1. Charles Loring Brace, "The Little Laborers of New York City," *Harper's New Monthly Magazine* 47 (August 1873): 330; Charlene Joy Talbot, *An Orphan for Nebraska* (New York: Atheneum, 1979).

2. James Magnuson and Dorothea G. Petrie, *Orphan Train* (New York: Dial Press, 1978). This book was adapted for a 1979 CBS television movie. For description, see *Topeka Capital-Journal*, Dec. 16, 1979, *TV Time Magazine*, p.2. Television gave more exposure to placing out on a 1988 NBC segment of "Unsolved Mysteries," which recounted the search for placed-out siblings. See "OTHSA to Assist National TV Series," *Crossroads* 4 (Summer 1988): 1. For fictional accounts, see Joan Lowery Nixon, *A Family Apart* (New York: Bantam Books, 1987) and *Caught in the Act* (New York: Bantam Books, 1988).

3. *Peoria* (Ill.) *Daily Press*, Feb. 6, 1855.

4. *Rock Island* (Ill.) *Republican*, Mar. 31, 1855; Brace, "The Little Laborers," 330; Charles Loring Brace, *The Dangerous Classes of New York and Twenty Years' Work Among Them*, 3rd ed. (New York: Wynkoop & Hallenbeck, 1880; reprinted, Montclair, N.J.: Patterson Smith, 1967), 242.

5. *The Children's Aid Society of New York: Its History, Plan and Results* (New York: Wynkoop & Hallenbeck, 1893), 34.

CHAPTER I

1. Fanny S. French, "The Beggar Child and Church," *Ladies' Repository* 18 (October 1858): 607; Horatio Alger, Jr., *Jed the Poorhouse Boy* (New York: Trade Publishing Co., 1899). For other examples, see "The Orphan's Faith," *Godey's Magazine and Lady's Book* 64 (January 1862): 52; "Mother's Last Words," quoted in Lou Taylor, *Mourning Dress: A Costume and Social History* (London: George Allen and Unwin, 1983), 166.

2. Horatie Alger, Jr., *Julius the Street Boy* (New York: Trade Publishing Co., 1894), 3.

3. Margaret C. Gillespie, *History and Trends: Literature for Children* (Dubuque, Iowa: Wm. C. Brown, 1970), 88; Bernard Wishy, *The Child and the Republic: The Dawn of Modern American Child Nurture* (Philadelphia: University of Pennsylvania Press, 1968), 11–12 and 23; Carl N. Degler, *At Odds: Woman and Family in America from the Revolution to the Present* (New York: Oxford University Press, 1980), 67; Catharine Beecher, *Religious Training of Children,* quoted in Lyman Beecher Stowe, *Saints, Sinners, and Beechers* (Indianapolis: Bobbs-Merrill Co., 1934), 99.

4. Mrs. A. J. Graves, "Woman in America," in *Root of Bittnerness: Documents of the Social History of American Women,* ed. Nancy F. Cott (New York: A. Dutton, 1972), 144–45; William H. Pyle, "A School of Motherhood," *School and Society* 31 (February 22, 1930): 268. See also Alice Kessler-Harris, "Women, Work, and the Social Order," in *Liberating Women's History: Theoretical and Critical Essays,* ed. Berenice A. Carroll (Urbana: University of Illinois Press, 1976), 330–44; Barbara Welter, "The Cult of True Womanhood, 1820–1840," *American Quarterly* 18 (Summer 1966): 151; Shulamith Firestone, *The Dialectic of Sex: The Case for Feminist Revolution* (New York: Bantam Books, 1972), 86 and 91. Popular literature points to a development of a Cult of Childhood; the "Cult" was given name and form in F. A. Steel, "The Cult of the Child," *Littel's Living Age* 237 (April–June 1903): 761. See also Marilyn Irvin, "The Cult of Childhood in Nineteenth-Century America" (master's thesis, Sangamon State University, 1981).

5. Ann Porter, "Cousin Helen's Baby," *Godey's Magazine and Lady's Book* 39 (October 1849): 235–38; "Children Gone," *Ladies' Repository* 35 (May 1875): 426; Taylor, *Mourning Dress,* 164–66. For other sentiments on early death, see Mrs. H. E. Francis, "A Mother's Trial," *Godey's Magazine and Lady's Book* 64

(September 1862): 276; "'Awa, Awa': Hugh Miller on the Death of His First Child," *Ladies' Repository* 18 (April 1858): 200.

6. Philippe Ariès, *Centuries of Childhood: A Social History of Family Life*, trans. Robert Baldick (New York: Alfred A. Knopf, 1962), 329.

7. Graves, "Woman in America," 144; *First Annual Report of the Executive Committee of the Children's Mission to the Children of the Destitute* (Boston: Benjamin H. Greene, 1850), 5; *Farmer's Wife* (Topeka, Kans.), Mar. 1892, p.2. This Populist newspaper is a mixture of radical political rhetoric written by women, drawings of the latest fashions—which few farmers' wives could imitate—and sections on child care, including the "Alliance Children's Home Kindergarten" for women's "primary instruction" in their most important job. For examples, see *Farmer's Wife*, Oct. 1891, p.5 and Jan. 1892, p.1.

8. "Little Children," *Godey's Magazine and Lady's Book* 48 (March 1854): 207; Elizabeth Pleck, *Domestic Tyranny: The Making of Social Policy against Family Violence from Colonial Times to the Present* (New York: Oxford University Press, 1987), 78; "Health and Beauty," *Godey's Magazine and Lady's Book* 38 (May 1849): 370; Kate Douglas Wiggin, *Children's Rights* (Cambridge, Mass.: Cambridge Press, 1892), 12. *Godey's* demonstrates an increased emphasis on children. In the 1830s, *Godey's*, in twenty-four issues, mentioned children only three times as topics of interest and portrayed them in illustrations only six times. In the 1840s and 1850s, articles and illustrations with children as the focus were more numerous, and by 1870s less was written about children but they appeared in 55 percent of all illustrations; 10 percent of these showed children without any adult.

9. Mrs. Lydia Child, *The Mother's Book* (Boston: Carter and Hendee, 1831; reprinted, New York: Arno Press and the New York Times, 1972), 3.

10. Jacob Riis, *The Children of the Poor* (New York: Scribner's Sons, 1892; reprinted, New York: Arno Press and the New York Times, 1971), 155; *The Children's Aid Society of New York*, 4; Fresh Air Fund advertisement, *New Yorker*, Aug. 14, 1989, p.71.

11. Brace, *The Dangerous Classes of New York*, 17; Wiggin, *Children's Rights*, 65; Sarah B. Cooper, "Kindergarten for Neglected Children," *American Journal of Education* 31 (1881): 206–8; *Manual of Law and Rules for the Government of the Soldiers' Orphans' Home at Atchison, Kansas* (Topeka: Kansas Publishing House, 1891), 10; Timothy Miller, "Charles M. Sheldon and the Uplift of

Tennesseetown," *Kansas History: A Journal of the Central Plains* 9 (Autumn 1986): 129; *The Magic City: Chicago World's Columbian Exposition, 1893* (St. Louis: Historical Publishing Co., 1894), Children's Building photographs, in "Lady Managers" section.

12. John Kent Folmar, ed., *"This State of Wonders": The Letters of an Iowa Frontier Family, 1858–1861* (Iowa City: University of Iowa Press, 1986), 41; Ella Guernsey, "Letters from the People," *New Era* 1 (April 1885): 121–22.

13. David E. Schob, *Hired Hands and Ploughboys: Farm Labor in the Midwest, 1815–60* (Urbana: University of Illinois Press, 1975), 180; diary entry, Nov. 7, 1819, p.38, Mary Leggett Papers, Manuscripts, Illinois State Historical Library (hereafter cited as Manuscripts, ISHL); Christiana Holmes Tillson, *A Woman's Story of Pioneer Illinois*, ed. Milo Milton Quaife (Chicago: Lakeside Press, R. R. Donnelley and Sons Co., 1919), xv; Julia Antoinette Losee Preston, "Washtub over the Sun," *Palimpsest* 68 (Spring 1987): 4.

14. James R. Shortridge, *The Middle West: Its Meaning in American Culture* (Lawrence: University Press of Kansas, 1989), 28; J. A. Riis, "Christmas Reminder of the Nobelist Work in the World," *Forum* 16 (January 1894): 631. See also *Illinois State Journal* (Springfield), Mar. 2, 1858; Richard H. Abbott, "The Agricultural Press Views the Yeoman: 1819–1859," *Agricultural History* 42 (January 1968): 35–48; Shortridge, *Middle West*, 29; Henry Nash Smith, *Virgin Land: The American West as Symbol and Myth* (Cambridge: Harvard University Press, 1950), 123. That the West allowed an egalitarian society that promoted frontier individualism to exist was an 1892 thesis by Frederick Jackson Turner in "The Significance of the Frontier in American History," reprinted in Martin Ridge, ed., *Frederick Jackson Turner: Wisconsin's Historian of the Frontier* (Madison: State Historical Society of Wisconsin, 1986), 43–44. For individual testimonials to a western, classless society see Arthur E. Bostwick, *The Different West: As Seen by a Transplanted Easterner* (Chicago: A. C. McClurg & Co., 1913).

15. William F. Deverell, "To Loosen the Safety Valve: Eastern Workers and Western Lands," *Western Historical Quarterly* 19 (August 1988): 269–85; Norman J. Simler, "The Safety-Valve Doctrine Re-Evaluated," *Agricultural History* 32 (October 1958): 250–57; Thomas Bender, *Toward an Urban Vision: Ideas and Institutions in Nineteenth-Century America* (Lexington: University Press of Kentucky, 1975), 24 and 46–47.

16. "First Annual Report," (1854) in *Annual Reports of the Children's Aid Society, Nos. 1–10, Feb. 1854–Feb. 1863* (New York: Arno Press and the New York Times, 1971), 4 and 6 (hereafter cited as *Annual Reports*); *First Annual Report of the Children's Mission to the Children of the Destitute,* 9; "Forty-Sixth Annual Report of the Children's Aid Society [1898]," Orphan Trains file, Manuscripts, Kansas State Historical Society (hereafter cited as OT, KSHS).

17. W. P. Letchworth, "Dependent and Delinquent Children: Institutions in New York in 1877," *American Journal of Education* 28 (1878): 913; "Report of the Commissioner of Education for the Year 1877," *American Journal of Education* 29 (1879): 182–208; David J. Rothman, *The Discovery of the Asylum: Social Order and Disorder in the New Republic* (Boston: Little, Brown and Co., 1971), 187–89 and 221; Michael B. Katz, *Poverty and Policy in American History* (New York: Academic Press, 1983), 201–17; J. S. Holliday, "An Historian Reflects on Edgewood Children's Center," *California History* 64 (Spring 1985): 123 and 126; *Philadelphia as It Is, 1852* (n.p., ca. 1852), 268–77.

18. Grace Abbott, ed., *The Child and the State* vol.2 (Chicago: University of Chicago Press, 1938), 63; Homer Folks, *The Care of the Destitute, Neglected, and Delinquent Children* (Albany, N.Y.: J. B. Lynon Co., 1900; reprinted, New York: Arno Press and the New York Times, 1971), 24 and 35–36; "The Poor of Newton, Set Up and to be Struct off to the lowest Bidder per week for one year," Apr. 12, 1793, Apr. 14, 1794, copies from record book courtesy Bernadine Barr, Stanford University.

19. *Cobbey's Annotated Statutes of Nebraska, Supplement of 1905* (Beatrice: J. E. Cobbey, 1905), sec.5449, p.121. "Editor's Table," *Godey's Magazine and Lady's Book* 53 (August 1856): 46. See also Page Smith, *The Rise of Industrial America,* vol.6 (New York: McGraw-Hill Book Co., 1984), 368 and Rothman, *The Discovery of the Asylum,* 163–72. For delinquency definitions, see "Report of the Judge of Neosho County, State of Kansas, F. F. Cain, Juvenile Judge," Gov. George H. Hodges Correspondence, box 10, folder 2, Archives, Kansas State Historical Society (hereafter cited as Archives, KSHS).

20. Brace, *The Dangerous Classes of New York*; Riis, *Children of the Poor*; Wiggin, *Children's Rights,* 65; "Premiums on Pauperism," *Frank Leslie's Illustrated Newspaper* 33 (January 20, 1872): 290; "Our Homeless Poor," *Frank Leslie's Illustrated Newspaper* 34 (July 13, 1872): 277.

21. *Illinois State Journal,* Mar. 27, 1858, p.2. Accounts of revivals, camp meet-

ings, and spiritual renewal can be found in many newspapers of the late 1850s. As examples, see *Indianapolis Daily Journal,* Nov. 3 and 6, 1857 and Mar. 18, 1858; *Illinois State Journal,* Mar. 5, 1856, p.3; *Peoria* (Ill.) *Daily Democratic Union,* Mar. 19, 1858, p.2; *Vermilion County Press* (Danville, Ill.), July 28, p.2, Aug. 18, p.2, 1858, and Jan. 11, 1860, p.2. See also Richard C. Wade, *The Urban Frontier: The Rise of Western Cities, 1790–1830* (Cambridge: Harvard University Press, 1959), 134–35.

22. Brian Harrison, "Philanthropy and the Victorians," *Victorian Studies* 9 (June 1966): 353–74. For de Tocqueville see Phillip Shaw Paludan, *"A People's Contest": The Union and the Civil War, 1861–1865* (New York: Harper & Row, 1988), 339.

23. *Aurora* (Ill.) *Daily Beacon,* Apr. 20, 1857; *The Old Brewery, and the New Mission House at the Five Points by Ladies of the Mission* (New York: Stringer and Townsend, 1854), 302; Marilyn Irvin Holt, "Placing Out in Illinois: Emigration for the Poor, 1855–1863," *Transactions of the Illinois State Historical Society* (1988), 37; Vivienne Harter to author, phone interview, Oct. 17, 1990.

24. William A. McKeever, *Farm Boys and Girls* (New York: Macmillan Co., 1913), 295.

25. Brace, "The Little Laborers," 330; Brace, *The Dangerous Classes of New York,* 242; "First Annual Report," (1854) *Annual Reports,* 4; Arthur Charles Cole, *The Era of the Civil War, 1848–1870* (Chicago: A. C. McClurg & Co., 1922), 15.

26. *Illinois Bounty Land Register* (Quincy), Oct. 16, 1835.

27. *Indianapolis Daily Journal,* Mar. 21, 1857, p.2.

28. *Illinois Daily Journal* (Springfield), July 12, 1853 and Apr. 2, 1855. *Daily Pantagraph* (Bloomington, Ill.), Jan. 5, 1858. For Ohio and Wisconsin references, see Schob, *Hired Hands and Ploughboys,* 3, 191, 193, 194, 196 and 200. *Indianapolis Daily Journal,* Mar. 6, 1858, p.2. *Illinois Daily Journal,* Apr. 2, 1855. "Adopting Boys," *Orphan's Advocate* (November 1851): 2. H. E. Stearns to Gov. John P. St. John, Aug. 9, 1879, Gov. St. John Correspondence, box 14, folder 5, Archives, KSHS. Thomas B. Hubbard to Gov. Arthur Capper, January 8, 1915, Gov. Capper Correspondence, box 2, folders 82–98, Archives, KSHS. See also Holt, "Placing out in Illinois," 38; McKeever, *Farm Boys and Girls,* 44; and Catharine Beecher, "The Peculiar Responsibilities of American Women," in *Root of Bitterness,* ed. Nancy F. Cott, 176.

29. "The Farmer's Wife," *Central Farmer and the Nonconformist*, Omaha, Nebr., Jan. 17, 1901.

30. Elliott West, *Growing Up with the Country: Childhood on the Far Western Frontier* (Albuquerque: University of New Mexico Press, 1989), 79; Viviana A. Zelizer, *Pricing the Priceless Child: The Changing Social Value of Children* (New York: Basic Books, 1985), particularly ch.2.

31. Indenture Papers, 1849–60, Hamilton County Courthouse, McLeansboro, Ill.; Indenture Papers, Sangamon County, Illinois, 1839–50, Manuscripts, ISHL; Rothman, *The Discovery of the Asylum*, 185; *Statutes of the Territory of Kansas, 1855* (Shawnee M & L School, 1855), ch.6, secs. 8 and 10, and ch.43, sec.5.

32. *Prairie Farmer*, 5 (March 1855): 104; *Republican and Gazette* (Sterling, Ill.), Nov. 3, 1860, p.2. See also Schob, *Hired Hands and Ploughboys*, 183; Clare L. McCausland, *Children of Circumstance* (Chicago: R. R. Donnelly & Sons Co., 1976), 7.

33. J. C. Mohler and I. D. Graham, "High Points in Kansas Agricultural History," in *History of Kansas, State and People*, comp. William E. Connelly (Chicago: American Historical Society, 1928), 962–64; Robert W. Richmond, *Kansas: A Land of Contrasts* (St. Charles, Mo.: Forum Press, 1974), 127–29 and 131–34.

34. Mohler and Graham, "High Points in Kansas Agricultural History," 961; Richmond, *Kansas: A Land of Contrasts*, 149; *The Annals of Kansas, 1886–1925*, vol.1 (Topeka: Kansas State Historical Society, 1926), 312–13; "Beet Sugar Industry," *Central Farmer*, Omaha, Nebr., Apr. 11, 1901; Sara A. Brown and Robie O. Sargent, "Children in the Sugar Beet Fields of the North Platte Valley of Nebraska, 1923," *Nebraska History* 67 (Fall 1986): 256.

35. R. M. Allen, vice-president, Standard Cattle Co., Ames, Nebraska, to Governor Stanley, Feb. 7, 1902, Gov. Stanley Correspondence, box 1, folder 10, Archives, KSHS.

36. Emma Brace, ed., *The Life of Charles Loring Brace Chiefly Told in His Own Letters* (New York: Scribner's Sons, 1894), 202.

37. Josiah Strong, *Our Country: Its Possible Future and Its Present Crisis* (1886; rev. ed., 1891; reprinted, Cambridge: Belknap Press of Harvard University Press, 1963), 37.

38. Margaret B. Bogue, *Patterns from the Sod*, Land Series, vol.1 (Springfield:

Illinois State Historical Library, 1959), 17; Paul Wallace Gates, *The Illinois Central Railroad and Its Colonization Work* (Cambridge: Harvard University Press, 1934), 223–41; Richmond, *Kansas: A Land of Contrasts*, 110–11, 148–49, and 151; "Report of the Atchison, Topeka and Santa Fe Railroad Company and Leased Lines to the Railroad Commissioners, State of Kansas, 1883," p.5, Archives, KSHS; "Records of the Western-Trunk-Line Association: Joint Through Emigrant Movables Tariff, No. 86," pp.1–3, pamphlet, Union Pacific Museum, Omaha, Nebr. Specific emigrant guides are too numerous to mention (examples are in English, German, Danish, and Swedish) and may be found in railroad and historical society collections. For a Nebraska guide, see Edwin A. Curley, *Nebraska: Its Advantages, Resources, and Drawbacks* (New York: American News Co., 1876); routings and rates for first, second, and third class fares are listed on pages 47–51.

39. Mildred Throne, "Suggested Research on Railroad Aid to the Farmer, With Particular References to Iowa and Kansas," *Agricultural History* 31 (October 1957): 50–56; Constance Libbey Menninger, "The Gospel of Better Farming According to Santa Fe," *Kansas History: A Journal of the Central Plains* 10 (Spring 1987): 43–66; Cole, *Era of the Civil War*, 49.

40. Brace, *The Dangerous Classes of New York*, 249; "Recent Trip West," *The Little Wanderers' Advocate* 5 (April 1869): 50.

41. Miriam Z. Langsam, *Children West: A History of the New York Children's Aid Society, 1853–1890* (Madison: State Historical Society of Wisconsin, 1964), 24 and 25; Roberta Star Hirshson, *"There's Always Someone There. . .": The History of the New England Home for Little Wanderers* (Boston: the author and New England Home for Little Wanderers, 1989), 44. In Santa Fe Collection, Manuscripts Department, Kansas State Historical Society (hereafter cited as Manuscripts, KSHS), the subject of one photo is identified as an "orphan train"; Union Pacific Railroad files contain clippings on placing out. See reference to UP files in *Crossroads* 4 (Summer 1988): 4.

42. U.S. Bureau of the Census, *Historical Statistics of the United States, 1789–1945: A Supplemental to the Statistical Abstract of the United States* (Washington, D.C.: U.S. Department of Commerce, 1949), 200–5.

43. "Brother Searches for Hoffman Sisters," *Crossroads* 1 (Fall 1987): 6.

44. McKeever, *Farm Boys and Girls*, 26.

CHAPTER 2

1. James Grant Wilson and John Fiske, eds., *Appleton's Cyclopaedia of American Biography*, vol.1 (New York: D. Appleton and Co., 1900), 344; Allen Johnson, ed., *Dictionary of American Biography*, vol.2 (New York: Charles Scribner's Sons, 1929), 539–40; Langsam, *Children West*, 5; Bender, *Toward an Urban Vision*, 136–39.

2. Brace, *Life of Charles Loring Brace*, 153–54, 256n, and 377. Among Brace's works are *The Best Method of Disposing of Our Pauper and Vagrant Children* (n.p., 1859); *The Races of the Old World: A Manual of Ethnology* (n.p., 1863); and *Gesta Christi; or, A History of Humane Progress under Christianity* (n.p., 1882). These and others are noted in Brace, *Life of Charles Loring Brace*, and Johnson, *Dictionary of American Biography*. For evolutionist arguments related to treatment of the poor, see Smith, *The Rise of Industrial America*, 140–59.

3. Riis, "Christmas Reminder of the Nobelist Work in the World," 626; Brace, *Life of Charles Loring Brace*, 153–54; Brace, *The Dangerous Classes of New York*, 457.

4. Brace, *The Dangerous Classes of New York*, 452–53; *The First Annual Report of the Children's Mission to the Children of the Destitute*, 8; Associated Charities of Boston, *A Directory of the Charitable and Beneficent Organizations of Boston*, 6th ed. (Boston: Old Corner Bookstore, 1914), 82; Langsam, *Children West*, 17–18; Brace, *Life of Charles Loring Brace*, 172; Priscilla Ferguson Clement, "The City and the Child, 1860–1885," in *American Childhood: A Research Guide and Historical Handbook*, eds. Joseph M. Hawes and N. Ray Hiner (Westport, Conn.: Greenwood Press, 1985), 258.

5. Holliday, "An Historian Reflects on Edgewood Children's Center," 123 and 124. Edgewood's antecedent was the San Francisco Orphanage Asylum Society established by women of several church congregations in 1851.

6. Abbott, *The Child and the State*, 157–62; Ivy Pinchbeck and Margaret Hewitt, *Children in English Society*, vol.2 (London: Routledge & Kegan Paul, 1973), 546–69; Langsam, *Children West*, 6 and 17; Loren N. Horton, "A Sphere of Moral Philanthropy: Prison Reform in the Victorian Period," *Hope & Glory* 1 (Spring 1987): 32; Ethel Verry, "Eighty Years Ago," *Survey* 56 (June 15, 1926): 384; Richmond, *Kansas: A Land of Contrasts*, 160; R. A. Leach, "Industrial and General Characteristics, Poor Law Administrator, and Charities," in *The*

Organization of Charities, Being a Report of the Sixth Section of the International Congress of Charities, Corrections, and Philanthropy, 1893, ed. Daniel C. Gilman (Baltimore: John Hopkins Press, 1894), 325–26. British transportation of prisoners practically ended after 1867, but that of women and children continued; England still transported children in the 1950s. See Horton, "A Sphere of Moral Philanthropy," 35; Pinchbeck and Hewitt, *Children in English Society,* 554–56.

7. *The Children's Aid Society of New York,* 3. See also Johnson, *Dictionary of American Biography,* 2:540; Brace, *Life of Charles Loring Brace,* 201. For Brace as pro-urban see Paul Boyer, *Urban Masses and Moral Order in America, 1820–1920* (Cambridge: Harvard University Press, 1978), 96–101; Bender, *Toward an Urban Vision,* 148–49; Clement, "The City and the Child," 261–62. The Children's Aid Society archives holds at least three diaries of "visitors" who went about locating those who needed assistance and encouraging children to attend the society's industrial schools or to take shelter in the lodging houses. Unfortunately, these diaries are unavailable to researchers. Ethel J. Lambert, archivist, Children's Aid Society, to author, Dec. 20, 1990.

8. Brace, *Life of Charles Loring Brace,* 158; *The Children's Aid Society of New York,* 4; Langsam, *Children West,* 4.

9. Brace, *Life of Charles Loring Brace,* 158.

10. "First Annual Report," (1854) *Annual Reports,* 9; *The Children's Aid Society of New York,* 39–40; Bruce William Bellingham, "'Little Wanderers': A Socio-Historical Study of the Nineteenth Century Origins of Child Fostering and Adoption Reform, Based on Early Records of the New York Children's Aid Society," (Ph.D. diss., University of Pennsylvania, 1984), 110–12 and 128–31.

11. "First Annual Report," (1854), *Annual Reports, passim*; Langsam, *Children West,* 21–22 and 25; *Illinois Daily Journal,* Aug. 4, 1855; "First Orphan Train 'Set Sail' in 1854," *Crossroads* 7 (Spring 1989): 8. Quotes are from "Orphan Trains West," exhibit brochure, Oct. 1987, Southwestern Michigan College Museum, Dowagiac, Michigan.

12. Donald Dale Jackson, "'Orphan trains' transported kids to fresh starts in West," *Minneapolis Star and Tribune,* Sept. 17, 1986, p.4CX.

13. Ibid.; "Brother Searches for Hoffman Sisters," 6; "Dunnaways Chose A Fiesty Boy," *Crossroads* 2 (Winter 1987–88): 6.

14. "Children's Aid Society Annual Report," *New York Times*, Nov. 27, 1901, p.9; "Fifty-Eighth Annual Report, 1910," p.116, Orphan Train File, Nebraska State Historical Society (hereafter cited as Orphan Train, N S H S); "Gilbert Eadie Shares His Life," *Crossroads* 7 (May 1989): 4.

15. Henry Kuhn to Whitelaw Reid, Aug. 9, 1883, Henry Kuhn Letterbook, Manuscripts, K S H S. For Reid's involvement see *Republican-Democrat* (Ravenna, Ohio), Apr. 14, 1880, and *Hornellsville* (N.Y.) *Weekly Tribune*, Apr. 29, 1881.

16. "Children's Aid Society—Annual Report, 1886," p.74, and "Fifty-Eighth Annual Report, 1910," p.116, Orphan Train, N S H S; Harry Colwell, "A New York Orphan Comes to Kansas," *Kansas History: A Journal of the Central Plains* 8 (Summer 1985): 112.

17. Francis H. White, "Placing Out New York Children in the West," *The Charities Review: A Journal of Practical Sociology* 2 (February 1893): 217–18 and 225; *The Children's Aid Society of New York*, 40. White gave the number as seventy-five thousand; *The Children's Aid Society of New York* gave the higher figure. Of the total, over six thousand had been returned to parents or institutions.

18. Charles Loring Brace, "The Little Laborers," 330; *Jacksonville* (Ill.) *Journal*, Apr. 26 and May 24, 1860; *Catalogue of the Officers, Alumni, and Former Students of the Illinois College, 1829–1912* (Jacksonville, Ill., 1912), 31.

19. Langsam, *Children West*, 63; *Leonardville* (Kans.) *Monitor*, June 17, 1886; *Elk County Citizen*, (Howard, Kans.), July 13, 1899; "New York Orphans Come to Burlington," *Coffey County Footprints* 5 (March 1987): 2.

20. Brace, "The Little Laborers," 330.

21. "Aurora man relives past journey on Orphan Train," *News-Register*, (Aurora, Nebr.), Dec. 2, 1987, p.2; "P. Mary Young," Orphan Train, N S H S.

22. Brace, *The Dangerous Classes of New York*, 268–69; "She Was Put Out on a Farm in Kansas," *Crossroads* 7 (May 1989): 11; "Children's Aid Society—Annual Report, 1913," Orphan Train, N S H S; "Sixth Annual Report," (1859) *Annual Reports*, 50 and 79–80; Riis, "Christmas Reminder of the Nobelist Work in the World," 631.

23. "Nebraska towns mentioned in Annual Reports of the Children's Aid Society," Orphan Train, N S H S; White, "Placing Out New York Children," 218–19; *Leonardville Monitor*, June 17, July 8 and July 22, 1886; Colwell, "A New

York Orphan Comes to Kansas," 110; *Wichita* (Kans.) *Eagle-Beacon,* Dec. 22, 1979; Harriet Creager, "History Hints," *Wilson County Historical Society Newsletter* 6 (March 1979): 4; "Orphan Train Sisters Find Good Parents," *Crossroads* 4 (Summer 1988): 5; "Searching," *Crossroads* 7 (May 1989): 6; *Illinois Daily Journal,* Aug. 4, 1855; *Monmouth* (Ill.) *Atlas,* Aug. 10, 1855; *Weekly Pantagraph* (Bloomington, Ill.), Feb. 6, 1856; *Jacksonville Journal,* May 24, 1860; "Sixth Annual Report," (1859) *Annual Reports,* 50.

24. *Twenty-Fifth Annual Report of the Children's Home, 1885* (Cincinnati: Cincinnati Children's Home, 1886), 9.

25. *Thirty-third Annual Report of the Children' Aid Society, November 1885* (New York: Wynkoop, Hallenbeck & Co., 1885), 23–24.

26. Ibid., 22–23.

27. "Children's Aid Society—Annual Report, 1884," Orphan Train, NSHS; John R. Harmon, "One Orphan's Odyssey," *Midwest Living* (December 1988), p.34, Orphan Train File, South Dakota Historical Society (hereafter cited as Orphan Train File, SDHS); "Aurora man relives past journey on Orphan Train," 2; "Third Annual Report" (1856), *Annual Reports,* 50.

28. For Hill see Martha Nelson Vogt and Christina Vogt, *Searching for Home: Three Families from the Orphan Trains* (Grand Rapids, Mich.: Triumph Press, 1983), iii, 12–13, 48, and 49; "She Was Put Out on a Farm in Kansas," 11; *Salina* (Kans.) *Daily Union,* July 2, 1912, p.8 (this refers to her as Laura Anna Hill); "Searching," 3. For Swan, see "TV Program Sparks Orphan's Memories," *Crossroads* 7 (May 1989): 2; "Baby Jean a Town 'Curiosity'," *Crossroads* 3 (Spring 1988): 4; "Orphans Help Populate County," clippings from *Sabetha Herald,* 1908, OT, KSHS. For Comstock see M. Vogt and C. Vogt, *Searching for Home,* 56 and 80–83; "Placing-Out Agent Clara Comstock," *Crossroads* 4 (Summer 1988): 4. For South Dakota placement see *Aberdeen* (S. Dak.) *Daily American,* Mar. 4, 1914, p.2; "Orphan Train Sisters find Good Parents," 5. For Morgan see "Brother Searches for Hoffman Sisters," 6; "Letter from Former Aid Society Agent," *Crossroads* 1 (Fall 1987): 7; "They Pretended to Be Twins," *Crossroads* 2 (Winter 1987–88): 2.

29. Brace, *The Dangerous Classes of New York,* 268; *Thirty-third Annual Report of Children's Aid Society, November, 1885,* 21 and 24; *The Children's Aid Society of New York,* 34; "Finding Homes for the Homeless," *American Monthly Review of Reviews* 20 (August 1899): 224; "P. Mary Young," Orphan Train, NSHS.

30. For agreement see Brace, "The Little Laborers," 330, and Langsam, *Children West*, 18 and 23. For indentures see *Chicago Daily Journal*, Mar. 21, 1856; *Belleville* (Ill.) *Weekly Democrat*, Apr. 17, 1858; Indenture papers, Fayette County, Ill., Aug. and Dec. 1860, Archives, Sangamon State University (hereafter cited as Indenture papers, Archives, ssu). For Mary see, "Third Annual Report," (1856) *Annual Reports*, 50.

31. "Ninth Annual Report," (1862) *Annual Reports*, 48; "Eighth Annual Report," (1861) *Annual Reports*, 49; *Thirty-third Annual Report of Children's Aid Society, November, 1885*, 22; "Fifth Annual Report," (1858) *Annual Reports*, 79.

32. *Elk County Citizen*, July 13, 1899.

33. White, "Placing Out New York Children," 216; *The Children's Aid Society of New York*, 40; Brace, *The Dangerous Classes of New York*, 300–3.

34. Langsam, *Children West*, 53; Nina Swanson, "The Development of Public Protection of Children in Kansas," *Collections of the Kansas State Historical Society, 1919–1922* 15 (1923): 256; Elinor Nims, *The Illinois Adoption Law and Its Administration*, Social Services Monograph no. 2 (Chicago: University of Chicago Press, 1928), vii, 9, 11, and 12; Abbott, *The Child and the State*, 164; Elinor Nims, "Experiments in Adoption Legislation," *Social Service Review* 1 (June 1927): 241–48.

35. *Aberdeen Daily American*, Mar. 4, 1914, p.2; "Children's Aid Society—Annual Report, 1921," p.94, and "Children's Aid Society—Annual Report, 1923," p.89, Orphan Train, nshs; "Forty-Sixth Annual Report of the Children's Aid Society [1898]," ot, kshs; Colwell, "A New York Orphan Comes to Kansas," 111–12; "One Orphan's Odyssey," Orphan Train File, sdhs; "Searching," 6; "She Was Put Out on a Farm in Kansas," 11; Osage County Historical Society, *One Hundred Fifty Years: From Trail to Sail, Osage County, Kansas* (The author, 1976), 26; Bonita Mulanax, "Orphan Trains to the Midwest," (paper, History of Kansas course, Kansas State University, Apr. 19, 1989, copy in author's possession), 11, quoting Viola L. Parks to Mrs. Ione L. McCollough, Sept. 26, 1946; *The Story of Graham School* (N.p., ca. 1950), 9, 12, and 14; Maurice V. Odquist, *The History of Graham* (N.p., ca. 1960), 5. The Orphan Asylum Society of New York, predecessor of present-day Graham Home at Hastings-on-Hudson, New York, was for Protestant children only until 1957; it abandoned in-state indenture in 1905.

36. Brace, *The Dangerous Classes of New York,* 232–33, 265, and 284–85; "Children's Aid Society—Annual Report, 1883," Orphan Train, NSHS.

37. Brace, *The Dangerous Classes of New York,* 228–29, 235, and 265; George R. Crooks, "Emigration of Children to the West," *Harper's Weekly* 24 (July 31, 1880): 486–87.

38. Riis, "Christmas Reminder of the Nobelist Work in the World," 633; "Children's Aid Society Annual Report," *New York Times,* Nov. 27, 1901, p.9.

39. Joseph W. Snell, ed., "Roughing It on Her Kansas Claim: The Diary of Abbie Bright, 1870–1871," *Kansas Historical Quarterly* 37 (Autumn 1971): 235, 239–40, and 244. Bright recorded her Indiana teaching experiences prior to making her Kansas claim.

40. *Aurora Daily Beacon,* Apr. 20, 1857, p.2; "Third Annual Report," (1856) *Annual Reports,* 35; Langsam, *Children West,* 28–30; Brace, *The Dangerous Classes of New York,* 249; Degler, *At Odds,* 135; Clement, "The City and the Child," 263.

41. Brace, *The Dangerous Classes of New York,* 272; Langsam, *Children West,* 28; "Forty-Sixth Annual Report of the Children's Aid Society [1898]," OT, KSHS.

42. *Ninth Annual Report of the New York Association for Improving the Condition of the Poor* (New York: John F. Trow, 1852), 29; *Semi-Centennial. Fiftieth and Fifty-First Annual Reports of the New York Association for Improving the Condition of the Poor* (New York, 1894), 28; Riis, *Children of the Poor,* 156.

43. Robert P. Howard, *Illinois: A History of the Prairie State,* (Grand Rapids: William B. Eerdmans Publishing Co., 1972), 244–45; Carrie Prudence Kofoid, *Puritan Influences in the Formative Years of Illinois History* (Springfield: Illinois State Journal Co., 1906), 41; *The Thirty-Second Report of the American Home Missionary Society* (New York: John A. Gray, Printer, 1858), 81; Union County Indentures, Manuscripts, ISHL; *Egyptian Republic,* (Centralia, Ill.), Mar. 29, 1860; Gates, *Illinois Central,* 238–39.

44. Robert H. Bremner, *The Public Good: Philanthropy and Welfare in the Civil War Era* (New York: Alfred A. Knopf, 1980), 87; Paludan, *"A People's Contest,"* 181, 183, and 185; Edith Abbott, "The Civil War and the Crime Wave of 1865–70," *Social Service Review* 1 (June 1927): 219.

45. Paludan, *"A People's Contest,"* 156; Victor Hicken, *Illinois in the Civil War* (Urbana: University of Illinois Press, 1956), viii; Brace, *Life of Charles Loring Brace,* 245.

46. Brace, *The Dangerous Classes of New York,* 242; Brace, *Life of Charles Loring Brace,* 258; Langsam, *Children West,* 27.

47. Wishy, *The Child and the Republic,* 81–82.

48. *The Children's Aid Society of New York,* 39–40; "Kansan Seeking Mother's Sisters," *Crossroads* 4 (Summer 1988): 2; Charles Loring Brace, *The New West: or, California in 1867–1868* (London: G. P. Putnam & Son, 1869), 348. Riis, "Christmas Reminder of the Nobelist Work in the World," 629 and 631.

49. "Finding Homes for the Homeless," 224.

50. *New York Times,* June 12, 1916, p.18.

51. Brace, *The Dangerous Classes of New York,* 268; *Elk County Citizen,* July 13, 1899; "Finding Homes for the Homeless," 224; *New York Times,* Nov. 27, 1901, p.9. *National Cyclopaedia of American Biography,* vol.29 (New York: James T. White, 1941), 133; *National Cyclopaedia of American Biography,* vol.31 (New York: James T. White, 1944), 127. For a letter sent to Robert Brace as head of the emigration department see "Children's Aid Society—Annual Report, 1912," p.103, Orphan Train, N S H S; a boy in Texas was responding to Brace's correspondence.

52. Osage County Historical Society, *One Hundred Fifty Years,* 26, quoting Virginia Howard who, at age eight in 1910, was placed in Osage City, Kansas. Second quote is from Donald Gerald Pate, sent to Rogers, Arkansas, in 1915; he left his placement home at age thirteen to escape harsh treatment. See "Society President Tells Father's Story," *Crossroads* 3 (Spring 1988): 6.

CHAPTER 3

1. *Chicago Daily Journal,* Feb. 6, 1856, p.2; "Searching," 7; White, "Placing Out New York Children," 220. The New England Home for Little Wanderers, still in operation, saw another form of child relocation during World War II, housing British refugee "blitz kids." See "The New England Home for Little Wanderers," informational letter, 1989, New England Home for Little Wanderers.

2. *Ninth Annual Report of the Executive Committee of the Children's Mission to the Children of the Destitute* (Boston: John Wilson and Son, 1858), 24; Langsam, *Children West,* 17–18; Joseph Tuckerman, *On the Elevation of the Poor* (Boston: n.p., 1874), 62, 174–75, and 182; Rothman, *The Discovery of the Asylum,* 175–79.

3. *First Annual Report of the Children's Mission to the Children of the Destitute*, 1, 13, and 14.

4. Ibid., 8–9.

5. Ibid.; *Eighth Annual Report of the Executive Committee of the Children's Mission to the Children of the Destitute* (Boston: Benjamin H. Greene, 1857), 3–5, 12, and 16; *Ninth Annual Report of the Executive Committee of the Children's Mission to the Children of the Destitute*, 3.

6. *Eighth Annual Report of the Executive Committee of the Children's Mission to the Children of the Destitute*, 17.

7. *Ninth Annual Report of the Executive Committee of the Children's Mission to the Children of the Destitute*, 3, 4, 6, 7, and 9; *Fifty-first Annual Report: The Children's Mission to the Children of the Destitute, 1900* (Boston: Children's Mission, 1900), 7–10.

8. Clint Clay Tilton, "Gurdon Saltonstall Hubbard and Some of His Friends," *Transactions of the Illinois State Historical Society* 40 (Springfield: Illinois State Historical Society, 1933): 124; Kofoid, *Puritan Influences*, 30; *Urbana* (Ill.) *Union*, Feb. 21, 1856, p.2.

9. *Urbana Union*, Feb. 21, 1856; *Weekly Pantagraph*, Feb. 6, 1856, p.1; Cole, *Era of the Civil War*, 15; Holt, "Placing Out in Illinois," 36.

10. *Urbana Union*, Feb. 21, 1856.

11. "Seventh Annual Report," (1860) *Annual Reports*, 60–61; "Brother Searches for Hoffman Sisters," 6.

12. *Weekly Pantagraph*, Feb. 6, 1856; *Vermilion County Press*, Jan. 25, 1860, p.2.

13. *Vermillion County Press*, Jan. 11, 1860, p.2.

14. Indenture papers, Archives, ssu; *New York Juvenile Asylum, Fourth Annual Report* (New York: New York Juvenile Asylum, 1856), 25; *Ninth Annual Report of the New York Association for Improving the Condition of the Poor*, 39; *Semi-Centennial*, 24–25; "Report of the Commissioner of Education for the Year 1877," 202–3; Henry Bernard, "Public High School in a Graded System," *American Journal of Education* 28 (1878): 231; Rothman, *The Discovery of the Asylum*, 214 and 234–35.

15. McCausland, *Children of Circumstance*, 20; *Chicago Daily Journal*, Mar. 21, 1856; *Semi-Centennial*, 13 and 25; "Orphans and Orphan Asylums," Orphans, vertical file, Illinois State Historical Library (hereafter as cited Orphans, ishl).

16. For example of indenture papers, see Indenture papers, Archives, ssu; *News-Gazette* (Champaign, Ill.), Aug. 6, 1989, p.1E.

17. *Chicago Daily Journal*, Mar. 21, 1856; *News-Gazette*, Aug. 6, 1989, p.1E; Indenture papers, Archives, ssu; "Asylum Children in McLeansboro, Illinois," *Illinois State Genealogical Society Quarterly* 17 (Fall 1985): 148–49; "Asylum Children," broadside (1888), Orphans, ishl.

18. *Ninth Annual Report of the New York Association for Improving the Condition of the Poor*, 11–12 and 23–24; *Semi-Centennial*, 28–29.

19. Paludan, *"A People's Contest,"* xv. Paludan's prologue, "Anxious Conversations: The North Confronts Industrialization," pp.xiii–xxii, is an excellent discussion of industrialization in the pre-Civil War North.

20. *Republican and Gazette*, Oct. 27, 1860, p.3.

21. Edwin T. Freedley, *Philadelphia and Its Manufacturers, 1857* (Philadelphia: Edward Young, 1858), 186 and 241; Holt, "Placing Out in Illinois," 39; *Ninth Annual Report of the New York Association for Improving the Condition of the Poor*, 20–21.

22. "Fifth Annual Report," (1858) *Annual Reports*, 14–15. For newspaper examples, see *Cairo* (Ill.) *Weekly Times and Delta*, Nov. 25, 1857, p.1; *Monmouth Atlas*, Nov. 27, 1857; and *Vermilion County Press*, Aug. 25 and Sept. 1, 1858; *Indianapolis Daily Journal*, Nov. 6, 1857, p.2. For female labor see Gerda Lerner, "The Lady and the Mill Girl: Changes in the Status of Women in the Age of Jackson," in *Women and Womanhood in America*, ed. Ronald W. Hogeland (Lexington, Mass.: D. C. Heath and Co., 1973), 90–102.

23. *Weekly Belleville* (Ill.) *Advocate*, Nov. 20, 1857, p.4; *Daily Pantagraph*, Mar. 22, 1858, p.2; Cole, *Era of the Civil War*, 15; Arthur Charles Cole, "Illinois Women of the Middle Period," *Transactions of the Illinois State Historical Society* 27 (Springfield: Illinois State Historical Society, 1920): 85.

24. *Peoria Daily Democratic Union*, Mar. 8, 1858, p.2; *Weekly Pantagraph*, Jan. 6, 1857, p.2; *Daily Pantagraph*, Jan. 5, 1858, p.2; *Our Constitution* (Urbana, Ill.), Mar. 13, 1858, p.2.

25. *Peoria Daily Democratic Union*, Mar. 8, 1858, p.2; *Daily Pantagraph*, Mar. 27, 1858, p.3; *Morgan Journal*, Mar. 11, 1858, p.2.

26. *Morgan Journal*, Mar. 11, 1858, p.2; *Urbana Union*, Mar. 18, 1858, p.3; *Our Constitution*, Apr. 3, 1858, p.1; Christine Stansell, *City of Women: Sex and Class in New York, 1789–1860* (New York: Alfred A. Knopf, 1986), 175–80. For an

example of mail-order bride literature, see Walter Hart Blumenthal, "Back Soon—Gone to Get A Wife," *The Westerners New York Posse Brand Book* 7, no. 2 (1960): 5–6.

27. *Daily Pantagraph*, Feb. 1 and 4, 1858; *Our Constitution*, Apr. 3, 1858; *Illinois State Journal*, Mar. 13 and 20, 1858; Holt, "Placing Out in Illinois," 40.

28. *Daily Pantagraph*, Apr. 2, 1858, p.3; Holt, "Placing Out in Illinois," 40.

29. James Grant Wilson and John Fiske, eds., *Appleton's Cyclopaedia of American Biography*, vol.2 (New York: D. Appleton and Company, 1900), 411; Eliza W. Farnham, *Life in Prairie Land* (New York, 1855; reprinted, Nieuwkopp, Netherlands: B. DeGraff, 1972), v; Barbara J. Berg, *The Remembered Gate: Origins of American Feminism* (New York: Oxford University Press, 1978), 246.

30. For women choosing prostitution, see Gary L. Cunningham, "Moral Corruption and the American West," (Ph.D. diss., University of California, Santa Barbara, 1980), 52 and 158–65. For nursing and the Civil War see Philip A. Kalisch and Beatrice J. Kalisch, *The Advance of American Nursing* (Boston: Little Brown and Co., 1978), 62; and Minnie Goodnow, *Outlines of Nursing History*, 4th ed. (Philadelphia: W. B. Saunders, 1930), 139. For Mercer, see *New York Times*, Oct. 2, 1865, p.4; Charles W. Smith, ed., "Asa Shinn Mercer: Pioneer in Western Publicity," *Pacific Northwest Quarterly* 27 (October 1936): 348 and 355; and Stewart H. Holbrook, *The Yankee Exodus: An Account of Migration from New England* (New York: Macmillan Co., 1950), 242–52.

31. Berg, *The Remembered Gate*, 227–29; *The Old Brewery*, 36; James D. McCabe, Jr., *Lights and Shadows of New York Life; or, The Sights and Sensations of the Great City* (Philadelphia: National Publishing Co., 1872), 401.

32. "Third Annual Report," (1856) *Annual Reports*, 35; Earl Schenck Meiers, et al., eds., *Lincoln Day by Day: A Chronology, 1809–1865* (Springfield: Lincoln Sesquicentennial Commission, 1960), 2:275.

33. *Daily Pantagraph*, Mar. 23, 1858, p.3; *Sterling* (Ill.) *Republican*, June 13, 1857, p.2; *Belleville Weekly Democrat*, Apr. 17, 1858, p.2.

34. *Illinois Daily Journal*, Aug. 4, 1855, p.2; *Sterling Republican*, June 13, 1857, p.2; *Belleville Weekly Democrat*, Apr. 17, 1858, p.2.

35. *Belleville Weekly Democrat*, Apr. 17, 1858, p.2.

36. Reverend N. Mead, "The 'Five Points' Mission: Its Present Condition and Future Prospects," *Ladies Repository* 18 (April 1858): 201.

37. Bender, *Toward an Urban Vision*, 139; Wilson and Fiske, *Appleton's Cyclopaedia of American Biography*, 1:344; McCabe, *Lights and Shadows of New York Life*, 416; Sarah Ann Maxwell, "Sarah's Story Concludes," *Crossroads* 14 (January 1990): 12; "Children's Aid Society—Annual Report, 1921," Orphan Train, NSHS.

38. McCabe, *Lights and Shadows of New York Life*, 418 and 420–21.

39. "The Pattern Was Created in New England 125 Years Ago," brochure, New England Home for Little Wanderers; "Home for Little Wanderers, Baldwin Place, Boston, Mass.," *Frank Leslie's Illustrated Newspaper* 30 (July 30, 1870): 311–12; *Baldwin Place Home for Little Wanderers, The Wanderers' Advocate* 7 (June 1871): 82–85, 94; Hirshson, *"There's Always Someone There"*, 36–37.

40. Hirshson, *"There's Always Someone There,"* 36–37 and 41–44; "Plan of the Work," *New England Home for Little Wanderers Advocate and Report* 14 (January 1890): 1; *Fortieth Annual Report and Quarterly Advocate* 41 (May 1905): 47–49, and 62.

41. Hirshson, *"There's Always Someone There,"* 43–44; *Fortieth Annual Report and Quarterly Advocate*, 48.

42. *First Annual Report of the Children's Mission to the Children of the Destitute*, 6–7.

43. McCabe, *Lights and Shadows of New York Life*, 652–53; Bremner, *The Public Good*, 87; Langsam, *Children West*, 47–49.

44. A. Blake Brophy, *Foundlings on the Frontier: Racial and Religious Conflict in Arizona Territory, 1904–1905* (Tucson: University of Arizona Press, 1972), 8–10.

45. Ibid., 6–7; Brace, *The Dangerous Classes of New York*, 408; "The Nursery and Child's Hospital," *Frank Leslie's Illustrated Newspaper* 48 (June 14, 1879): 253; "The City Health," *Frank Leslie's Illustrated Newspaper* 48 (July 12, 1879): 306; "The Foundling-Hospital and Idiot-Asylum on Randall's Island, East River," *Frank Leslie's Illustrated Newspaper* 30 (April 2, 1870): 45–46. See also Smith, *The Rise of Industrial America*, 367–68, for tenement infant mortality figures in 1888; cited is a rate of 62.9 per 1,000 in the ninety-four worst tenements, and in one Italian section, known as Mulberry Bend, one in every three infants born in 1888 died.

46. *New York Foundling Hospital, Annual Report* (New York, 1873), chart for Condition of Infants upon Entering Hospital; Smith, *The Rise of Industrial*

America, 367; Brophy, *Foundlings on the Frontier,* 10; Jan Arman, "Orphan Train Rider and His Music," *Crossroads* 7 (May 1989): 3.

47. "Santa Claus among the Foundlings," *Frank Leslie's Illustrated Newspaper* 33 (January 20, 1872): 295; Brace, *The Dangerous Classes of New York,* 414–15; "Infant Asylums, Considered in the Light of Advanced Medical Science," *Frank Leslie's Illustrated Newspaper* 34 (April 27, 1872): 103; Ariès, *Centuries of Childhood,* 374.

48. "Nebraska Bound, 1912–1962, a Foundling Family feature," *Mater Dei* 8 (July 1962): 2–3; "Eighty-four-year-old wants facts about his early life," newspaper clipping, Orphan Train File, SDHS.

49. Brophy, *Foundlings on the Frontier,* 27–28. For western orders see James A. McGongle, "Missions among the Indians in Kansas: Right Reverend John B. Miege, S. J., First Catholic Bishop in Kansas," *Transactions of the Kansas State Historical Society, 1905–1906* 9 (1906): 156; "Galveston Community College buys properties of St. Mary's Orphange," *Texas Catholic Herald,* July 28, 1967, newspaper clipping, Catholic Archives of Texas (hereafter cited as Catholic Archives).

50. Brophy, *Foundlings on the Frontier,* 32; Hendrix, "The Orphan Train," 32, Orphan Train File, SDHS; "The Alice Lewis/Generosa Forquer Story," *Crossroads* 5 (Fall 1988): 2. For mentions of the tagging system used by the placed out, see "Searching," 6; Arman, "Orphan Train Rider and His Music," 3; and "Placing Out History Preserved by OTHSA," *Crossroads* 7 (May 1989): 12.

51. *Ellis County News* (Hays, Kans.), Aug. 12, 1948.

52. *Hope* (Kans.) *Dispatch,* Nov. 28, 1901, p.4.

53. *Ellis County News,* Aug. 12, 1948.

54. Ibid.; "Little Orphan Lady Wins Big Victories," *Crossroads* 7 (May 1989): 9.

55. Arman, "Orphan Train Rider and His Music," 3.

56. *Garden City* (Kans.) *Telegram,* Aug. 2, 1983; Peggy Deane Toffier Pounder, "Milton Peter Toffier," *Crossroads* 4 (Summer 1988): 7; "Brothers Reunited by Louisiana Writer," *Crossroads* 3 (Spring 1988): 7; "Texan Responds to Newspaper Article," *Crossroads* 2 (Winter 1987–88): 7; "The Alice Lewis/Generosa Forquer Story," 2; "There She Is!," *Crossroads* 5 (Fall 1988): 5 and 8; "Natalie Hanson Rode to Chicago," *Crossroads* 5 (Fall 1988): 10; "Searching," 6–7. For Aid Society numbers see *The Children's Aid Society of New York,* 38.

57. Howard, *Illinois: A History of the Prairie State,* 255.

58. *Indianapolis Daily Journal,* Apr. 26, May 8, June 7, and June 12, 1858; B. R. Sulgrove, *History of Indianapolis and Marion County, Indiana* (Philadelphia: L. H. Everts & Co., 1884), 382–83; *"The World's" History of Cleveland: Commemorating the City's Centennial Anniversary* (Cleveland: Cleveland World, 1896), 197–98.

59. White, "Placing Out New York Children," 220; "The Children's Home of Cincinnati, Ohio," *Crossroads* 1 (Fall 1987): 1; *The Children's Aid Society of New York,* 39; "The Pattern Was Created in New England 125 Years Ago," brochure, New England Home for Little Wanderers; H. W. Beckwith, *History of Montgomery County, Together with Historic Notes on the Wabash Valley* (Chicago: H. H. Hille and N. Iddings, 1881), 111–14; "Our Seventieth Birthday," *The Children's Home Record, 1934* and *The Bicentennial Guide to Greater Cincinnati: A Portrait of Two Hundred Years* (Cincinnati Historical Society, 1988), Children's Home of Cincinnati files, Cincinnati Historical Society (hereafter cited as Children's Home of Cincinnati files). White did not specify which Cleveland orphanages placed out, but a likely candidate is the city-supported Children's Aid Society that ran the Cleveland City Industrial School for destitute children. See *"The World's" History of Cleveland,* 197.

60. White, "Placing Out New York Children," 220; *Twelfth Annual Report of the Children's Aid Society of Indiana,* 8.

61. *Chieftain* (Tecumseh, Nebr.), July 8, 1893. This is the only located reference to this society. A search of Chicago Historical Society materials and Chicago city directories did not uncover mention of the organization; it may have been one of the black market adoption agencies targeted for elimination early in the twentieth century. For Nebraska institutions see "Auditor's Report for Year ending 1890," in *Forty Years of Nebraska: At Home and in Congress,* ed. Thomas Weston Tipton (Lincoln: State Journal Co., 1902), 164.

62. *The White Hall Orphan's Home Society* (N.p., ca. 1907), 2, Orphan, ISHL.

63. White, "Placing Out New York Children," 225; *The Children's Aid Society of New York,* 32 and 33.

CHAPTER 4

1. Michael Patrick, Evelyn Sheets, and Evelyn Trickel, *We Are a Part of History: The Story of the Orphan Trains* (Santa Fe: Lightning Tree, 1990), 113 and 147; "One Orphan's Odyssey," 34, Orphan Train File, SDHS; Jackson,

"'Orphan trains' transported kids to fresh starts in West"; "Orphans Help Populate County," clippings from *Sabetha Herald*, 1909, OT, KSHS; *World-Herald* (Omaha, Nebr.), Dec. 15, 1921.

2. "Brother Searches for Hoffman Sisters," 6; "Dunnaways Chose a Fiesty Boy," 6.

3. Brace, *The Dangerous Classes of New York*, 462; Langsam, *Children West*, 25 and 56–57; Brace, *Life of Charles Loring Brace*, 348.

4. Langsam, *Children West*, 57; Bender, *Toward an Urban Vision*, 145; Brace, *Life of Charles Loring Brace*, 348.

5. Brace, *The Dangerous Classes of New York*, 463.

6. Brace, *Life of Charles Loring Brace*, 348; White, "Placing Out New York Children," 219–20; *The Children's Aid Society of New York*, 39; "Children's Home Society Celebrates Centennial," Orphan Train File, SDHS; *Wichita Eagle-Beacon*, Dec. 22, 1979; "Forty-Sixth Annual Report of the Children's Aid Society [1898]," OT, KSHS.

7. *The Children's Aid Society of New York*, 34.

8. *Thirty-third Annual Report of the Children's Aid Society, November 1885*, 24.

9. Ibid., 21.

10. White, "Placing Out New York Children," 220; "The Spectator," *Outlook* (May 11, 1912), 80–81. For White, see letter and attached materials to Annette Fry, Feb. 26, 1972, and *Clifton News*, Nov. 23, 1944, clipping, OT, KSHS. For Yost see Annette Riley Fry, "The Children's Migration," *American Heritage* 26 (December 1974): 81.

11. Riis, "Christmas Reminder of the Nobelist Work in the World," 631; Robert Sobel and John Raimo, eds., *Biographical Directory of the Governors of the United States, 1789–1978*, vol.3 (Westport, Conn.: Meckler Books, 1978), 1171–72.

12. *National Cyclopaedia of American Biography*, vol.42 (New York: James T. White & Co., 1958), 107; Ted C. Hinckley, *The Americanization of Alaska, 1867–1897* (Palo Alto, Calif.: Pacific Books, 1972), 129, 133, 156, and 225.

13. Brace, *The Dangerous Classes of New York*, 263 and 264.

14. "Children's Aid Society—Annual Report, 1883," "Children's Aid Society—Annual Report, 1912," p.103, "Children's Aid Society—Annual Report, 1913," and "Children's Aid Society—Annual Report, 1923," p.89, Orphan Train, NSHS.

15. Brace, *The Dangerous Classes of New York*, 234–35, 266.

16. "Forty-Sixth Annual Report of the Children's Aid Society [1898]," OT, KSHS; *The Children's Aid Society of New York,* 40.

17. "She Was Put Out on a Farm in Kansas," 11.

18. Bellingham, "'Little Wanderers'," 94 and 140; "Asylum Children in Mc-Leansboro, Illinois," 148–50; Pauline Christiansen, "Anna Van Cura Finds Kansas Home," *Crossroads* 4 (Summer 1988): 6; "P. Mary Young," Orphan Train, NSHS.

19. "Eighth Annual Report," (1861) *Annual Reports,* 62.

20. Patrick, Sheets, and Trickel, *We Are a Part of History,* 88–89.

21. "Children's Aid Society—Annual Report, 1886," p.74, Orphan Train, NSHS; *The Old Brewery,* 302; "New York Orphans Come to Burlington," 2.

22. *Indianapolis Daily Journal,* Mar. 6, 1858, p.2; Langsam, *Children West,* 26 and 58–59; Brace, *The Dangerous Classes of New York,* 234.

23. "Third Annual Report," (1856) *Annual Reports,* 50; Brace, *The Dangerous Classes of New York,* 258; pamphlet "Let's Move Them Out of the Shacks" (Dallas, ca. 1921), 1 and 8, Catholic Archives; "Where Is the Child's Home?," *Orphan's Advocate and Social Monitor* (July 1853): 53.

24. Folks, *Care of the Destitute,* 104; Walter I. Trattner, *Homer Folks: Pioneer in Social Welfare* (New York: Columbia University Press, 1968), 20–26; Riis, "Christmas Reminder of the Nobelist Work in the World," 630; Brace, *The Dangerous Classes of New York,* 446.

25. Brace, *The Dangerous Classes of New York,* 35, 234, and 244; Langsam, *Children West,* 9 and 28–30; Holt, "Placed Out in Illinois," 42; "Forty-Sixth Annual Report of the Children's Aid Society [1898]," OT, KSHS. Langsam noted that organizations such as the Aid Society had a "Protestant frame of reference" in which Catholics and Jews were excluded from governing boards and organizational structures. Some Foundling Hospital placing-out accounts mention baptismal records; see for examples "Texan Responds to Newspaper Article," 7, and Arman, "Orphan Train Rider and His Music," 3.

26. Brophy, *Foundlings on the Frontier, passim,* particularly pages 3, 11, 13–15, 27–28, 30, 60–61, 63, 67–77, and 101: for *Los Angeles Examiner* headline, see page 67; for *Boston American* quote see page 71. The more sympathetic story appeared in "Foundlings in Arizona," *New York Times,* Nov. 6, 1904, p.6; this story concentrated on the territory's undisciplined population, particularly Anglos, who had the nerve to want statehood.

27. John Rowe Townsend, *Written for Children: An Outline of English-language Children's Literature* (Boston: Horn Book, 1974), 73.

28. White, "Placing Out New York Children," 225; Hirshson, *"There's Always Someone There"*, 43.

29. "'Orphan trains' children get together as adults," *Minneapolis Star and Tribune*, Sept. 17, 1986, p.4CX; *Anchor* (Northwood, Iowa), July 1913, quoted in "Placing-Out Agent Clara Comstock," 4; M. Vogt and C. Vogt, *Searching for Home*, 56 and 72.

30. Langsam, *Children West*, 65.

31. Patrick, Sheets, and Trickel, *We Are a Part of History*, 91.

32. "'Orphan trains' children get together as adults"; Arno Dosch, "Not Enough Babies to Go Around," *Cosmopolitan* 49 (September 1910): 431. Zelizer, *Pricing the Priceless Child*, 193–94, notes that the largest demand for girls was among Protestant and Catholic families; while families hoped that a first-born would be a son, adoptive families asked for girls, perhaps believing them more pliable in their growing-up years.

33. Pounder, "Milton Peter Toffier," 7.

34. Langsam, *Children West*, 60.

35. "Children's Aid Society—Annual Report, 1886," p.74, and "Children's Aid Society—Annual Report, 1921," Orphan Train, NSHS.

36. Langsam, *Children West*, 62–63.

37. Ibid., 66.

38. "Report of the Children's Aid Society, 1911," p.15, and "Report of Miss A. L. Hill of an Inspection of All Children Placed Since 1911 in Family Homes in or Near McPherson, Kansas," 1924, OT, KSHS.

39. Wade, *Urban Frontier*, 120–21; Bessie Louise Pierce, *A History of Chicago, 1848–1871*, vol.2 (New York: Knopf, 1940), 440–47; Lana Ruegamer, "'The Paradise of Exceptional Women': Chicago Women Reformers, 1863–1893," (Ph.D. diss., University of Indiana, 1982), 84.

40. Bender, *Toward an Urban Vision*, 146–47.

41. "A Talk on Orphans," *New York Times*, Mar. 14, 1910, p.6; "Orphan's Chance in Life," *New York Times*, Mar. 16, 1910, p.8. For another discussion of the institutionalized child, see "Rabbi Hirsch's Views of the Institutionalized Type," *New York Times*, Apr. 16, 1910, p.10.

42. Louisa Lee Schuyler, "The State Charities Aid Association of the State of

New York, 1872–1893," 57 and 63–64, in *The Organization of Charities, Being a Report of the Sixth Section*; Langsam, *Children West*, 58 and 59; Amos W. Butler, "The Indiana Plan for Supervision," in *Public Welfare in the United States: The Annals*, ed. Howard W. Odum (Philadelphia: American Academy of Political and Social Services, 1923), 123; *The White Hall Orphan's Home Society*, 2, Orphan, ISHL; Charles Richmond Henderson, *Introduction to the Study of the Dependent, Defective and Delinquent Classes* (Boston: D. C. Heath & Co., 1906), 104.

43. Langsam, *Children West*, 65; Kay Hively, "Little Strangers from the East," *Ozarks Mountaineer* 35 (February 1987): 43; *Annotated Code of Nebraska, 1901* (Beatrice: J. E. Cobbey, 1901), ch.2, secs. 1732–43, pp.374–76.

44. Annette Fry materials, Feb. 26, 1972, OT, KSHS; M. Vogt and C. Vogt, *Searching for Home*, vii; Bellingham, "'Little Wanderers'," 111.

45. Brace, *The Dangerous Classes of New York*, 230–31.

46. Kirke Mechem, ed., *The Annals of Kansas, 1886–1925*, vol.1 (Topeka: Kansas State Historical Society, 1954), 339 and 347; Swanson, "Public Protection," 263; *Session Laws of Kansas, 1901* (Topeka: Kansas State Printing Plant, 1901), ch.106, secs. 15 and 17.

47. G. Whiting Swayne to Governor William Stanley, Nov. 26, 1901, and Dec. 6, 1901, Gov. Stanley Correspondence, box 3, folder 1, Archives, KSHS.

48. Rev. Chr. [Christian] Krehbiel to Governor Stanley, June 4, 1901, Gov. Stanley Correspondence, box 3, folder 1, Archives, KSHS. For Halstead Indian Industrial School see *Halstead Independent, Souvenir Edition*, Aug. 12, 1937, p.32, and Donald J. Berthrong, "From Buffalo Days to Classrooms: The Southern Cheyennes and Arapahos and Kansas," *Kansas History: A Journal of the Central Plains* 12 (Summer 1989): 106–7. A search of Kansas State Board of Charities files, and Secretary of State Records, "Official Bonds and Trademarks, 1899–1939," book no. 4, 1901–1904, Archives, KSHS, showed no placing-out organization making payment of bond or registering with the State of Kansas, although from the source noted in footnote 49, it would appear that payment was made to some state entity.

49. Henry J. Allen to Governor Stanley, May 19, 1902, Gov. Stanley Correspondence, box 3, folder 10, Archives, KSHS.

50. Swanson, "Public Protection," 256; *Session Laws of Kansas, 1903* (Topeka: Kansas State Printing Plant, 1903), ch.361, sec.1.

51. *Report of the Joint Committee on Home-Finding Societies, Forty-eighth General Assembly, 1915* (Springfield: Schnepp & Barnes, 1915), 39.

52. Strong, *Our Country,* ix, 42, 56–7.

CHAPTER 5

1. "Texan Responds to Newspaper Article," 7.

2. *Jacksonville Journal,* Apr. 26, 1860, p.3; "Shipping the Poor West," *Illinois State Genealogical Society Quarterly* 17 (Fall 1985): 149–50, quoting *New York Herald,* Jan. 1886; *New York Times,* Nov. 27, 1901, p.9.

3. *The Children's Aid Society of New York,* 39–40.

4. Henry H. Riley, *Puddleford, and Its People* (New York: Samuel Hueston, 1854); Holliday, "An Historian Reflects on Edgewood Children's Center," 125; Margaret Marshall, "Of Such Is the Middle West," unpublished paper, Manuscripts, KSHS; "Orphans Help Populate County," newspaper clipping, *Sabetha Herald,* 1909, OT, KSHS.

5. Sister Marian Healy, S.C., New York Foundling Hospital, to author, Sept. 19, 1989; Helen Steinman, New York Children's Aid Society, to author, Oct. 4, 1989, quoting Fry, "The Children's Migration." Fry, whose grandfather was Agent Charles R. Fry, wrote that the board continued limited placing out after 1929 (p.81). The 1930 annual report did not mention such placements, but Fry possibly saw in-house directives not available to other researchers. For other Aid Society programs see "Fresh Air Work," *New York Times,* July 8, 1928, p.4; "War on Malnutrition," *New York Times,* Sept. 1, 1928, p.7; "$3,625,000 Child Aid Asked," *New York Times,* May 20, 1930, p.6; and "Before Autumn Comes," *New York Times,* Aug. 20, 1930, p.18.

6. Theodore Dreiser, *Sister Carrie* (Modern Library, 1900; reprinted, Cambridge, Mass.: R. Bentley, 1971); Theodore Jorgensen and Nora O. Solum, *Ole Edvart Rölvaag: A Biography* (New York: Harper and Brothers, 1939), 353–54.

7. Katharine P. Hewins, "Division of Responsibility Between Family and Children's Agencies," *Family* 3 (November 1922): 179. Langsam, *Children West,* 66; Richard K. Conant, "The Massachusetts Department of Public Welfare," 119, in *Public Welfare in the United States*; Edith Abbott and Sophonisba P. Breckinridge, "The Administration of the Aid-To-Mothers Law in Illinois," 7–8 and 12–17, and Mary F. Bogue, "Administration of Mothers' Aid in Ten Localities," 1–3, in *The Family and Social Service In the 1920's: Two Documents,*

eds. David J. Rothman and Sheila M. Rothman (New York: Arno Press and the New York Times, 1972); Arthur C. Wakeley, ed., *Omaha: The Gate City and Douglas County, Nebraska* (Chicago: S. J. Clarke Publishing Co., 1917), 361; Emma Octavia Lundberg, "Progress of Mothers' Aid Administration," *Social Service Review* 2 (September 1928): 435. Reformers feared that under socio-economic changes the family unit would dissolve; the Progressive era's duty was to ensure family cohesiveness and rehabilitation. See Steven Mintz and Susan Kellogg, *Domestic Revolutions: A Social History of American Family Life* (New York: Free Press, 1988), ch.4; Linda Gordon, *Heroes of Their Own Lives: The Politics and History of Family Violence, Boston 1880–1960* (New York: Viking Penguin, 1988), 72–75.

8. Bellingham, "'Little Wanderers,'" 58–78 and 288–96; Patricia Ann Schene, "Accountability in Nonprofit Organizations: A Framework for Addressing the Public Interest," (Ph.D. diss., University of Colorado, 1990), 101–2.

9. Howard, *Illinois: A History of the Prairie State*, 399–400; "The Conference of Charities and Correction," *School and Society* 1 (February 20, 1915): 288; "Baby Boarders," *Survey* 54 (April 15, 1925): 83–84.

10. Brophy, *Foundlings on the Frontier*, 10; "The New England Home for Little Wanderers," informational letter, 1989, New England Home for Little Wanders; *The Bicentennial Guide to Greater Cincinnati*, Children's Home of Cincinnati file; *Fifty-First Annual Report: The Children's Mission*, 6–8; *The Children's Mission to Children, Seventy-Sixth Annual Report, 1925* (Boston: Children's Mission to Children, 1925), 3. For in-city relief examples see "Brooklyn Children's Aid Society Gives Free Pasteurized Milk," *New York Times*, July 6, 1901, p.6, and "Tenement Reform Conference," *New York Times*, Feb. 20, 1901, p.7.

11. Brace, "The Little Laborers," 330; Writers' Program, w p a, *Oklahoma: A Guide to the Sooner State* (Norman: University of Oklahoma Press, 1941), 47; Edith Hess, "State Regulation of Woman and Child Labor in Kansas," *Collections of the Kansas State Historical Society, 1919–1922* 15 (1923): 297; Zelizer, *Pricing the Priceless Child*, 64–65. By 1927 less than three-fifths of the fourteen- and fifteen-year-olds with work permits in industrial cities had completed eighth grade; one-fourth had completed only through sixth grade. See "Child Labor," *School and Society* 31 (June 7, 1930): 761.

12. Owen R. Lovejoy, "What Remains of Child Labor," in *Children and Youth in America*, vol.2, ed. Robert Bremner (Cambridge: Harvard University Press,

1971), 705–6; "The Federal Child-Labor Law," *School and Society* 6 (September 1, 1917): 256–57; Howard, *Illinois: A History of the Prairie State*, 400.

13. "Child Labor, the Home and Liberty," *New Republic* 41 (December 3, 1924): 32–33; Zelizer, *Pricing the Priceless Child*, 65–66.

14. As an example, Hamlin Garland in *Boy Life on the Prairie* (1899; reprinted, New York: Frederick Ungar Publishing Co., 1959), 29, wrote that school lasted from December to March, when little farm work could be done. As noted by West in *Growing Up with the Country*, 189, children were kept home for many reasons, sometimes the distance to school was one of them.

15. Smith, *The Rise of Industrial America*, 151; McKeever, *Farm Boys and Girls*, 295–96; J. E. Hagerty, "The Universities and Training for Public Leadership and Social Work," 206–12, in *Public Welfare in the United States*; Bleecker Marquette, "Positions of Social Work in the Fields of Public Education and Public Health," 177–84, and Edith Shatto King, "The Scope and Nature of Positions in the Field of Non-Governmental Social Agencies," 172–76, in *Public Welfare in the United States*; Herbert B. Adams, *Notes on the Literature of Charities*, Fifth Series, Johns Hopkins University Studies in Historical and Political Science (Baltimore: Johns Hopkins University, 1887), 7–48.

16. Hirshson, *"There's Always Someone There,"* 52 and 64–65; Emily Cooper Johnson, ed., *Jane Addams: A Centennial Reader* (New York: Macmillan Co., 1960), 89–90.

17. *Children's Mission to Children, Seventy-Sixth Annual Report, 1925*, 5.

18. Percy G. Kammerer, "The Relation of the Church to Social Work," *Family* 8 (June 1927): 121–22; Richard C. Cabot, "The Inter-Relation of Social Work and the Spiritual Life," *Family* 8 (November 1927): 211–17; Dr. B. S. Winchester, "Spiritual Factors in Family Life," *Family* 8 (December 1927): 279–81; Regina G. Kunzel, "The Professionalization of Benevolence: Evangelicals and Social Workers in the Florence Crittenton Homes, 1915 to 1945," *Journal of Social History* 22 (Fall 1988): 21 and 24–26; Paula Baker, "The Domestication of Politics: Women and American Political Society, 1780–1920," *American Historical Review* 89 (1984): 636.

19. Miller, "Charles M. Sheldon," 128–29 and 132–34.

20. Reverend Worth M. Tippy, "The Field of the Church in Social Work and Public Welfare," 68–70, in *Public Welfare in the United States*.

21. *The Story of Graham School*, 5; *Encyclopedia of American Biography, New*

Series (New York: American Historical Society, 1937), 179; "What Shall Be Done with Our Orphan Asylums?," *Review of Reviews* 72 (July 1925): 92–93. Reeder and Folks were allied when Reeder was director of the Child Welfare Division of the American Red Cross during World War I. Folks then joined the post-World War I American Relief Administration (ARA), which gave aid to European refugees, particularly children; both men saw work in Serbia. American social worker involvement in the ARA suggests that they may have considered child relocation such as that later used with World War II's English "blitz" children, but evidence suggests that Herbert Hoover, head of relief efforts and himself an orphan, dismissed the idea. See Homer Folks to Louis Strauss, Apr. 17, 1919; ARA Paris Office letter to Folks, Apr. 19, 1919; and ARA Paris Office letter to Major F. K. Heath, Apr. 26, 1919, American Relief Administration, European Unit, Records, 1919–1923, Hoover Institution, Stanford University.

22. R. R. Reeder, "Our Orphaned Asylums," *Survey* 54 (June 1925): 285.

23. Bessie A. McClenahan, *The Iowa Plan for the Combination of Public and Private Relief,* Studies in Social Sciences Series, vol.5, no. 3 (Iowa City: University of Iowa, 1918), 8 and 68; Pleck, *Domestic Tyranny,* 131; Frank Dekker Watson, *The Charity Organization Movement in the United States: A Study in American Philanthropy* (New York: Macmillan Co., 1922), 265; *Compiled Statutes of the State of Nebraska; With Amendments, 1882 to 1905* (Lincoln: State Journal Co., 1905), no. 2145, sec.149, pp.559–60. The 1876 population reported in the twenty homes were 2,514 males and 1,632 females; the largest number in any institution were 360 males and 242 females at the Ohio Soldiers' and Sailors' Orphan Home in Xenia. See "Report of the Commissioner of Education for the Year 1877," 190.

24. S. P. Breckinridge, "Summary of the Present State Systems for the Organization and Administration of Public Welfare," 93–94, in *Public Welfare in the United States*; Gerald C. Rothman, *Philanthropists, Therapists and Activists: A Century of Ideological Conflict in Social Work* (Cambridge, Mass.: Schenkman , 1985), 22–23 and 26; Minutes, Women's Board of Associate Charities, Feb. 13, 1889 to Jan. 3, 1894, Archives, NSHS.

25. Breckinridge, "Summary," 93–94; "Chicago Spikes the Baby Farmer," *Survey* 65 (December 15, 1930): 326.

26. For a quote representative of the organizations' goals, see "Nebraska

Legislative Act, 1887, Relating to Nebraska Industrial Home and Women's Board of Associate Charities," in Tipton, *Forty Years of Nebraska,* 172.

27. Johnson, *Jane Addams,* 90 and 94.

28. Wm. H. H. Young to Governor William Stanley, July 17, 1899, and E. L. Hillis to Governor Stanley, Mar. 12, 1901, Gov. Stanley Correspondence, box 2, folder 2, and Thomas B. Hubbard to Gov. Arthur Capper, Jan. 8, 1915, Gov. Capper Correspondence, box 2, folders 82–98, Archives, K S H S. The Soldiers' Orphans' Home, organized in 1885, took in children fourteen years of age or younger. See *First Biennial Report of the Soldiers' Orphans' Home, at Atchison, Kansas* (Topeka: Kansas Publishing House, 1888), 4, and *Second Biennial Report of the Soldiers' Orphans' Home, at Atchison, Kansas* (Topeka: Kansas Publishing House, 1890), 19. Another Kansas charity, the Children's Home Society, indentured children in the Mother Bickerdyke Home and Hospital, the State Industrial School for Boys, the Soldiers' Orphans' Home, and the Industrial School for Girls. See Bessie E. Wilder, comp., *Governmental Agencies of the State of Kansas, 1861–1956* (Lawrence: Governmental Research Center, University of Kansas, 1957), 32.

29. Neva R. Deardorff, "Bound Out," *Survey* 56 (July 15, 1926): 459; "Indentured Children," *School and Society* 26 (November 26, 1927): 674.

30. "An Early Adventure in Child-Placing, Charles Loring Brace: Editorial Note," *Social Service Review* 3 (March 1929): 78.

31. Judge J. T. Clark, president, Kansas Children's Home Society, to Gov. William Stanley, Feb. 24, 1900, Gov. Stanley Correspondence, box 3, folder 1, Archives, K S H S. See also Reeder, "Our Orphaned Asylums," 285.

32. Dale W. Broeder and Frank J. Barrett, "Impact of Religious Factors in Nebraska Adoptions," *Nebraska Law Review* 38 (May 1959): 643. For an example of a religious protection statute see *Cobbey's Annotated Statutes of Nebraska, Supplement of 1905,* p.126.

33. Fry, "The Children's Migration," 81; "Orphans Help Populate County," newspaper clippings, *Sabetha Herald,* 1908, 1909, O T, K S H S.

34. "Nebraska Bound," 3–4; "Ninth Annual Report" (1862) *Annual Reports,* 48; Riis, "Christmas Reminder of the Nobelist Work in the World," 630.

35. Jackson, " 'Orphan trains' transported kids to fresh starts in West."

36. Colwell, "A New York Orphan Comes to Kansas," 121–23.

37. "Second Annual Report," (1855) *Annual Reports,* 4.

Bibliographical Essay

*A*s WORK on this book progressed, the bibliography developed into divisions under subject headings: children, placing out, women, agriculture, railroads, social work and institutions, and general histories dealing with state and local history, urban development, and western expansion. The divisions were helpful to me, but would be less valuable to others since sources were categorized by the material immediately relevant to the story of placing out. For example, a volume on nineteenth-century family life might be categorized under children rather than women or social work, depending on the material most useful to my research. If anything, the only point such categories would demonstrate to a reader is the multidisciplinary nature of the subject; one that required the use of such diverse volumes as Phillip Paludan's excellent *"The Peoples' Contest": The Union and the Civil War* (New York: Harper & Row, 1988), Charles Loring Brace's *The Dangerous Classes of New York and Twenty Year's Work Among Them* (1880; reprinted, New Jersey: Patterson Smith, 1967), and David Schob's valuable *Hired Hands and Ploughboys: Farm Labor in the Midwest, 1815–60* (Urbana: University of Illinois Press, 1975).

No attempt will be made here to list all materials consulted. The sociological, public welfare, and public education periodical material, particularly from early twentieth-century issues of *Family, Survey,* educator John Dewey's *School and Society,* and *Social Service Review,* would fill pages, as would literature directly related to specific social workers, educators, and their programs. The material on Jane Addams, for example, is extensive and includes not only her own writings such as *Twenty Years at Hull-House* (New York: Macmillan Co., 1910) and "Social Settlements in Illinois," *Transactions of the Illinois State Historical Society* 11 (1906): 162–71, but a number of biographies and evaluations of Addams and her work. It must be added, however, that review of literature for the times is invaluable. Just as popular press materials in *Godey's Lady's Book* give a view of material values and middle-class trends in child rearing, the social welfare and educational literature provides insight to development of and controversy over various theories. Some real gems of studies and analyses are found, such as "Children's Bureau War-Time Program for Child Welfare," *School and Society* 6 (December 15, 1917): 707, and Marshall E. St. Edward Jones, "Foster-Home Care of Delinquent Children," *Social Service Review* 10 (September 1936): 450–63, to name two not cited in text.

In this essay, I shall note a selected number of works important to my research, comment on other sources, and suggest areas for study within the broader subject of child transportation.

To obtain data and develop a comprehensive picture of the placing-out system, one must look at the annual reports and periodicals of placing out organizations. Published reports and case studies are not always easily accessed from the institution in question but they can be found in other repositories and sources: some New York Children's Aid Society reports, for example, were found in various state historical society collections, as well as in the collected volume *Annual Reports of the Children's Aid Society, Nos. 1–10, Feb. 1854–Feb. 1863* (New York: Arno Press and the New York Times, 1971) and the *New York Times;* and reports for the Children's

Mission to the Children of the Destitute were found at the Boston Athenaeum. Also of value are popular press stories such as those that appeared in *Frank Leslie's Illustrated Newspaper* and *Harper's Weekly*, the writings of Charles Loring Brace and his contemporaries, social work periodicals, and newspaper stories that on a local level provide eyewitness accounts, often the names and ages of those placed, and the names of families who took a child. Sometimes libraries have newspaper clipping files, but the largest body of my research for localized accounts was collected from reading reel upon reel of microfilm. The reference to libraries also brings up the point that, thankfully, many state and local historical societies have recognized the subject of orphan trains and have reference files on the subject. With a note of caution, it must be added that these are limited, and do not usually include all possible materials in an agency's collections relating to the subject.

For overviews there are also articles published today in popular history journals; those not cited elsewhere include Donald Dale Jackson, "It Took Trains to Put Street Kids on the Right Track Out of the Slums," *Smithsonian* 17 (August 1986): 95–103, and Leslie Wheeler, "The Orphan Trains," *American History Illustrated* 18 (December 1983): 10–23. And, a growing number of volumes are devoted to oral histories of the placed out; to my mind one of the best remains one of the first published, Martha Nelson Vogt and Christina Vogt, *Searching for Home: Three Families from the Orphan Trains* (Grand Rapids: Triumph Press, 1983).

Oral histories are a focus for the Orphan Train Heritage Society of America, Inc., founded in 1987 and situated in Springdale, Arkansas. The society's newsletter, *Crossroads,* provides a forum through which individual stories are told and in which those seeking information about family can receive some direction in their searches. The newsletter is helpful in identifying organizations that placed out children and noting persons who are collecting data on the orphan trains, particularly in localized areas. The society sponsors a yearly reunion, and there are others held in Nebraska, Illinois, Missouri, and Minnesota—states that once received the placed out.

In many areas of the country individuals and organizations are pursuing the subject of placing out. On an individual level, Eloise Thomsen of Omaha, Nebraska, has over the last twelve years compiled a registry of the placed out. Through her work, over six hundred names, plus many personal histories, have been preserved. At Southwestern Michigan College in Dowagiac, Michigan, Stanley Hamper, museum director and curator, continues to compile the names of those sent to Dowagiac and the county in which it is located. By his count, as many as three hundred New York Children's Aid Society children came to that community between 1854 and the 1870s. One avenue followed by Hamper has been the use of census records when materials from the New York Children's Aid Society have not been available. Census records identify children whose last names are not those of the family in which they reside; but as Hamper points out, these children could be farmhands, domestics, or dependents who were not necessarily sent out by the Aid Society.

Hamper's use of census materials suggests other research possibilities. Indenture, adoption, and juvenile court records held in state, university, and county archives do lend themselves to study; the same is true of governors' records and those of state charities. These are often incomplete or, in the case of charity files, sometimes unavailable because rules of confidentiality still apply. I found this to be true at the state level as well as with materials held by the New York Children's Aid Society and the Foundling Hospital. With private institutions there is sometimes an access problem because they have little or no staff. To be fair, institutions, and not just charities, often do not find it important to have professional archivists or conservators on staff to process or maintain records. Another problem, of course, are records no longer extant. In one

Illinois county, I found that New York Juvenile Asylum indentures had been destroyed; when the courthouse ran out of space years ago, a judge ordered materials taken to the city dump. In my search, I met a man whose grandfather had been one of those Asylum children; the man had personally scoured the dump with the hope of retrieving the records, but to no avail. On another note, the records of Charles Loring Brace, particularly his letters, are believed by descendants to have been culled for more famous names and then destroyed by the institution to which they were given; thus, forbidding a more insightful look at the man.

Basic secondary sources are the volumes on children and childhood history. Philippe Ariès, *Centuries of Childhhood: A Social History of Family Life* (New York: Alfred A. Knopf, 1962), Bernard Wishy, *The Child and the Republic: The Dawn of Modern American Child Nurture* (Philadelphia: University of Pennsylvania Press, 1968); and Lloyd De Mause, *The History of Childhood* (New York: Psychohistory Press, 1974) are important to anyone beginning a study of childhood; De Mause may be disconcerting when he describes childhood as a nightmare from which man is just awakening, and some may find Ariès and Wishy somewhat dated in light of more recent studies. These volumes, however, provide a backbone for study and research. There are also Mark Poster's *Critical Theory of the Family* (New York: Seabury Press, 1978); Eli Zaretsky's *Capitalism, The Family, and Personal Life* (New York: Harper and Row, 1976); Kathryn Sather's "Sixteenth and Seventeenth Century Child-Rearing: A Matter of Discipline," *Journal of Social History* 22 (Summer 1989): 735–43; and the edited volumes Michael Gordon, ed., *The American Family in Social-Historical Perspective* (New York: St. Martin's Press, 1983) and Donald Scott and Bernard Wishy, eds., *America's Families: A Documentary History* (New York: Harper & Row, 1982).

These lead to the obvious, but implicit, point that childhood is bound to the history of family and the roles of women. Here, the following are of interest but certainly not inclusive of the available literature: Carl N. Degler, *At Odds: Women and Family in America from the Revolution to the Present* (New York: Oxford University Press, 1980); Letty Cottin Pogrebin, *Family Politics: Love and Power on an Intimate Frontier* (New York: McGraw-Hill, 1983); Steven Mintz and Susan Kellogg, *Domestic Revolutions: A Social History of American Family Life* (New York: Free Press, 1988); Elizabeth Pleck, *Domestic Tyranny: The Making of Social Policy against Family Violence from Colonial Times to the Present* (New York: Oxford University Press, 1987), a volume that also could be classified under women's history or social welfare theory; Andrew Billingsley and Jeanne M. Giovannoni, *Children of the Storm: Black Children and American Child Welfare* (New York: Harcourt, Brace, Jovanovich, 1972) and Gilbert G. Gonzalez, "Segregation of Mexican Children in a Southern California City: The Legacy of Expansionism and the American Southwest," *Western Historical Quarterly* 16 (January 1985): 55–76, are also easily placed under social welfare and education theory, but additionally call to mind the importance of research into family life among specific ethnic or racial groups.

Complimentary to these volumes are studies that have focused on women in social reform movements. Among those not cited elsewhere are Estelle Freedman, "Separatism as Strategy: Female Institution Building and American Feminism, 1870–1930," *Feminist Studies* 5 (Fall 1979): 512–29; Jill Conway, "Women Reformers and American Culture, 1870–1930," *Journal of Social History* 5 (Winter 1971–72): 166–74; and June O. Underwood, "Civilizing Kansas: Women's Organizations, 1880–1920," *Kansas History: A Journal of the Central Plains* 7 (Winter 1984–85): 291–306. Freedman argued that institutional work created an environment in which women bonded, creating a new feminist attitude. Conway and Underwood, however, concluded that women's participation in such work did not change women's or society's traditional view of this work as an extension of domestic home duty. To expand on

these studies, one may also consider Winfield Scott Montogom-
ery's *Fifty Years of Good Works of the National Association for the
Relief of Destitute Colored Women and Children* (Washington, D.C.:
National Association for the Relief of Destitute Colored Women
and Children, 1914); located in the Rare Book and Special Collections Division, Library of Congress, this commemorative history
of national charity work for the "relief, uplift, and salvation" of
destitute black women and children does not analyze women's roles
as do the journal articles cited, but it does offer provocative material
for today's scholars interested in women's social service roles and
their influence on other women.

Viviana A. Zelizer's *Pricing the Priceless Child: The Changing
Social Value of Children* (New York: Basic Books, Inc., 1985) focuses
on urban, eastern examples, but her discussion of the "productive"
child fits nicely with Elliott West's *Growing Up with the Country:
Childhood on the Far Western Frontier* (Albuquerque: University of
New Mexico Press, 1989), which notes the economic contributions
of children and is important for its use of diaries, letters, and
memoirs that bring out the child voice. Also exploring the use of
childhood memories and writings is Yuko Takahashi's "Frontier
Children: Childhood Experiences in Kansas, 1860–1900," *American Review* 22 (March 1988): 170–91.

Reviewing *Growing Up with the Country,* Annette Atkins in
"The Child's West: A Review Essay," *New Mexico Historical Review* 65 (October 1990): 477–90, notes that publications on western
life have given notice to childhood experience, but within the
subjects of expansion or women's history. Among these volumes are
Julie Roy Jeffrey's *Frontier Women: The Trans-Mississippi West,
1840–1880* (New York: Hill and Wang, 1979); Lillian Schlissel's
Women's Diaries of the Westward Journey (New York: Schocken,
1982); Sarah Deutsch, *No Separate Refuge: Culture, Class, and Gen-
der on an Anglo-Hispanic Frontier in the American Southwest, 1880–
1940* (New York: Oxford University Press, 1987); Susan Armitage

and Elizabeth Jameson, eds., *The Women's West* (Norman: University of Oklahoma Press, 1987); and Lillian Schlissel, Vicki L. Ruiz, and Janice Monk, eds., *Western Women: Their Land, Their Lives* (Albuquerque: University of New Mexico Press, 1988). To this list could be added John D. Unruh, Jr., *The Plains Across: The Overland Emigrants and the Trans-Mississippi West, 1840–60* (Urbana: University of Illinois Press, 1979) and Merrill J. Mattes, *The Great Platte River Road* (Lincoln: University of Nebraska Press, 1969); neither contains an index heading for children but both refer to them, including material on those orphaned during the journey.

Rather miscellaneously I want to note a few publications, not cited elsewhere, that provided background and suggested avenues for evaluating children's history. These include David Grylls, *Guardians and Angels: Parents and Children in Nineteenth Century Literature* (Boston: Faber and Faber, 1978); John von Hartz, *New York Street Kids: 136 Photographs Selected by the Children's Aid Society* (New York: Dover Publications, 1978); N. Ray Hiner and Joseph M. Hawes, eds., *Growing Up in America: Children in Historical Perspective* (Urbana: University of Illinois Press, 1985); Eileen Simpson, *Orphans, Real and Imaginary* (New York: Weidenfeld & Nicholson, 1987); R. M. Schieder, "Loss and Gain? The Theme of Conversion in Late Victorian Fiction," *Victorian Studies* 9 (September 1965): 28–44; Nancy F. Cott, "Notes Toward an Interpretation of Antebellum Childrearing," *Psychohistory Review* 7 (Spring 1978): 4–20; N. Ray Hiner, "The Child in American Historiography," *Psychohistory Review* 7 (Summer 1978): 13–23; and Kathleen W. Jones, "Sentiment and Science: The Late Nineteenth Century Pediatrician as Mother's Advisor," *Journal of Social History* 17 (Spring 1983): 79–96. The nineteenth-century literature included Reverend Daniel A. Payne, *A Treatise on Domestic Education* (Cincinnati: Cranston & Stowe, 1889) and "Home Training for Children," *Monthly Religious Magazine* 10 (January 1853): 24. Here also must be added publications that deal with ideas of the agrarian myth: Robert G. Athearn, *The Mythic West in Twentieth-Century America* (Lawrence: University Press of Kansas, 1986); James M. Marshall, *Land Fever: Dispossession and the Frontier Myth* (Lexington: University Press of Kentucky, 1986); and Daves Rossell, "Tended Images: Verbal and Visual Idolatry of Rural Life in America, 1800–1850," *New York History* 69 (October 1988): 425–40.

The subject of placing out, the orphan trains, can claim little literature devoted specifically to the subject. Miriam Z. Langsam's *Children West: A History of the New York Children's Aid Society, 1853–1890* (Madison: State Historical Society of Wisconsin, 1964) and A. Blake Brophy's *Foundlings on the Frontier: Racial and Religious Conflict in Arizona Territory, 1904–1905* (Tucson: University of Arizona Press, 1972) are important exceptions. As well, Bellingham's doctoral dissertation, cited in this work used New York Children's Aid Society case studies. Not cited but of interest is Kristine E. Nelson's "The Best Asylum: Charles Loring Brace and Foster Family Care," (Ph.D. diss., University of California, Berkeley, 1980), which expands on Langsam's earlier work.

Useful in setting placing out within perspectives of sociological thought and urban development were Richard C. Wade's *The Urban Frontier: The Rise of Western Cities, 1790–1830* (Cambridge: Harvard University Press, 1959); David J. Rothman's *The Discovery of the Asylum: Social Order and Disorder in the New Republic* (Boston: Little, Brown & Co., 1971); Thomas Bender's *Toward an Urban Vision: Ideas and Institutions in Nineteenth Century America* (Lexington: University Press of Kentucky, 1975); Paul Boyer's *Urban Masses and Moral Order in America, 1820–1920* (Cambridge: Harvard University Press, 1978); and Robert H. Bremner's *The Public Good: Philanthropy and Welfare in the Civil War Era* (New York: Alfred A. Knopf, 1980). Also of importance were Dan Cantrall, "The Illinois State Board of Public Charities and the County Poorhouses, 1870–1900: Institutional Ideals vs. County Realities," *Transactions of the Illinois State Historical Society* (1988): 49–58; Amy

G. Srebnick's "True Womanhood and Hard Times: New York and Early New York Industrialization," (Ph.D. diss., State University of New York at Stoney Brook, 1979); and Christine Stansell's *City of Women: Sex and Class in New York, 1789–1860* (New York: Alfred A. Knopf, 1986), which builds upon her "Women of the Laboring Poor in New York City, 1840–1857," (Ph.D. diss., Yale University, 1979). Stansell provides some material on Charles Loring Brace, the Children's Aid Society, and other charitable organizations that worked with women and children. Finally, of interest for social theory and control are Nathan Huggins, *Protestants Against Poverty: Boston's Charities, 1870–1900* (Westport, Ct.: Greenwood Publishing, 1971) and Anthony Platt, *The Child Savers: The Invention of Delinquency* (Chicago: University of Chicago Press, 1969).

The study of placing out provides some suggestions for research in the whole subject of child transportation. It is not too extravagant to say that from the Children's Crusade of the Middle Ages through present-day efforts by parents to remove their children from war-torn countries to safer environments, there have been circumstances that resulted in some form of child transportation. England's system for resettling children and women, the impact of reformers such as Homer Folks and R. R. Reeder on child saving efforts among refugees of World War I, the rush to remove Jewish children from Nazi domination, and the "blitz" kids of the Second World War are just a few of the possibilities to develop further understanding of child migration and its impact on social thinking and history.

Ivy Pinchbeck and Margaret Hewitt, *Children in English Society* (London: Routledge & Kegan Paul, 1973) remains an important two-volume set on English transportation and programs for the poor in general, and more recently Kenneth Bagnall's *The Little Immigrants: The Orphans Who Came to Canada* (Toronto: Macmillian Press, 1980) has added to the literature. Periodical material on transportation and gang labor includes the nineteenth-century "Experiment with Boy Laborers in Herefordshire," *Littell's Living Age* 19 (October 1848): 165–66, and the twentieth-century A. Roger Ekirch's, "Great Britain's Secret Convict Trade to America, 1783–1784," *American Historical Review* 89 (December 1984): 1285–91. (Just as television gave to audiences the movie *Orphan Train*, Hollywood has depicted convict transportation; the 1953 movie *Botany Bay* was presented as a "colorful seafaring yarn" about British convicts on their way to Australia in 1790.) Studies that recognize the British farm pupil system in America also deserve note; these include Curtis Harnack, *Gentlemen on the Prairie* (Ames: Iowa State University Press, 1985) and Larry A. McFarlane, "The Fairmont Colony in Martin County Minnesota in the 1870s," *Kansas History: A Journal of the Central Plains* 12 (Autumn 1989): 166–74. Harnack deals with the system near Le Mars, Iowa, whereas McFarlane looks at the plan that sent middle-class British youths to Minnesota.

One may argue that there are still elements of child transportation. States remove their charges, the delinquent, troubled, and addicted, to out-of-state institutions, and projects for at-risk interurban youngsters, such as Outward Bound, still use the country environment as a way in which to teach self-confidence and self-reliance. Sociological literature today in abundance addresses many facets of American social welfare in practice and theory, reflecting as did earlier published materials the ongoing debates of what best serves the child. In fact, those discussions continue in such forums as the March 1991 national seminar held in Kansas City, Missouri, on developing modern-day orphanages, a proposal with many supporters. Some may say that present-day practices have divorced themselves from the past, but studies such as Paul Gerard Anderson's, "The Origin, Emergence, and Professional Recognition of Child Protection," *Social Service Review* 61 (June 1989): 222–44 and

Patricia Ann Schene's dissertation, "Accountability in Nonprofit Organizations: A Framework for Addressing the Public Interest" (cited in text) demonstrate ties to earlier beliefs and practices.

It is painfully simplistic to state that placing out is intricately woven into the history of children, women, family, public welfare, and western expansion. The point remains, however, that it is, and the sources cited here and in the notes (although I will not claim to have exhausted *every* volume on women or settlement or welfare history) demonstrate the variety of places and varying contexts in which children, childhood, and placing out are addressed.

Index